SECOND OPINION

A doctor's dispatches from the British inner city

Theodore Dalrymple

Monday Books

First published in book form in the UK in 2009 by Monday Books
Articles originally published in *The Spectator* magazine, 1997 to 2009

A CIP catalogue record for this title is available from the British
Library

ISBN: 978-1-906308-12-4

Typeset by Andrew Searle
Printed and bound in the UK by CPI Mackays, Chatham ME5 8TD

www.mondaybooks.com
info@mondaybooks.com

To the memory of William Beveridge

Preface

ALL HIS LIFE, said De Gaulle, he had a certain idea of France; and I for a long time had a certain idea of England. This idea included the population's cool and ironic detachment from its own experience, that permitted it to face adversity with great good humour and modesty rather than by resort to histrionics, and a polite restraint that was a precondition of depth of character. This restraint seemed to me heroic in an undemonstrative way; it was also the guarantor of an implicit subtlety. No doubt there were drawbacks to the English character, for example a constipated inability to express emotion; but where emotion is concerned, I prefer constipation to its opposite, for emotional incontinence ends by being indistinguishable from fraud, fakery and hysteria.

Whether or not there was any truth to my idea, or perhaps I should say ideal, of England, it is certainly not true now. The English are known almost everywhere in Europe rather for their militant vulgarity, their lack of restraint, their arrogant loudness, their ferocious and determined drunkenness, their antisocial egotism, their aggression and quick resort to violence, the grossness of their appetites, the prideful ugliness of their appearance and their total lack of finesse in any department of human existence whatever. (A visit to a continental resort at which the English foregather will quickly convince anyone sceptical of the accuracy of this depiction.)

It is as if the English have undergone a *gestalt* switch where their understanding of character is concerned. Those qualities that formerly were admired are now decried; those qualities that formerly were decried are now admired. Crudity has become almost a badge of political virtue, for to exhibit it is taken by many as a sign of their own solidarity with the people.

Nowhere are the deeply unattractive characteristics of contemporary English character more evident than in the lower reaches of society. However, I do not like the concept of an underclass, for it implies that there exists a section of the population – five or ten per cent, shall we say – that is completely distinct from the rest of the population and shares none of its characteristics, either in taste or behaviour. Increasingly, in fact, the British middle class resembles nothing so much as an underclass with money. Its social behaviour, cultural tastes, modes of dress and so forth increasingly approximate to those of the underclass. The problems of English (and the rest of British) society are more than merely social or economic, therefore: they are cultural or civilisational. This means that there is no possible solution by social engineering alone of the type so beloved of our bloated, bullying and incompetent state apparatus.

In these pages, I have described what I have seen and heard while working as a doctor in a hospital and the nearby prison in a British inner city. My sample of English humanity is a selected one, no doubt, but it is by no means small: it involves experience of thousands, and perhaps even tens of thousands, of cases. And each case told me about the lives of several people with whom he or she was connected. Moreover, there is no reason to think that what I saw and heard is unique to where I saw and heard it, that if I had worked elsewhere I should not have encountered very similar cases, and in the same numbers.

What follows might seem to some to be unvarnished or even exaggerated, but in fact I have somewhat blurred and softened the picture rather than heightened it. I once kept a diary in which I recorded all that I saw and heard during my work, but I gave up, not through laziness but simply because what I recorded was far too horrifying for anyone (including myself) to read. It was literally unbearable, in fact: all the more so because what I was recording was human brutality unforced by coercion, and in the absence of such extenuating circumstances as real hunger and deprivation. The situation is far worse than I describe.

Wordsworth said that poetry is emotion recalled in tranquillity; what follows is horror and desperation recalled in tranquillity. Many people – I know from experience – will dismiss what I say first by denying its truth and then by denying its significance. 'Twas ever thus, they will say; think of late Victorian Whitechapel, they will say, where Jack the Ripper operated. Or for that matter, Gin Lane.

But even if Victorian Whitechapel was really as bad as they think it was – remember that Jack the Ripper's victims were often found by policemen walking alone in Whitechapel, armed only with a lamp and a whistle, which I doubt they would dare to do nowadays – should we, after more than a century of enormous technical progress, be comparing ourselves with people who were but the slightest accident away from death, whose productivity was but a fraction of ours, and the great majority of whom necessarily lived in the greatest material discomfort by comparison with us? Have we no sense, have we no feeling, have we no shame?

The following pieces appeared in *The Spectator* between 1997 and 2009, under the headings 'Second Opinion', 'Medicine And Letters' and 'Global Warning'. During the great majority of that time, until his early retirement from the NHS, Theodore Dalrymple practised as a doctor and psychiatrist in a hospital in the inner-city and at a nearby prison.

He Knew I Knew
He Knew I Knew

EVERYONE KNOWS WHAT doctors do: they diagnose and treat illness. First, a patient comes to the doctor and complains of symptoms. Then the doctor examines him and perhaps performs some laboratory or other tests. Finally, having arrived at a diagnosis, the doctor applies the correct treatment, be it pharmacological or surgical. From the purely abstract point of view, it is all rather simple and straightforward.

In practice, however, complications sometimes arise. For example, last week there was a patient in my ward who told me that he had been off sick from work for the past year.

'With what sickness?' I asked. Normally in these circumstances this question produces puzzlement, as if it were a complete irrelevance. But this particular patient was well prepared.

'Backache,' he said. 'I've got severe pain in my back.'

I confess I was surprised. He looked a fit young man to me, and he moved around with perfect ease, not like a man crippled by back pain. Moreover, he had a number of cuts and bruises on him, the result of having been beaten up by a gang of children who had tried to mug him in the street and whom he had unwisely chased. People with back pain are quite often mugged, of course, but they rarely run after their muggers. Perhaps this man was emboldened by the fact that his hobby was martial arts: again, an odd choice of pastime for someone with incapacitating backache.

I telephoned his general practitioner with my suspicions, thinking that perhaps he had been deceived by his patient into signing him off sick. I told the doctor my grounds for suspecting that his patient's backache was not as bad as he claimed. It turned out, however, that I was telling the doctor nothing he did not already know.

'Yes,' he said, 'he has never struck me as having been in much pain.'

'But he has been off sick for the past year,' I said, my voice tinged with outrage.

'Yes,' said the doctor, 'but the last patient whom I made fit to work when he didn't want to return to work picked up my computer and threw it at me. We ended up having a fight on the floor.'

I understood at once. It isn't only sick notes that are procured by threat, of course: round here all mind-altering substances – tranquillisers and antidepressants – are prescribed not for the patient's sake but to forestall an attack on the doctor, who gives that patient whatever he wants to remove him from his presence as quickly as possible, before the patient spits at or punches him.

Things are a little better in the prison, I'm glad to say. There the doctor is free to do what he thinks is best for the patient, thanks to the proximity of several very large men at his beck and call.

Last week, a patient arrived in the prison, a fit (though presumably not very skilful) young burglar.

'Are you on any treatment?' I asked him.

'Yes,' he said. 'DF 118, diazzies and amitrippiline.'

An opiate analgesic, an addictive tranquilliser (diazepam) and an antidepressant (amitriptyline).

'Why?' I asked.

'Backache,' he replied.

'Ah, a burglar with a backache.' I said.

He smiled at me, and I smiled back. Then we had a good chuckle together. I knew, he knew I knew, I knew he knew I knew, and he knew I knew he knew I knew.

'Nice one, Doctor,' he said as he left the room, in excellent spirits.

Everyone Does It

WHY DO PEOPLE do the things they do, especially when they are so bad for them? A patient of mine last week offered me the complete explanation, when I asked him why he had taken heroin for the last eight years, with the exception of the time he had spent in prison.

'Everyone does it,' he said.

'I don't,' I said.

'Everyone I know.'

So there you have it: in this age of unbridled self-expression, when (to quote our esteemed Minister of Education) the three Cs, culture, creativity and community – or is it compassion, caring and crying in public? – have replaced the three Rs, everyone does what everyone else does. But things are not quite as bleak as they seem; there is more variation than at first sight appears.

'Do you have brothers and sisters?' I asked

'Yes, two brothers and two sisters.'

'Do any of them take heroin?'

'No,' he replied.

'So it's not quite true, then, that everyone you know takes heroin?'

Suffice it to say that he did not greet my exposure of the contradiction between what he said and the truth with the pleasure that a disinterested searcher after knowledge might have expressed.

'I've been trying to give up for years,' he said. 'But it's everywhere.'

Then he uttered the heartfelt cry of despair that thousands of middle-class housewives since time immemorial have uttered.

'I just can't get the help.'

I moved on. My next patient had spent the last 20 minutes chatting cheerfully on his mobile phone. Having made arrangements for the evening, he wore a complacent grin, and it surprised me to learn that the night before he had taken an overdose.

'What did you take?' I asked.

'Temazzies,' he said.

Temazzies belong to the same class of drugs as diazzies – and nitrazzies, lorazzies, bromazzies, flurazzies and oxazzies. You can tell that people love them by the fact that they give them a familiar name. No one does this for, say, the vincristine that treats their leukaemia. And the property for which all the -azzies are so highly esteemed is their ability to dull the mind and empty it of thought: which is, after all, the great object of most English life, especially in its recreational phase. If someone were to start a Society for the Prevention of Thought, he would swiftly make a fortune from the subscriptions.

I broke my vow never to use the argot of the streets.

'Why did you take the temazzies?' I asked.

'This bloke gave them to me in the pub.'

'But why did you take them?'

'Well, what else was I supposed to do with them?'

'But why? Did you know what they were?'

'I'd seen him take them before. He took them regular, by the handful. They never did him no harm.'

'But I still don't quite understand why you took them.'

'Well, I had alcohol in my head, didn't I?'

I suppose every event must have a cause but, when it comes to human conduct, not every action must have a reason.

'Would you do it again?' I asked.

'It depends how I was feeling. And whether there was any temazzies about.'

Gold Front Tooth Syndrome

I TRUST THAT I shall not be called cynical when I mention that the first question to be answered by a doctor on examining a prisoner with abdominal pain is whether the patient is trying to get out to hospital, either as relief from the monotony of the prison regime or because it is easier to escape from hospital than from prison. The last prisoner who gave it a go ended up with a broken leg, because he escaped from his hospital bed still wearing his socks and he slipped on our hospital's shiny stone floor. I am not sure whether he brought a case against the hospital, which after all has a duty of care towards its escaping prisoners, but I wouldn't mind betting that the thought occurred to him.

Nevertheless, I always examine very carefully prisoners who claim to have abdominal pain. After all, even notorious E-men (the prison term for escapees) are not immortal, and can suffer medical emergencies. Sod's law states that the one prisoner you don't examine properly will be the one who turns out to have something seriously wrong with him.

So when I was asked to see a young man called Aziz who was complaining of serious abdominal pain, I resolved, as I always do, to examine him properly, despite the fact that he was laughing and joking with the other prisoners, gave the thumbs-up sign to them on his way to the examination room, and continued to walk with the self-assured vulpine lope of the urban predator.

In fact, I recognised him at once as a severe case of Gold Front Tooth Syndrome. There has been a frightening epidemic of golden dentistry in our inner cities: one sees the gleam of it in every nook and cranny in the prison, mainly among youths of Jamaican and Pakistani descent, though it seems to be spreading fast among the whites. I suspect that half the crime in this country is committed not to purchase drugs, as the conventional wisdom holds, but gold front teeth.

There are, of course, several styles of gold front teeth. There is, for example, the whole row of gold teeth, which may sometimes be replacements for the originals amateurishly extracted with baseball bats. Then there is the golden rim around one, two or three teeth, and the golden edge that is to a normal tooth what an iron toe-cap is to a normal shoe.

Sufferers from Gold Front Tooth Syndrome are recidivists who see nothing wrong in what they do and are even proud of it. They are cheerful and never commit suicide, unlike other prisoners. Lack of self-esteem is the least of their problems. The girlfriends they are about to abandon are always pregnant: indeed, pregnancy is to their girlfriends what designer stubble is to certain celebrities. They walk with their legs slightly apart and their arms swinging in front of them. They have springs in the balls of their feet.

Aziz was a fulminating case: no hope for him, I am afraid (or rather, for those with whom he comes in contact 'on the out'). Otherwise, though, there was nothing wrong with him. I told him so.

'You mean I'm not going out to hospital?' he said.

'No,' I replied.

'I thought you was here to help me,' he said. 'You're just flogging me off.'

'No I'm not,' I replied. 'I wouldn't get anything for you.'

Later, I saw a woman who complained of headaches and unhappiness.

'I'm in a battered relationship,' she said.

It was not her first such, of course. She had three children by three different men, all of whom had abandoned her, but not before strangling her a little, blacking her eye a few times and knocking her unconscious.

'And how are the children?' I asked.

They were fine, she said, except that the eldest had begun to steal cars, which is the modern equivalent of measles, although it is unlikely that a vaccine will be found against it.

'Does your current boyfriend live with you?' I asked.

'No, he's in prison,' she replied.

'What for?'

'Kidnap.'

'Of whom?'

'A man. He owed him some money.'

'He's been in prison before?'

'Yes, lots of times.'

'And he's violent to you?'

'Yes. You see, he's very jealous. He doesn't like me to talk to no one. That's how the rows start.'

'Has he had his hands round your throat?'

'Yes, a few times. But he's never squeezed hard.'

'And what else?'

'Well, he's give me a broken rib, and he's slashed me across the back with a smashed glass. But don't get me wrong, doctor, he's not a bad person. He's brilliant with the kids.'

'And of course you visit him in jail?'

'Yes, otherwise there'd be a row between us.'

'He sounds as if one day he might kill you.'

'It's funny you should say that. I've often thought he's the one of all of them who'll kill me.'

'But he's not a bad person?'

'No, not really.'

Each man kills the thing he loves, but each woman is killed by the thing she loves.

The Poetry Of The Welfare State

WHEN I WAS 12 years old, I had an English teacher whom I admired to the point of hero-worship, one of whose aphorisms was that poetry was man's natural form of expression. It was prose, in his view, that was unnatural. I came to think this an absurd and overwrought idea, but now I am not so sure. Age, of course, makes us more rigid in our beliefs; but experience makes us more flexible.

Yes, it is true that people, and not necessarily the best-educated among us, often speak in poetry. For example, I was in the prison last week when I heard a few lines of the purest verse. A female officer had refused to give an inmate more tablets than the doctor had prescribed, to which he responded with the words, 'Listen, you bitch, I'm gonna cut your tits off and nonce your children.'

What command of language, what rhythm, what verbal inventiveness! This was the first time I had heard the noun 'nonce' (sex offender) used as a verb. Imagine it in verse form:

Listen, you bitch.
I'm gonna cut your tits off
And nonce your children.

This is the very lyricism of the slums, the poetry of the welfare state.

Perhaps it was on account of the rhythmical quality of his outburst that he was not punished for it; in any case, it would be quite wrong to inhibit self-expression, and possibly damaging to the psyche also.

Drugs, of course, are a well-known aid to self-expression, but they are used for other purposes as well. For example, in the hospital that same week I had a patient who was admitted with what was described in the notes as an overdose of cocaine (what is the correct dose?). He had been taking cocaine for years, and I asked him why he started.

8

'I was just trying to shut down, trying to take everything away. Now I take it and take it until something happens, until my mind stops working overtime.'

I guessed from his tattoos – ACAB (All Coppers Are Bastards) on his knuckles, a policeman hanging from a lamppost on his left ankle and a cannabis leaf on his upper arm – that he had sometimes been in conflict with the law, and I asked him about his latest imprisonment.

'It wasn't for violence, it was for a verbal.'

Now, however, he had a health problem.

'Doctor,' he said, 'I've got severe anger loss.'

He meant, of course, that he was always going into one and losing it.

The patient in the next bed had taken an overdose because his girlfriend had left him and he was on bail for having assaulted her.

'I know I've given her a good slap now and again,' he protested, 'but a slap's just a slap.'

They'd fallen out over the care of their child.

'I told her it's my baby's inside you, I don't want you to fucking get rid of it. But I still have feelings for her, even though she's a crackhead and a smackhead.'

I asked him about his relations with his parents.

'My father don't speak to me no more,' he said.

'Why not?' I asked.

'He says I tried to run him over.'

'And did you?'

'No, of course I fucking didn't. I've been brought up old-fashioned, to respect my olders. If I'd run him over, I'd've put my hands up to it, wouldn't I?'

There Is Only One Way To Escape British Squalor

WHY THE BRITISH want to reproduce themselves is a question which is as puzzling in its own way as that of the origin of life. Their existence is so wretched, so utterly lacking in anything reasonably resembling a purpose, so devoid of those things that make human life worthwhile (I am merely paraphrasing what thousands have told me) that it is a marvel that they should go in for children. I suppose the nearest I can come to an explanation is that they hope a child will supply the want that they feel: the triumph of hope over experience, for they soon discover that a British child merely adds chores to emptiness.

However, there is a small sub-group of our population that recognises the undesirability of reproducing itself: I mean, of course, some fathers, or perhaps I should say, to be more accurate, baby-fathers. Between fathers, in the old sense, and baby-fathers there is a great gulf fixed. A baby-father is an inseminator merely: the term derives from Jamaican culture, or – again to be more accurate – I should say behaviour.

A true baby-father neglects his offspring, except to buy it a pair of shoes now and again when he wants access to 'his' baby-mother, to have sex with her and beat her up either afterwards or before. I mustn't generalise, of course: not all baby-fathers are the same, and some believe that prevention is better than neglect. In accordance with this wise view, they attempt to prevent their babies from ever being born, by procuring miscarriages.

There are two main techniques for bringing about this desirable end: they pull their baby-mothers by their hair to the top of the stairs and push them down, or they kick them in the stomach. Of course these methods are not mutually exclusive, and some use both. That'll teach women to conceive, or (as they say) fall pregnant.

Some baby-mothers never learn, however. Last week I met a baby-mother whose baby-father had thrown her down the stairs and kicked her in the stomach while she was pregnant, yet subsequently had – I use her own words – 'two kids for him'. Of these, one had narrowly missed being kicked into touch, as it were: my own hospital saved the pregnancy after the kicking. Now that we believe that adopted children have a right to know who their biological parents are, should children who narrowly miss being aborted by their fathers have a similar right to knowledge?

That same day, I was preparing to go abroad for a short and much-needed rest from British state-promoted squalor. I went to bed late – half-past one – after finishing a couple of medical reports before my departure. At 4.20 a.m. came an urgent and insistent ringing on my doorbell. Blearily I answered it to a drunk woman in her thirties, swaying in a miasma of stale alcohol.

'Can I use your phone to call the police?' she asked. 'I've been raped.'

I asked her in, dialled the number and handed her the receiver. She was too drunk to explain coherently what had happened. A few minutes later, the police arrived. Seeing them, she said, 'Oh, let's forget it.'

A policewoman spoke into her radio. 'She's homeless. She appears to be destitute.'

The woman was mortally offended.

'I'm not a prostitute, I'm not!' she cried.

There is, it seems, only one way to escape British squalor, and that is to escape Britain. Closing your front door behind you is not enough.

Pure And Unvarnished Truth

IN THE PREFACE to *Martin Chuzzlewit*, Dickens replied to those who accused him of being a mere caricaturist. What is caricature to one man, he said, is pure and unvarnished truth to another.

He was certainly right, at least with regard to language. Though few recognise it, people in this country are still speaking pure Dickensian, for which I thank God. To listen to my patients complaining in Standard English would be the purest torture.

Of course, the beauty of Dickensian speech depends wholly upon the existence of Standard English, but that is another matter. There would be no uplift, no soaring of the spirit, in Mrs Gamp feeling so dispoged, if there were no correct way to speak. No doubt there is an educational theorist somewhere who will object that there is nothing wrong with dispoged, because Betsy Prig knew exactly what Sairey Gamp meant by it; but this is an argument not worth dispoging of.

A single phrase often makes my day. I think I have not lived entirely in vain if I have heard something poetic, inventive, original and wrong. An avalanche of drivel may bury a verbal gem, and so one must listen attentively. A moment's lapse of concentration and it is lost for ever, irrecoverable. I try to impart this wisdom to my students, but few if any listen.

I once had a patient who could hardly open his mouth without uttering a perfectly formed malapropism. Alas, he is no more: but when I get to heaven, I expect him to greet me there, still complaining that the antibionics have given him a gastric stomach.

Last week, I was talking to a man about the reason he was in prison. He had beaten up his baby-mother's latest boyfriend.

'Why?' I asked.

'He was baby-sitting and he was cracked out of his face.'

'Cracked out of his face': how succinct and expressive, so much more vigorous than, say, 'intoxicated by an excess of crack cocaine'. I asked him what he had done.

'I didn't want no crackhead looking after Gemma, so I took her upstairs – they're on the brown, like, so they're nice and quiet – and then I went downstairs to sort him out.'

Being 'on the brown', by the way, is taking heroin.

I asked him whether he had ever been violent before.

'My first sentence was for violence.'

'What did you do?'

'I beat up my best mate.'

'Why, if he was your best friend?'

'I caught him shagging my ex-missis, the one before my baby-mother. They was banging away, so I went and got a piece of scaffold.'

I asked him whether he had ever been violent to his baby-mother.

'When we argued, it was aggressive.'

It? What was the 'it' to which he referred? In this context 'it' technically means the relationship between a man and a woman, at least one of whom is violent.

'What do you mean?' I asked.

'Well, I mean we was having a bit of a scrap in the street and her mother comes running up to me and tries to head-butt me.'

'And did she succeed?'

'No, she couldn't, she was pissed up. She's always on the piss.'

'But did she attack you often?'

'Only when she was pissed off with me.'

How Terrible It Must Be
To Live In Switzerland

I ARRIVED ON my ward last week just in time to hear a woman on the television shriek, 'It's disgusting!'

I agreed with her completely, of course, though I never found out what it was that had disgusted her. Since everything these days disgusts me, I think it follows in strict logic that I was in full agreement with her.

Disgust, I have noticed as I grow older, is a pleasure that never palls. I spend many happy hours discussing my disgust and its objects with my friends, who are all of like mind. How terrible it must be to live in Switzerland, where everything is perfect and nothing is disgusting. What on earth do the Swiss find to talk about? Remove disgust from my conversation, and I should fall silent.

Watching television from adjacent beds in the ward were two young people, the first of whom had metal studs in his lips, ears, eyebrows and tongue. His arms were tattooed with pseudo-Maori and Japanese designs, as if he hoped to be mummified after death and exhibited in the Museum of Mankind. He was in hospital because he was suffering from some of the less-desired effects of what are popularly known as 'recreational' drugs. Before passing out under their influence, he had managed – also under their influence, he said – to beat his girlfriend so badly that she ended up in our intensive care unit.

I wanted to find out whether he was what I call a recreational beater of girlfriends. 'I've only ever done it once before, doctor,' he said.

'When was that?'

'I was out of my skull on drugs at the time, doctor. It wasn't really me talking, it was the drugs.'

This, I suppose, is the 21st century equivalent of spirit possession.

'Doctor, I think I need help with my temper.'

'How about not taking drugs?'

'That's easier said than done.'

In the bed next to his was a young woman with lime-green hair and a black eye. She also had a ring through her nose – I dare say that, had I asked, she would have told me she was easily led. That would probably have explained why she had LOVE and HATE tattooed on her knuckles.

I interviewed her in my room. She had been sexually abused as a child in the normal fashion – that is to say, by her mother's boyfriend – and ever since puberty she had consorted with jealous, drunken, drug-taking, violent criminal men. She was in hospital because she'd taken an overdose of sleepers. This was after Leroy (her third boyfriend of that name) had half-strangled her. I asked whether he half-strangled her often.

'No, only once before. That was a long time ago.'

'How long?'

'I don't know.'

'Go on, have a guess.'

She looked for inspiration at the reproduction on my wall: the portrait of Giovanna Tornabuoni by Domenico Ghirlandaio. It jogged her memory. 'About a month.'

'He sounds dangerous to me,' I said.

'Our relationship's always been violent,' she said, as if in complete contradiction to my remark.

'Why do you stay with him?'

'Leroy's the best thing that ever happened to me.'

'You mean the second best,' I said.

'What do you mean?' she asked.

'I saw you exchanging telephone numbers with the man in the bed next to yours.'

Men Of No Talent

HAVING SPENT SO LONG, if not in the lower depths exactly, at least among their inhabitants, it is not surprising, perhaps, that I see the lower depths wherever I go. My experience haunts me, and I am on the lookout for them. For example, not long ago I was in a bookshop in a chic part of Paris when I picked up a book by a young woman who called herself simply Leila. The title of the book was *Mariée De Force* (Forced Marriage), and the cover showed the eyes of a young woman peering out of a slit in a black veil.

The book recounts the life of a young woman, born in France of Moroccan parents. Everything she recounted reminded me of my young female patients of Pakistani origin: everything, in fact, was exactly the same. She was allowed no freedom at all; if she failed to obey her male relatives with the alacrity of a slave or, worse still, showed the slightest sign of independence, she was accused of prostitution and then beaten into obedience. Her brothers defended her 'honour' – that is to say, their own right to lord it over a female slave called a wife, while indulging themselves elsewhere to their hearts' content – by spying on her constantly and denouncing her to her parents. And her father perpetuated the whole horrible social system by forcing her to marry a Moroccan boy who wanted to marry her so that he could live in France. 'It was a rape pure and simple,' she said, 'to which he wanted me to submit.'

The book caused me to tremble with rage, so many times had I heard the story from my own patients. I had to move on to another book in the shop, or everyone would think I was a lunatic escaped from the asylum. I picked up a book by the Hungarian novelist Sándor Márai called *Mémoires de Hongrie*. In the first few pages there was an anecdote that explains the current state of Britain better than anything else I know: reading it was like having a Eureka experience.

Márai had a dinner party in Budapest in March 1944, shortly before the arrival of the Red Army. There wasn't much food, but he had wine. One of the guests, a Nazi sympathiser, said that it was necessary to 'remain faithful to our allies'. Márai tried to contradict him, and was surprised by his reply.

'I'm a National Socialist,' he said. 'You can't understand, because you have talent. But I, who haven't any, need National Socialism.' A little while later he added, 'The age belongs to us, we the men who have no talent!'

Who, on reading that, could fail to think of the whole inflated apparatus of British government, especially if he had worked in the National Health Service?

On a train back home, I sat next to a young woman with a pleasant expression, whose manner was definitely not that of the slut class. Her mobile telephone rang, and it seems that even good girls these days do not mind discussing their private affairs in public. She was having difficulty with her boyfriend, who was clearly the jealous type.

'You're not going to be in a mood with me tomorrow, are you?' she asked. 'What do you mean, you don't know? I haven't had no text messages, and I haven't spoken to no-one neither… Steve, please don't be like that, don't be arsey with me… I haven't been ignoring you all day, you know my phone don't work on the Tube.'

When the conversation was over, I spoke to her. 'I hope you don't mind,' I said, 'but I couldn't help overhearing. I'm a doctor, and I hear stories like that every day. You should leave him. You will do so in the end, so you might as well now. Don't waste your life on him, he isn't worth it.'

'I know,' she said, and laughed. 'You're right.'

But she won't leave him, not yet. She'll prefer to be beaten up a few times first.

My Wife Says I Don't Talk Enough

IT IS IN LISTENING to other people talk that you learn to appreciate silence. What higher praise of a man could there be than that he is taciturn? People have only to talk for a short time for it to become obvious that the greatest of human rights is not freedom of opinion, but freedom *from* opinion. It is a mercy that there are so many languages that one does not understand.

While in Venice recently I joined a queue for an exhibition in the Doge's Palace. It was very long, and the conversation behind me obtruded itself upon my consciousness.

It was between a middle-aged couple, formerly of Detroit, Michigan, but now of Sarasota, Florida (out of the frying pan into the warm bath, as it were), and a young Canadian woman, the large number of whose earrings in her upper ear served as her Declaration of Independence.

They had formed the equivalent of a shipboard friendship and the young Canadian poured out her soul to the American couple. She had been travelling in Italy for some time and had arrived in Venice the night before. She gave her initial impressions of the city that has enchanted so many people before her.

'I was so happy to arrive here,' she said. 'It was the first hotel I'd been in with a bathtub.'

'Wow!' said the Floridan couple in concert.

'I wish I could describe it to you,' the Canadian continued. Then her wish came true. 'It's like, deep and wide. It's awesome. It has two showerheads, one in the place where you normally expect one to be and one on the side. I mean, I just loved it when the two were going together. I filled up the tub and lay there for hours.'

Then came a description of the shower in Sorrento, a town that she had found quite 'westernised'.

'There were ants in it,' she said. 'I mean, you can't have that kind of fun in Canada.'

'I'm not so sure,' said the man from Sarasota, not wishing to impugn the possibilities of enjoyment in the northern climes. 'If you go to the right places…'

'Yes, if you go to the right places,' agreed the Canadian. 'I guess I've just never been to them.'

However, she had been to the right places in Italy all right, including the public conveniences.

'In Florence,' she said, 'I never had to pay more than 50 cents, sometimes only 25.'

'Wow!' remarked the couple again.

'But in Venice I've always had to pay one euro.'

I was about to interject that in that case perhaps she should not carry a bottle of mineral water with her, when I reminded myself that I was not my sister's keeper.

'But if you go to the glass-blowing factory in Murano,' she said, 'it's free.'

Gosh, I thought, for someone who has been in Venice only since last night, she's fitted in a lot.

'That's useful to know,' said the woman from Sarasota.

My wife says I don't talk enough. In that case, I think I must be almost unique.

He Took The Precaution
Of Stabbing Him

FROM TIME TO TIME, our ward looks more like a police lock-up than a haven of healing. By every bed there are two policemen preventing the escape of the patient, and usually watching television at the same time. Sometimes they and their captives chat amicably; at other times there is a sullen silence between them.

Last week we had one of the jollier type of suspects in our ward. He was what is known in the trade as a body packer: a man (or woman) who transports heroin or cocaine by swallowing packets and recovering them from the other end of his digestive tract a few days later, in the privacy of a lavatory. This is the modern equivalent, I suppose, of the transport of nitroglycerine in *The Wages of Fear*: for one burst packet of cocaine means certain death. I am not sure whether the jolly body packer was unaware of the danger he was in, or merely set a low value on his own life.

The police, of course, were interested in his faeces. The law states, however, that an Englishman's poo is his property, and to search it without the owner's consent requires a search warrant. I had mistakenly supposed that, once shed, it was in the public domain. One learns these arcane things through experience.

I spoke in private to the body packer about his life. He prefaced his remarks by admitting that he was no angel, in case I was under any misapprehension on that score. If I had been, his gold front tooth alone would have disabused me. His body bore the scars of various fights: he had been 'cut' many times, though he had no bullet wounds as yet, and therefore wasn't a real man. I asked him whether he was violent.

'No,' he said. 'I'm peaceful. But I don't like parties where there's a lot of bare niggers.'

20

'Bare niggers?'

'Niggers with attitude, bad boys. Then I can get aggressive, and things happen.'

His latest knife-fight had been with an old adversary.

'The boy was a typical boy who acts bad, who comes on bad.'

'Who is he?'

'His nickname's Snake.'

'Why?'

''Cause he's like a python, he's got a deadly sting.'

'Pythons are not poisonous,' I said. Imprecision in such matters brings out the pedant in me.

'Well, Snake is.'

One day they had a minor contretemps in the street. Snake, who was with some friends, drew away and immediately started calling people on his mobile phone.

'What was he saying?'

'He was getting people to come and get me kidnapped, or hole me up.'

'Hole you up?'

'Yes, shoot me, put holes in me.'

Next time he saw Snake, he took the precaution of stabbing him a few times. Snake had asked for it: he had taunted him by saying, 'Come here, pussy, come here. Bring it on.' So he did.

'And now? What's going to happen next?'

'I've had these phone calls from friends of Snake.'

'What do they say?'

'We know where you live, you're fucked wherever you are, you're fucked if you're in prison and you're fucked if you're not.'

No wonder he was so cheerful on the ward. Eat, drink and be merry, for tomorrow we die.

Nietzsche Had The Advantage Of Suffering From Neurosyphilis

ALL FLESH IS GRASS, of course – that goes without saying – but, round here, it is also batteries, coins, razor blades, bleach, 'wraps' of cocaine and heroin, and anything else that can pass down the human gullet. Some people come to the hospital, indeed, with entrails like a small hardware store. The surgeons are forever retrieving bits and pieces from the guts of the disgruntled. In our district, getting down to the nuts and bolts is no mere metaphor.

There has been an epidemic of swallowing lately. One poor deluded soul swallowed a battery because he thought he was a robot and needed power. Another poor deluded soul thought he could elude the attentions of the police by swallowing the evidence, in this case heroin wrapped in condoms. He refused to have blood tests until his solicitor was present.

In the prison the day before, a prisoner informed me that he had swallowed a bottle of washing-up liquid. I asked him why.

'My cellmate said he'd beat me up if I didn't.'

This, of course, brings us to the interesting question as to why anyone would demand of another that he drink a bottle of washing-up liquid. I suppose it would take a Nietzsche to answer that particular question; but then Nietzsche had the inestimable advantage, from the point of view of explaining human behaviour, of suffering from neurosyphilis.

The things people do to themselves! I suppose by now I shouldn't be surprised at it, but having grown up in an ordered world in which I was by far the least rational person I knew, I am still shocked by the insouciance with which people destroy themselves. That doesn't prevent them from blaming others, of course.

Drug addicts are among the most enthusiastic, or at any rate most successful, of self-destroyers. You'd think that British housing estates were concentration camps to see the state in which the young men who live in them arrive for a sojourn at Her Majesty's expense. They come in hollow-chested, sallow-skinned, sunken-eyed, rotten-toothed; one rubs one's eyes and wonders what century one is in. Prison is a health resort by comparison with a British housing estate.

The arms of drug addicts are so horrible that I avert my eyes. You'd also think our housing estates were infested by vicious tsetse flies that confined themselves to biting along the line of the veins of the arm. Quite often such arms bear dark, purplish-black lumps, rather like buboes, where an abscess is forming when the addicts have missed the vein and injected into the tissue instead. And of course they're all on methadone – known round here as 'meffs' – as well. Just as alternative medicine is actually additional (additional, that is, to the orthodox variety), so round here methadone does not supplant heroin; it supplements it.

Last week a prisoner told me that, 'on the out, like', he was prescribed '80 ml of meffs a day'. I pointed out to him that the numerous injection sites on his arms suggested to me (I told him that one didn't have to be Sherlock Holmes to deduce it) that he took heroin as well. And methadone, I said, was supposed to be taken as a substitute for heroin, not as a top-up.

'Yeah, but it's prescribed to stop me feeving, doctor,' he said.

'And what are you in here for?' I asked.

'Feft,' he replied.

One Long, Boring, Grinding Day After Another

WHO HATH WOE? who hath sorrow? who hath contentions? who hath babbling? who hath wounds without cause? who hath redness of eyes?

No prizes for guessing the answer: they that tarry long at the wine, of course, especially what the Bible calls 'mixed wine', the ancient equivalent of our White Lightning, snakebite and Special Brew. The current favourite among the park-benchers, if I may so call them, is 8.4 per cent cider, an appalling liquid which comes in two- and three-litre bottles known technically as 'rubber ducks'.

'Why are they called that?' I asked a patient who belonged to the park-bench culture.

'I don't really know. It's because they float in the bath or the pond, I suppose.'

'Not with two or three litres of cider in them.'

'But they never have two or three litres in them for long.'

True enough: I've seen many a rubber duck in the gutter, but never a full one.

'And when did you last work?' I asked.

He screwed up his eyes and scoured his brain, like an archaeologist scratching around in the sand for traces of remote antiquity.

'1976,' he said, after much delay.

'How have you kept yourself since then?'

'I've been on the Sick.'

'What illness?'

'Drink. It's not that I'm stupid, doctor, it's just that I'm addictable.' A sudden happy thought came to him, like a mitigating circumstance after an unexpected verdict of guilty. 'I did do a bit of work, though, for a couple of weeks.'

'Where?'

'In this factory. Only I couldn't do it for long, I kept getting nervous and shaking in the morning and being sick.'

'So either the work or the drinking had to go, and you chose the work?'

'Well, I didn't know about the morning drink in those days, doctor.'

Happily, his knowledge of morning drink had increased since then. He lived with an alcoholic woman – 'one of the best pianists in the country, doctor, when she's sober' – and together they rose early.

'We wake up and start drinking at 5 o'clock in the morning.'

'I suppose it's a question of the early bird catching the vermouth. And why did you come to hospital?'

'It was my doctor who sent me. His name abates me. He said I had no blood in me. I said it wasn't because I cut my wrists or anything, it must be because I keep throwing it up.' He shook his head sorrowfully. 'To tell you the truth, doctor, the drinking is abysmal.'

'Are you sure it's the drinking that's abysmal?' I asked.

'Of course, it doesn't help that she's an alcoholic too. She's a lovely woman, but put a drink in her and it's like playing with a snake.'

'Are you violent towards her?'

'Yes, but it's six of one and half a dozen of the other. She beat me up on video once, it's humiliating, me being a bloke and all that.'

'And are you going to stop?'

'Well, I'll have to, doctor. I mean when you're drinking it's just one long, boring, grinding day after another.'

'Unlike being at work,' I said.

Old Isaiah was right after all: woe unto them that rise early in the morning, that they may follow strong drink; that continue until night, till wine inflame them!

The Tweeded Pedants,
Of Whom I Am One

IF YOU WOULD like to see the kind of out-at-elbow tweed jackets once beloved of schoolmasters before they discovered the joys of earrings and the like, and still by far my preferred apparel, you must go to provincial book fairs.

They are smaller and less frequented than they used to be. It is a strange thing, but I am now usually at the lower end of the age spectrum of the people who attend the events that I enjoy. I have the not altogether unsatisfying impression that civilisation is collapsing around me. Is it my age, I wonder, or the age we live in? I am not sure. Civilisations do collapse, after all, but on the other hand people grow old with rather greater frequency.

There are two types of people who attend provincial book fairs: the tweeded pedants, of whom I am one, and the nylon-padded monomaniacs, who tend to smell unwashed and who collect books on (say) road building or double-decker buses of the world.

But we are all eyed with something approaching malevolence by many of the booksellers. They have all, I think, read, marked and inwardly digested that short but very great late Victorian work, *The Enemies of Books*, by William Blades. It has wonderful plates, including one of John Bagford, shoemaker and biblioclast, and another of a charwoman burning a Caxton in a fireplace. In a series of chapters on the destroyers of books that resembles a great chain of being, and that rises from the inorganic forces of destruction, fire and water, to those of insects and other vermin, and proceeds via bigotry to human boys, especially those aged between six and 12, and female servants who would clean books – 'Dust!' says Blades, 'it is all a delusion. It is not the dust that makes women anxious to invade the inmost recesses of your Sanctum, it is ingrained curiosity' – he finally reaches the worst and most ferocious enemies of books, book collectors, who are worse even than book-binders. That is the indelible lesson that most booksellers must have learnt from Blades.

I knew a bookseller who was so ill-disposed to his clientele that he often would not open his door to them, and those privileged persons that he allowed to enter were subjected to recordings of Schoenberg to ensure that they did not linger. He once refused to sell me a history of Sierra Leone – I was writing a book about Liberia at the time – because he thought my purposes in wishing to possess it were insufficiently serious. He thought my projected book frivolous. Several reviewers agreed with him, I am sad to say.

On this latest occasion, however, I found a congenial seller who did not find me totally unworthy of his stock.

I dithered over a very expensive but beautiful early edition of a famous 17th-century work, and finally agreed on a price, somewhat lower than that marked in pencil on the inside cover. 'You couldn't rub that out, could you?' I asked. 'My wife would be horrified.'

He took out a labour-saving device that I had never seen before, an electric rubber.

'You'd be surprised,' he said as it went to work, 'how many customers ask me to do that.'

I Was Just Trying It On To Get Some Sleepers

I PREFER ALCOHOLICS to drug addicts. They are more often people of character and are much more amusing. Even their special pleading (for themselves) is often funny, and they can be brought to see it. By contrast, drug addicts whine horribly and frequently turn nasty.

I see a lot of drug addicts. They clutch their abdomens with their arms in an effort to impress the doctor with the severity of their withdrawal symptoms, intestinal cramps being one of them. But as often as not the doctor has seen them laughing and joking with their peers shortly before.

Last week a drug addict came to see me in the prison.

'Will I get my meffadone?' he asked.

'No,' I replied.

'What about sleepers?'

'No, no sleepers either.'

'But I can't sleep. I haven't slept for three days. I got to get my head down.'

'No sleepers.'

'Then it's on your head,' he said. 'It'll be on your conscience.'

'What will?'

'You'll see.'

He meant suicide, of course. Were it not for the administrative inconvenience that his suicide would cause afterwards – not that it was very likely, except as a stupid gesture that got out of hand – I should have taken the Humean view that self-slaughter was his inalienable right. Instead, I gave orders that his clothes were to be removed and he was to be put in Home Office issue clothing, specially designed to prevent their being used for hanging.

The addict was horrified. 'That's not necessary, guv,' he said. 'I don't want to go into a strip cell.'

'But you're suicidal.'

'Naaaah!' he exclaimed. 'I was just trying it on to get some sleepers.'

'So you're a liar?'

'Yes,' he said.

'So how do I know that you can't sleep?'

He left the room, cured of his suicidal tendencies and his insomnia. As he did so, I thought how, if we ever rebuilt the Academy in modern England, we should inscribe the words 'Just Trying It On' instead of 'Know Thyself' over its portal.

Pusillanimous Doctors Versus Ambitious Dimwits

ANYONE WHO DOUBTS that, at least from the cultural point of view, the Soviet Union won the Cold War in Britain hands down should attend a conference organised for doctors about impending organisational changes in the National Health Service (and organisational changes are always impending in the NHS).

There he will be convinced that every doctor will soon have a political commissar working alongside him to remind him of his wider responsibilities to government and party.

Doctors in Britain are now roughly in the position of Tsarist generals, scientists and 'specialists' in the first phase of the Russian Revolution: necessary but distrusted, hated and feared, and to be eliminated altogether as soon as possible. The British revolution, however, has been carried out neither by the proletariat nor in the name of the proletariat: it is, rather, the revolution of the ambitious but ungifted, of whom there is a gross oversupply. For everyone is persuaded these days that there is only one thing worth having, and that thing is power.

Recently I attended, for the sheer fun of it, a conference about some forthcoming changes to the NHS. One of the lectures was given by a lady apparatchik from the Department of Health whose grimacing attempts at smiles, and whose bodily writhing as she tortured the English language with neologisms, acronyms and platitudes in the service of evident untruth, made Gordon Brown's bonhomie seem like a model of spontaneity. She knew what the assembled doctors thought of her, so in a sense she was being brave; at one point in what I suppose I must call her 'presentation' there was a single guffaw of contemptuous laughter.

It was an illuminating moment, a flash of lightning in a moonless night-time landscape.

For a moment I felt almost sorry for the speaker: you could see the panic on her face, a fear lest 150 doctors turn on her and demand explanations in comprehensible language.

Alas, doctors are far too well brought up and chivalrous (or is it pusillanimous?) to humiliate an ambitious dimwit in public; and so the ambitious dimwits live to plot their revenge and increase their power.

Once in the Equatorial Guinean capital of Malabo I spent a very happy afternoon counting the number of aid agencies whose white Land Cruisers passed me in the street (the only vehicles there were). I counted 27 agencies in all, which goes to show that corrupt dictatorships are the boon of aid agencies. And I had a friend who played a game of special cricket in his mind whenever he was in the company of an eminent but notoriously self-obsessed colleague. A run was scored every time the colleague said 'I'; there was a wicket whenever he uttered a sentence without mentioning himself. Needless to say, no innings was ever completed.

In like fashion, I spent the conference counting the acronyms. Of course, I may have missed a few after lunch, when my stomach was full of soggy quiche and a banana. Here is a list, probably not exhaustive; RIA, BIA, HEI, ASW, PQ, GSCC, IMCA, MCA, DOLS, PCT, LA, CSIP, AMHP, NWW, CPA, MDT, MHA, LPA, SCT, EMI, ECHR, EPA, SHA, AC, RMP, CRMO, NR, CTO, SOAD, RC. The best acronyms, of course, should provide no clue as to their meaning, and yet be bandied about as if the meaning were known to all. Once their meaning is known to all, however, their bureaucratic utility declines: for acronyms are to modern bureaucrats what incantations are to ancient shamans.

The Metaphorical
Urban Darkness

SCRATCH THE SURFACE and there is always tragedy, mixed, of course, with wickedness.

Because of the economic crisis, I was waiting at the bus station: £2.80 for a bus instead of £28 for a taxi home. I had 50 minutes to wait and was reading a book by Richard Yates. I was wondering why the literature of so optimistic a country as America was so deeply pessimistic (awareness of death is the answer, of the bust after the boom of life from which there is no upturn), when a lady in her eighties sat down beside me. She was tired. Her cheeks puffed and her lips pouted as one with chronic obstructive pulmonary disease.

'I prefer to take taxis,' she said to me, 'but I took one yesterday and I can't do it all the time. I've got a little in the bank, but you never know how long you'll last.'

These days, you don't know how long the bank will last, either, but I didn't say that.

She told me the story of her daughter, aged 44, whose consort, aged 57, had died of cancer a couple of months ago.

'He was perfectly fine until last Christmas, then he wasted away and he was like a little old man by the time he died. He was a lovely feller.' Her daughter hadn't bothered to get divorced from her first husband until it was clear that her consort, with whom she had lived ten years out of wedlock, was dying.

She finally got her divorce, and shortly before his death asked the registrar to marry them at home, he on his deathbed.

'The registrar telephoned her and said I'm sorry to have to tell you that there's been an objection to the marriage. I'm not allowed to tell you who it was.' But it was obvious: it was his former wife and their children, who were worried about the inheritance. They went round to the dying man's house two days before he died and created such a disturbance that the police had to be called, but they left before the arrival of the police. They had learnt that their objection to the marriage had made no difference, since he had long ago changed his will. Their parting words to the old lady's daughter as they left were, 'Enjoy your little house.' They were still making trouble.

The old lady caught a bus before mine, and a respectable old couple came and sat beside me. We were soon joined by a drunk in his late thirties, his clothes filthy.

His face had obviously kept many casualty departments busy in the past, and he had a cut with stitches over his left eyebrow.

Swaying and lurching towards the old couple, he asked them where his bus-stop was.

'That depends,' said the woman gently, 'where you're going.' This came to him with the force of revelation. He propped himself up against the glass of the bus-shelter and slid slowly down it on to his haunches.

'I'll have to think about it,' he said. 'Wait a bit.'

I thought of a line of Gloucester's in *Lear* and adapted it in my mind: I have no way, and therefore want no bus.

If it is possible to crawl to your feet, he did so. 'Want to hear a joke?' he asked. 'What do you call a rabbit with a bent dick?'

This was clearly a question that the old couple had not previously considered.

'A rabbit with a bent dick,' he said.

The bus arrived, he didn't get on it, and soon we were speeding along the literal darkness of the country lanes, instead of lingering in the metaphorical urban darkness.

You're Not Me

RECENTLY WHILE TRAVELLING on the London Underground, the opening words of Marx's *The Eighteenth Brumaire of Louis Bonaparte* ran through my mind like a refrain:

> 'Hegel remarks somewhere that all great world historic events and personages appear, so to speak, twice. He forgot to add: the first time as tragedy, the second time as farce.'

Why, you might ask, did this passage insinuate itself into my brain on the District Line between West Brompton and Earl's Court?

Standing opposite me was a young man badly dressed in black, on whose baseball cap was inscribed the word 'Victim'. On his black T-shirt were the words, 'I wish I could be you', which implied self-pity on an industrial scale. On his right forearm (from which, Sherlock Holmes-like, I inferred he was left-handed) were a series of parallel scars from self-inflicted injury. On his left forearm was tattooed a simplified reproduction of a picture by Gustav Klimt. All paintings appear twice: the first time as art, the second time as kitsch.

Reaching my destination, there was an announcement over the public address system. Because of the hot weather, it said, passengers are advised to carry a bottle of water with them while travelling, and passengers who felt unwell were advised to seek assistance. Who, I wondered, would help me with my profound sense of irritation?

I was on my way to lunch with an old doctor friend. He was in a lather of indignation, as usual, against the administration and its Newspeak. He was particularly exercised by the term 'quality assurance', the *locus standi* of yet another layer of bureaucracy.

'The problem is,' he said, 'that no one can be against quality.'

Then we started to utter slogans by turns.

'Down with quality!'

'Down with equity!'

'Down with easy access!'

'Down with world class!'

'Fewer patients, more paperwork!'

'Shorter consultations, longer lunches!'

The other customers in the restaurant of the Royal Academy – for that is where we were – must have thought we were lunatics with delusions of medical qualifications who had been let out for the day.

Later that afternoon, I waited for my wife at a pub near a well-known railway station. It was pleasant to sit outside with a drink, even if most of the other drinkers had shaven heads or pony-tails, or (in one case) both. The only woman around, before my wife arrived, was also a man.

He was clearly in the throes of the sex change, for he dressed like a woman, and had breasts, but spoke and behaved like a man. I wouldn't have mentioned this had he not spoken so volubly about something called a 'gender assignment certificate'.

Here indeed is a new field for bureaucracy to till. I suggest such certificates be made compulsory, like identity cards. There will be errors, of course, but such is the cost of progress.

I accidentally knocked an empty plastic bottle off my table and it fell at the feet of another drinker. I bent down to pick it up. 'I wouldn't bother if I were you,' he said.

'But you're not me,' I replied.

And then I thought of the man on the District Line: 'I wish I could be you.' Then I wouldn't mind wading through rubbish as I walked down the street.

Thrilled With My Own Importance

MY FIRST CONTACT with the police was through the works of Enid Blyton. I had broken my leg in the school playground and was put to bed with *The Big Noddy Book Number 6*, which had (as I recall) a glossy pink cover. Mr Plod the Policeman was one of the main characters, though I forget the exact nature of his participation in the story. He gave the impression of being amiable, but not as clever as Big Ears.

I first met a flesh-and-blood policeman shortly after some friends and I met a dirty old man in the park. I must have been about eight at the time. The old man had asked us to participate in an activity which I now recognise as disgusting, but which struck me then as merely pointless and peculiar. I told my mother all about it in a matter-of-fact way; to my surprise, I was put to bed once more and a policeman arrived to ask me questions soon afterwards.

How thrilled I was with my own importance! To think that a policeman (as they say in Nigeria, a *whole* policeman) should copy down in a notebook everything I said! It was my finest hour to date.

Let us now fast-forward the video-tape of my memory – to last week, to be precise. Suffice it to say that my attitude towards the police has become a little more nuanced in the intervening period. They appear to me now to be merely men who do a difficult job, with all the failings and temptations to which men who do difficult jobs are heir.

Well, last week I was trapped in one of those hi-tech security gates which make our prisons so difficult to get out of (I'm speaking now of the staff, you understand). Trapped with me were two large men with files under their arms, dressed in the kind of cheap double-breasted suits whose lapels curl almost immediately and which appear permanently crumpled.

Solicitors, I thought at first, my mind's lip curling like their lapels. But solicitors don't generally do weight-training, as these men obviously did, for their muscularity showed clean through their suits. Their shoes were a little too polished for solicitors, and too thick-soled into the bargain. There was something faintly menacing about the way they carried themselves, unlike solicitors, who tend to the Uriah Heep end of the spectrum of bodily habitus.

Eureka! I inwardly exclaimed. *Plainclothes police, beyond a doubt.* It had taken me thirty seconds to work it out.

Last week also, I had a young patient in the ward who had become deeply involved with drug-dealers. At first, they had supplied him with what he wanted; then they paid him to find new customers for them; but finally they said he must actually peddle the drugs himself, for he had failed to find sufficient new customers to justify what they had paid him, and therefore he was in debt to them. Failure to obey would result in the fire-bombing of his flat, or the kidnapping and murder of his infant son. This was debt-bondage, modern British style.

He wanted to speak to the Drug Squad and I called them to see him. They were large men, dressed in jeans and T-shirts. They both had earrings and one had a nose-stud. They had shaved heads, unshaved chins and they chewed gum.

'Hiya, Jason,' they said to Jason. 'What's going down?'

This, I thought, was pure Marie Antoinette playing at shepherdess. There was something indefinably wrong and unconvincing about their performance. I suppose I've grown more critical since I read *The Big Noddy Book Number 6*.

Goering Had Self-Esteem

THERE ARE FASHIONS in virtue as well as in dress, and some virtues are now as passé as the whalebone corset or the satin-lapelled frock-coat. Prominent among these unfashionable virtues is fortitude, which is now not merely unvalued but considered an outright vice. In an age of counselling, emotional incontinence is what we admire. Fortitude is regarded as a form of evasiveness, at best ridiculous, at worst vicious and immoral. He feels most who blubbers longest.

One of the most ardently-desired qualities these days is self-esteem. It seems to me that whoever wants self-esteem already has it, and in more than sufficient measure. I try to tell my patients that it is possible, even likely, that a person has too much self-esteem rather than too little. I cite the example of several prisoners of my acquaintance who, despite having committed the most terrible crimes, remain convinced of their inner rectitude and worth, and walk with a strut like the biggest turkey-cock in the farmyard.

'Goering had self-esteem,' I say to them, if I think they know who Goering was. 'And what does that tell you?'

'What?'

'That the correct measure of self-esteem is in a man's life. If you can have too little, you can also have too much. Thinking about the measure of self-esteem which is your due is like going to the Court of Appeal: your sentence may be reduced, but then again it may also be increased.'

It goes without saying that most people's self-esteem is much stronger without an exacting examination of the justification for it.

Sometimes, of course, the realisation of what one might call one's true wormfulness comes home to one, often in strange, unexpected or arcane ways. Recently a prisoner entered my room for a consultation. Try as I may to disregard a man's crimes when he consults me, sometimes it is beyond my power to do so, and this particular man was a man whose crimes were so heinous that it was difficult to recall in his presence that even the devil may sometimes require the alleviation of pain from haemorrhoids. This man had made a living for many years by cheating old ladies of their life savings, and he had finally bludgeoned one of them horribly to death and raped her – I suspect because she resisted his swindles.

'Doctor,' he said, in that peculiar hangdog, ingratiating, self-pitying whine of his. 'I'm hearing voices – voices in my head, like.'

'And what are they saying, these voices?'

'They're telling me I'm not a very nice person.'

If the hallucination fits, listen to it.

Last week, a young middle-class woman consulted me. She was not unattractive, but her expression was one of frivolous earnestness – that is to say, intense self-absorption. She approached the consultation like the oysters in *The Walrus and the Carpenter*, all eager for the treat. Here at last was an opportunity to talk about herself uninterruptedly and unconstrained by all those boring social conventions.

'What's your problem?' I asked.

'I hate myself.'

'And you've come for a second opinion?'

My Father Had The Worst Manners Of Any Man I Have Ever Met

I WAS PROCEEDING in an easterly direction down the hospital corridor one evening last week after work when my progress was impeded by a man and a young girl sauntering along even more slowly. The man had a bristly shaven head and a spider tattooed on his neck, so I knew at once that the little girl must be his stepdaughter. Men of his type don't have daughters except in the merest biological sense, only stepdaughters, and then not usually for very long. Little girls like her, on the other hand, are never short of stepfathers.

'Excuse me,' I said, making it known that I wished to pass them.

I half expected him to offer me a mouthful of what we in the prison call 'verbal', but what the few henpecked men in the vicinity call 'earache'. He had that pugnacious, uncouth, Gazza look which is so quintessentially English.

Somewhat to my surprise, however, he said nothing, but yanked the little girl's arm violently and pulled her like a recalcitrant sack of potatoes across him, nearly causing criminal damage with her to the wall on his left.

How charmingly, I thought, *the English bring up their children, with what refinement!* Thoughts of my own childhood naturally bubbled back into consciousness after many years of absence, and I began to laugh. For I recalled that, while walking in the street with my mother, she made me tip my school cap to any driver who stopped to let us cross the road.

Was this in the same country, I ask myself; was this in the same century? Reader, it was. It must be admitted, however, that any child who tried nowadays to follow my priggish example would, probably rightly, be accused at once of taking the piss and be run over instantly.

Even in those days, the seeds of decay had been sown. There was a conflict between my parents as to the meaning of good manners. My mother adhered to outward forms, my father to purity of heart and intention. Needless to say, this self-serving romantic conception gave him *carte blanche* to behave any way he liked, and he had the worst manners of any man I have ever met, at least this side of the shaven-headed, tattooed-neck brigade. He had an infallible instinct for saying the most offensive thing possible on every occasion. He believed this gave him a kind of rustic charm, when actually it made his company intolerable for more than a few moments.

Of course, savagery has progressed by leaps and bounds since those days. For example, a man came to me recently in the prison pretending in the most obvious fashion to be ill.

'What's the matter?' I asked. 'Are you in trouble on the wing?'

Before long he confessed that he was being bullied there. He had been beaten up more than once, and there was no prospect in sight of an end to the beatings.

'Why are they victimising you?' I asked.

'Because I'm not from round here,' he said. 'I'm from C___.'

C___ is a town about 20 miles distant. In today's Britain, the accident of having been born 20 miles away is a good enough reason to persecute someone, to injure and maybe even to kill him.

As I was talking to him, a crowd of prisoners outside the room gathered round a television to watch a football match in which the local team was playing. The other side scored a goal, and a deep, angry howl of protest went up which caused the roof to rattle.

'Fucking wankers!'

It Is Not The Earth Which
The Meek Inherit

THERE WORKS IN my hospital a man as unfortunate in his way as any I know. His misfortune is in his face: it is peculiarly thin and fish-like, about as unattractive as it is possible for a human face to be, this side of gross pathology. I think he works in the subterranean caverns of the hospital, among the pumps and the piping: certainly, he is always dressed in a boiler suit.

I see him often walking in the street, or rather slinking, his face turned from the world and towards the nearest wall, anxious lest he allow his fellow men to catch a glimpse of his piscine visage. I must have passed him in the corridor or the street a hundred times, but his eyes have always been averted from mine, as from everyone else's. He looks haunted and hunted, and I imagine he breathes a sigh of relief when he closes his front door behind him, safe from the gaze of the multitude.

I have long wanted to befriend him from a natural sympathy with such unmerited suffering. It is not fair – it is not just – that a man should suffer so through no fault of his own. I imagine, no doubt unreasonably, that he is possessed of talents which have never been allowed to flourish because of his physiognomy. But how can I approach him? No mouse cornered in a kitchen was ever more nervous than he: and what should I say to him? 'Sir, I realise that your unfortunate features have impeded the development of your social life. Permit me to be nice to you.'

The trouble is that in this area of the city any weakness is preyed upon or exploited with a ruthlessness which makes the savannahs of East Africa or the jungles of Brazil seem like a cathedral close in Edwardian England. Last week, for example, a patient of mine, a person of slow intelligence but exemplary character, offered a local shopkeeper a £10 note in exchange for some goods. The shopkeeper, who earlier in the day had been passed a counterfeit note, quickly exchanged this person's note for the counterfeit one residing in his till; then, feigning outrage, he called the police. No legal action was taken against my patient, but he lost his purchases and his £10 note alike. For him the loss of such a sum meant real discomfort.

No, this is not an area for the weak or the reticent. Round here, it is not the earth which the meek inherit, far from it, but a life of terror and abasement. A patient of mine, a mousy young lady of more than average intelligence, described how she − the child of ordinary working-class parents − had somehow conceived the desire to study Egyptology. But so consistent had been the bullying at school, and the ridicule of her peers and teachers alike ('What relevance has Egyptology to your life?'), that she rapidly became a nervous wreck, a state of mind in which the local glue-sniffers, who leave their polythene bags when exhausted of fumes upon her doorstep, had maintained her ever since − as, of course, had the operation of the social security system.

Nowadays, I cannot pass a council housing estate without reflecting upon the wealth of misery, of wasted talent and opportunities, of stunted ambitions, it must contain, and I don't know where to direct my anger: at humanity in general, at the English in particular, or at middle-class intellectuals who witter endlessly on about constitutions and the abolition of the monarchy, because they know nothing of, and care less about, the condition of the people living within a mile of their front door.

His Solicitor Thought He Might Have Some Kind Of Illness

IS THERE, OR could there be, anything more sacred than human life? How precious is our brief flowering or interlude between two eternities of oblivion. That is why the wisdom of ages has accorded to motherhood such deep and abiding respect.

Until now, that is. Last week I was examining a patient who was accused of having assaulted his girlfriend. His solicitor thought he might have some kind of illness that caused him to hit women. He, the solicitor, didn't want to be sued later for having left any stone unturned in the defence of the indefensible.

I asked the defendant about his previous girlfriends. At the age of 14 he had had two: a girl of 15 and a woman of 37. He being of Jamaican descent, and the girl of 15 being a Muslim of Pakistani descent, the relationship ended (for discretion is the better part of underage sex) when her brothers threatened to remove his arms with a machete. The 37-year-old was a white slut – the defendant's words, not mine. And that very week *The Guardian* published an article deploring the lack of interracial friendships in Britain!

He described his later girlfriends. His last was the only one he had hit.

'Any children?' I asked.

'Oh, I forgot,' he said, with the air of someone whose memory had been jolted as if by electricity. 'I missed out my baby-mother.'

'What happened to her?'

'We was together a long time, 18 months.'

Long enough to have two children, in fact; but then they fell out. 'We was arguing all the time, so we split up.'

'Do you see the children?'

'No, her new relationship doesn't want me around.'

My next patient was about the same age as the defendant: 22. In the course of the consultation he told me that he, too, had a child.

'And who's the mother?' I asked.

'Angie,' he replied.

'Angie who?' I asked.

He frowned and rolled his eyes. The thoughts in his skull were like a pinball rattling round a pinball machine.

'Angie… Angie… I can't remember,' he said at length.

My next patient honoured motherhood even more deeply, or at least widely. He had just broken up with his girlfriend.

'Baby?' I asked.

'Just born,' he said. 'A week ago.'

Unfortunately, he and she just weren't getting on, so he had to leave her a few days into his son's life.

'Any other children?' I asked.

'Four,' he said.

'Where are they?'

'All over the place.'

I think my habitual self-command must have failed. An eighth of my working life, after all, goes to pay for this kind of thing, and my face twitched a little.

'I know, I know,' he said.

In those four words, he confessed that everything that I thought was true, and that I was not merely a prejudiced bourgeois: that he knew that such behaviour was not only wicked and selfish, but that it would result in both a social disaster and personal catastrophe for his own children.

All that is necessary for evil to triumph is for the state to subsidise insouciance.

A Very Important Letter

LAST FRIDAY, AT midday precisely, I received a telephone call in my office. 'Hello, this is Human Resources here.'

I can't say I care much for being a Human Resource: it always sounds as if I might be bought up by Rio Tinto Zinc, or some other mining company. I can't help being reminded of the children's encyclopaedia I used to browse through when I was young which had a chemical breakdown of the human body, arranged in neat little piles of the various elements of which we are composed. If I remember rightly, there was enough phosphorus in the human body for a box of matches – or was it a single match? Either way, our Hospital Trust's financial situation is dire, bordering on bankruptcy: perhaps I am needed to light the Chief Executive's cigar. On the other hand, perhaps Human Resources means livers, kidneys and other transplantable organs with which the human body is so richly endowed. I gather the going price in some countries is considerable.

'Hello,' I said.

'Hello,' said a voice, obviously a Tracy of some description. 'Can you be at Trust Headquarters at 2.30 this afternoon? There's a very important letter for you which it is your responsibility to distribute to your staff.'

'An important letter? What's it about?'

'I can't tell you, I don't know, it's embargoed until 2.30 this afternoon.'

'Have I understood you correctly?' I asked. 'You propose that I should come to headquarters, on the other side of the city, in the middle of heavy traffic, to collect a letter, copies of which I must give to my staff?'

'Yes, it's very important.'

'And it's my responsibility to act as a postman?'

'It's your responsibility to distribute the letter to your staff, yes.'

'What about my out-patient clinic?' I asked.

'Your clinic?'

'Yes, my clinic, the one I've been doing every Friday afternoon for the last seven years. You want me to cancel it at an hour's notice in order to collect a letter?'

'I'm only giving you the message.'

'What do you think of the message?'

'What do I think of it?'

'Yes, is it clever or stupid?'

'I don't know.'

'Why can't you fax me the letter?'

'It's confidential.'

'Well, I'm not coming to collect it. I wouldn't collect it even if I could, but I can't.'

I suppose I need hardly add that a week later I still have not received this vital letter which it is my responsibility to distribute to my numberless staff. The birds are still singing and the leaves on the trees have come out, so it couldn't have been that important after all.

But what could it have been about, I wonder? There are so many unsolved mysteries in the world. For example, prostitutes have taken to standing on the street corner of the road in which I live. They are white girls, and I am told by my vigilant neighbour that their customers are all Indians. Their pimps, of course, are black. What is the politically correct response to this situation?

Darren Loved Donna, Which Is Why He Partially Strangled Her From Time To Time

MOBUTU SESE SEKO, it seems to me, is a much traduced man. In the field of social policy he was a most enlightened ruler and was greatly in advance of his time. For example, he lowered the age of consent to 13, legalised polygamy and endowed men with almost infinite rights over their women. He thus made *de jure* what, in an English slum, is merely *de facto*. His code of law, instead of limping lamely after social trends as British law invariably does, was on the contrary in the vanguard of social change – by definition a good thing.

Take the case of Donna, whom I saw last week. At the age of 14, Donna had given birth to Darren's daughter, predictably enough called Jade. Darren was 16 when he became a father, and the happy parents set up home together.

Darren soon grew tired of his responsibilities, but he nevertheless loved Donna, which is why he accused her all the time of having affairs, the slut, and why he partially strangled her from time to time, especially after he'd been at the glue, and why he broke her ribs and blacked her eyes. Once he pushed her all the way out of a closed window (on the ground floor) and Donna called the police, who told her that if only she'd remained indoors they could have done something but because she was out of doors they could do nothing. If she'd been indoors, of course, it would have been the other way round.

At the age of 19, Darren decided that he needed his 'own space', i.e. he moved in with another girl. But that did not prevent him from coming round to Donna from time to time, for respite care as it were, and there he would either make love to her or beat her up, or both. She once tried to lock him out, but he smashed the door down and broke her jaw, so she never tried again.

It is shameful that such a situation should be allowed to continue, with Darren being so uncertain of where he stands. I would suggest a Mobutuan law – possibly even a clause in a written constitution, since written constitutions have historically been the best guarantors of freedom – to the effect that men may physically chastise or beat up any woman with whom they have ever been in the slightest associated. Then, and only then, will the hypocrisy of the present situation be brought to an end.

Just in case anyone should run away with the idea that Darren's case was unique, let me describe Mohammed, aged 22, whom I met the same week, an alcoholic Muslim who broke into a house to burgle it, where he found Tracey, 15 at the time, all alone. Tracey wasn't getting on very well with her mum, Mohammed was charming, so she left the house with him. Six months later, Tracey was pregnant, though she still might not come to term because Mohammed kicks her in the stomach so much and so often. He doesn't allow her out of the house, he locks the doors when he's gone from his (now their) 11th-floor flat, and he demands that she dress, behave and act like a Muslim wife, that is to say obey him in everything.

I think a clause in a written constitution is needed to guarantee religious freedom.

The Pleasure To Be Had
From Flouting Rules
In A Rule-Mad Country

THE OTHER DAY, the 9.56 bus to the nearest train station was late and the people at the stop – of whom I was by far the youngest – began to grumble a little. Then, looming out of the mist, appeared the driver.

'I'm sorry, the brakes have failed,' he said. 'I'm not prepared to risk your lives and they won't be repaired until the next bus.'

The next bus – they are all decrepit round here, resuscitated from scrap heaps – was in an hour's time. Words such as 'typical', 'Third World', 'incompetence' and 'economic crisis' ran angrily through my mind.

'Thanks very much for letting us know,' said the old ladies at the stop with genuine gratitude at his concern for their lives, and then they went off happily in search of a cup of tea.

This morning the bus was on time. A man in his seventies with crutches stood at the first stop after I had got on. Opening the door, the driver called out to him, 'We don't stop here no more. You'll have to use them sticks to hobble to the next stop.' Everyone laughed. The man with crutches was a regular. At the next stop, a woman in her sixties with a progressive degenerative neurological condition got on and found her seat in front of me with jerks and stumbles.

'Don't mind me, dear,' she said to me. 'I'm only dancing.'

An admirable people! Not like those who have replaced them, such as I: querulous and brittle in their self-importance.

Near the front of the bus was a notice:

NO STANDING IN FRONT OF THIS LINE
DO NOT DISTRACT THE DRIVER WHILE THE BUS IS MOVING

The passenger with the crutches hung on manfully to a rail in front of the line and chatted with the driver the whole way. It did one's heart good to see rules in this rule-mad country flouted so without a second thought.

Above my head was another notice, this one with the NHS logo:

IF YOUR GP NEEDS YOU TO SEE A SPECIALIST YOU CAN
CHOOSE TO GO TO ANY HOSPITAL IN ENGLAND, INCLUDING
MANY PRIVATE AND INDEPENDENT ONES – FREE OF CHARGE

If your *GP* needs you to, *nota bene*, not if *you* need to, and not even if he advises you to. Then comes the real character-destroyer:

WHATEVER YOUR REASON, IT'S YOUR RIGHT

Ha! I saw my GP a few weeks ago. It took two weeks and many phone calls to get an appointment. Afterwards, I spent a happy hour or two trying to work out how long it would take in my little town to get to see the same doctor twice.

There are 12 doctors in the practice, in one of those new polyclinic buildings known affectionately to the profession as 'Darzai's khazis'. The women among them are usually on maternity leave and the men, nearing retirement, off sick, leaving the short-term locums. So I estimated that, with determination and effort, and bearing in mind the many imponderables, and ruling out exceptional luck, I might get to see the same doctor twice in nine months or so.

On the way back from the station I took a taxi. There was a notice inside:

IF YOU ARE SICK IT IS AN AUTOMATIC £25 FINE

Crime Pays – For The Professional Classes

THE ABSENCE OF a dynamic economy is a terrible thing. It means that, round here at least, evil is the root of all money.

I am not referring only or even mainly to pimps and drug-dealers. Far from it; I mean the professional classes. The worse the populace behaves, the more money they make.

This inspiring thought occurred to me in the prison last week. I happened to see there a colleague of mine. He is usually quite cheerful, but on this occasion looked a little crestfallen. Naturally, I asked him what the matter was.

'Lee's just been sentenced to life imprisonment,' he said.

I couldn't really see what was so terrible about that. The Lee in question had made it perfectly clear by his conduct that he had no intention of giving up his career of robbery and burglary. That he had at last received a sentence commensurate with his activities seemed to me – as a member of the general public – a cause for rejoicing rather than for lamentation. I confided my thoughts to my colleague.

'But don't you see?' he said. 'Lee gets caught about three or four times a year. Each time the court requests a medical report on him from me. Now they won't need one for a long time.'

I heard of a similar tragedy when I attended court later in the week. Another nice little earner – for the doctors, that is – had been sentenced to life imprisonment. His activities had almost single-handedly paid the school fees of another of my colleagues, who was far more devastated by the sentence than the recipient of it had been. The fact is that crime pays – for the professional classes called upon to deal with criminals.

This time I was in court only briefly. I happened to be present when the previous case was called.

'Are you William Jones?' the clerk of the court asked the man in the dock who, suffice it to say, had not dressed up for the occasion.

'No,' he said.

'Oh,' said the clerk of the court, a little flustered. 'I thought you were. Who are you, then?'

This was surely to get things the wrong way round: it should be sentence first, name afterwards. Whoever he was, he certainly looked guilty enough.

'I've tried to explain to you before,' said the defendant testily. 'I'm Bill Jones, not William.'

The judge looked sternly at him. He had infringed the court's monopoly on pedantry. However, no rebuke was forthcoming. The question the court had to decide was whether it was permissible for the chief prosecution witness to be cross-examined behind a screen on account of the defendant's violence.

The case having been adjourned, the jury for the case in which I was appearing was sworn in. If these were my peers, I'd rather be tried by being thrown in a pond to see whether I floated or sank; the chances of a true verdict would be considerably greater. What a collection! I begin to see why Mr Blunkett wanted to abolish jury trials: the British aren't up to them. Needless to say, they all wore trainers, even though ordinary decent shoes are no more expensive than trainers. And they were dressed in shiny nylon tracksuits of many colours. It gave you migraine just to look at them.

As the Iron Duke would have said, I don't know what they do to the criminals, but, by God, they frighten me!

Gross Misrepresentations Of
Our Country's Situation

WE SHOULD ALWAYS try to see ourselves as others see us, but not when the others are French. They are so biased against us that they can see nothing clearly: their animus obscures their view and makes it worthless.

This was proved to me yet again when I arrived in Paris recently. I always stay in the same hotel in that city, where I have developed my little habits. In the morning, I go out and buy *Le Monde*, which I read at breakfast in the same cafe. This particular morning, *Le Monde* carried a short commentary on the economic situation of Britain.

The satirical rogue who wrote it claimed that the fall in the value of the pound – 17 per cent against the euro in two months – was well justified by the economic situation of our tight little island. For, he said, the deficit in our balance of payments is 3 per cent of our gross national product. Moreover, he continued, the government is borrowing the equivalent of 8 per cent of the GNP this year, a figure that is likely to rise, and foreign currency markets don't like governments that maintain public deficits. True, inflation has fallen, but that is not likely to last long (said this vile Anglophobe) because the value of our importations is a third of the GNP. Mere prejudice led him to claim that inflationary pressures were building.

He admitted that the fall in the value of the pound might benefit our exports, but in the snide and underhand way typical of his nation, he went on to ask: which exports? Could anything establish his bad faith better than the ridiculous suggestion that, before we export something that others wish to buy, we have first to make it? One doesn't know whether to laugh or cry at the pathetic assertion that he makes to substantiate this ludicrous claim, that Albion – yes, always *la perfide Albion* – had de-industrialised further than any other country and that it no longer possessed either the productive capacity or the ability to innovate that would allow it to take advantage of the devaluation of its currency.

Does this man not realise that we have trained thousands, perhaps tens or hundreds of thousands, of our young people in media studies? Does he not know that equal numbers of young British girls, despite having a baby or two, have finished courses on hair and beauty (admittedly without much positive effect on their own appearance, but as the great Doctor Johnson pointed out a long time ago, you can criticise a table without being able to make one). Does the author of this scurrilous article masquerading as serious commentary think that, in a crisis, people will go without their televisions, their hair or their beauty?

Lo and behold, when I reached the end of the article I realised that it was not French at all, that it was a translation, presumably from the English, from something written by one Edward Hadas.

I am all in favour of freedom of criticism, of course but, as with all freedoms, there have to be limits. Surely there is no place in the modern world for such ill-informed, prejudiced nonsense by people who are little short of traitors. If we can legislate against religious hatred, surely we can legislate against gross misrepresentations of our country's situation?

Anyone Will Do Anything
For Ten Bags Of Brown

AS WE KNOW, human life is sacred and its worth is therefore above mere monetary considerations. The same cannot be said, however, of human injury, which, like every other commodity in demand, has a price that is determined by supply. And in prison that price is low, owing to a surplus of potential suppliers. There are, of course, distortions in the operation of the market, such as the activities of the prison officers, but the fundamental laws of supply and demand still hold good.

A man asked for asylum in the prison hospital last week. A few days earlier, someone had tried to slash him while he was out on the exercise yard. The would-be slasher had been offered two ounces of burn, that is to say tobacco, to do the job.

'Who was paying him?' I asked.

'Someone I knew on the out.'

'What did he have against you?'

'I was seeing his wife.'

Let it not be said that prisoners lack perseverance. The slashing having failed, the cuckolded husband had raised the reward to ten bags, that is to say ten bags of brown, that is to say ten bags of heroin, that is to say, in prison terms, serious money. Anyone will do anything for ten bags of brown.

My next patient was a good-looking young man who had somewhat spoiled his appearance by having his forehead tattooed. He said he wanted to commit suicide.

'What are you in for?' I asked.

'Threats to kill.'

'Threats to kill whom?'

'My girlfriend.'

'What are you supposed to have done?'

'Told her I would set her on fire.'

'Are you pleading guilty or not guilty?'

'Depends.'

'On what does it depend?'

'On circumstances.'

'What circumstances?'

'On all different circumstances.'

'Not on whether you did it or not?'

'I can't remember nothing about it.'

'Is that because you can't remember anything about the whole evening, or because the events were not memorable in themselves?'

'I can't remember nothing.'

'Then you're not in a strong position to deny the charge, are you?'

'I am if I can't remember.'

'And have you ever been to prison before?'

'Yes.'

'How many times?'

'Two or three.'

'Which, two or three?'

'Once for driving, once for burglary and once for a week on remand for a domestic.'

'A domestic?'

'Yes, my girlfriend said I held a knife or a gun to her head.'

'A knife or a gun?'

'Yes.'

'Which?'

'I can't remember.'

'Were you found guilty?'

'No.'

'Why not?'

'She dropped the charges.'

'On the grounds that you didn't do it?'

'She was lying.'

'Have you ever had your hands round her throat?'

'Only to get her off me.'

I telephoned her.

'Has he ever been violent towards you?' I asked.

'Yes, plenty of times. He said if he couldn't have me, no one else would. He's had guns and knives at my head.'

'Both guns and knives?'

'Yes.'

'And has he ever tried to strangle you?'

'Yes, twice.'

'How far did he get?'

'I was all dizzy and everything went silent – even the TV. I couldn't hear the programme no more, only my heartbeat.'

The TV went silent: that beats hollow the Marquis de Sade's argument in favour of strangulation, that it gives rise to sexual gratification.

The Struggle Continues

HURRAH FOR THE sexual revolution! How frustrating and dull life was before it! Men – I use the word loosely, to include women – were expected not to act upon all their sexual desires, and this of course turned them into hypocrites. Now every modern philosopher knows that there is nothing worse, morally speaking, than a hypocrite; besides, there is no torture more acute or terrible than frustrated desire.

This is perfectly obvious from my daily practice. For example, last week I saw a homeless young man who had injected himself with a consciousness-suppressing dose of heroin in the street, in order to obtain a roof over his head for the night. Really he preferred prison to hospital ('I've got no worries there'), but unfortunately the pedants insist that he break the law before sending him there. So much for the vaunted theory of personal autonomy and choice.

I asked him when he first took heroin.

'When my mum chucked me out.'

'When was that?'

'When I was 16.'

'And why?'

'Because I beat up her new boyfriend.'

'Why?'

'Because he was my best mate. He was the same age as me.'

You see what terrible consequences intolerance has? If only he had accepted his mother's choice, everything would have been all right. Indeed, who wouldn't want his dad for his best mate (or rather, his best mate for his dad)? As Pascal said, let us think clearly: for clear thought is the foundation of all morality.

I am glad to say, however, that the housing department has progressed beyond the hypocrisy inherent in making judgments.

That same day I saw a young woman as a patient who had been sexually (and physically) abused by her elder brother. He did it for a few years, raping her repeatedly while her mother was being beaten up downstairs by their drunken stepfather, who was old enough to be their brother.

Fortunately, she managed to get away: the council gave her a flat. A few months later, however, her brother decided to pay her a social call; that is to say, he demanded money from her. When she was so ungrateful as to remind him of their past life together, he grew angry and broke her arm, failing to break her leg only because it proved too strong for his powers of torsion.

She called the police and, marvellous to say, he was caught, charged and imprisoned pending trial. Three months later, when her arm had healed, she received another social visit from two of his friends, who broke her arm for a second time. Greater love hath no man than this: that he breaks the limbs of an enemy for his friend's sake.

Not altogether surprisingly, my patient did not feel entirely happy about the prospect of returning to her current accommodation. And she said that the person dealing with her case at the housing department was not very sympathetic about her wish to move away. I asked for her name.

'Charmaine.'

'Charmaine who?'

'I don't know, she didn't tell me.'

I phoned the office.

'No, we don't have no Charmaine here.'

'My patient says you do.'

'It must be at another branch.'

'My patient says she spoke to her at your branch.'

'I'll put you through to someone else.'

I asked that someone else for Charmaine.

'We don't have a Charmaine.'

'Yes you do.'

'Not in the back office, perhaps in the front office. I'll put you through.'

I asked once again to speak to Charmaine, and explained why. I was told I should speak to the manager.

'Can I speak to the manager, then?'

'She's can't speak to you now. She's busy. She'll call you back.'

'But when she calls me back, I'll be busy. If I take the same attitude, we'll never speak to one another.'

'No one's more important than anyone else.'

I exploded with impotent rage. See what my patient's narrow, bigoted intolerance of her brother's activities had led to? This proves the sexual revolution is only half-complete. As they used to say in Lusophone Africa, before the four horsemen had arrived in earnest, *A luta continua.*

The GMC Is Only
Obeying Orders

THESE THINGS ARE sent to try us: I'm speaking now of circular letters from the General Medical Council.

I recently received a second such letter about the Council's Ethnicity Census from the president of the Council:

> 'Toward the end of 2007, I wrote asking for your help with an important project designed to help us to understand better the diversity of doctors registered with the GMC. We were hugely encouraged by the response we received and now have ethnicity data for over 60% of all registered doctors in the UK. To complete the picture we still need your support and I would be grateful if you would provide the information we seek.'

What is the purpose of the GMC's racialist project?

> 'We are committed to ensuring that our processes and procedures are fair, objective, transparent and free from unlawful discrimination… That is why we need data for as high a proportion of registered doctors as possible.'

There is no explanation as to how such a census will ensure that the deliberations of the Council on individual cases will be rendered fairer by the possession of the data, and to try to find such an explanation on the Council's website is to enter a world of Kafka-esque euphemism, equivocation and evasion:

> 'We will use the data to analyse diversity issues. This analysis will, among other things, help us understand why proportionately more

international medical graduates appear before our Fitness to Practise Panels.'

Both in the letter and on the website, doctors are assured that the information gathered will be kept entirely confidential.

The GMC seems as blithely unaware of the recent scandals of supposedly confidential and highly sensitive information gathered by the government and left wholesale on trains, as it is unaware of at least two comparatively recent genocidal episodes that were made easier, or even possible, by ethnicity data on 100 per cent of the population. Furthermore, doctors did not cover themselves in ethical glory during either of those episodes, which suggests that prudence might be the better part of impudent busy-bodying.

Of course, the real reason for the Ethnicity Census is to be found in the letter. 'There is no statutory obligation on doctors to supply ethnicity data,' it says; but 'The census will... help us to fulfil our other general statutory duties and responsibilities under the Race Relations Act, 1976 (as amended) and other legislation.'

In other words, they are required to ask but no one is required to reply.

There is something deeply sinister to be found on the GMC's website, notwithstanding doctors' legal right to withhold the information sought. Even if doctors do not reply to the GMC's enquiry, there is no cause for the GMC to despair:

'We will be contacting those doctors for whom we do not have access to current ethnicity data, requesting they provide us with this information. We have successfully partnered with the NHS in England to obtain ethnicity data for doctors in their employ, significantly reducing the numbers of doctors who need to take part in this exercise.'

So much for confidentiality; and the prose reeks of bad conscience, as very well it might. I love in particular the phrase 'current ethnicity data', which conjures up the spectre of racial reclassification à la South Africa in the good old days.

But of course the GMC docs have a complete excuse. It is only obeying orders.

Even The Answers To Simple Questions Elude Me

WHEN I WAS YOUNG, I could explain everything, at least to my own satisfaction. With the passing of each successive year, however, my confidence in my understanding has waned to the point of not even understanding what it is to understand. The world has thus become utterly opaque and mysterious to me, especially that part of it called Man, God rot him.

What makes Man tick, exactly? That is the question. I just can't find out. Even the answer to so simple a question as 'Why does he take heroin?' eludes me. As for addicts, they don't know either, and evince no interest in the question. When asked, they are surprised: the question strikes them as bizarre. One might as well ask them why there is something rather than nothing.

One day last week I was consulted by three addicts in quick succession. I asked them all why they took heroin. The first, a woman, replied, 'It takes me out of the living world.' The second, a man, replied, 'I'm trying to get off it, but people keep coming to my door with it.' He used to be a security guard, he said, 'but that went all on top of me'. The third, also a man, replied, 'Because I'm an addict.' Since addicts take heroin, and he was an addict, he took heroin – otherwise he wouldn't have been an addict, would he?

Of these answers, the first was by far the most interesting: the need to escape the living world. If by this is meant the world in which we find ourselves, this is a need I myself feel daily; for I can never wait to escape from reality to representations of reality, either in books or in pictures. Since this is the case wherever I might happen to be at the time, I suppose it means that I have a basic dislike, or mistrust at least, of existence. I don't believe it – existence, I mean – augurs any good.

Enough of autobiography, however: the world, horrible as it is, is too interesting for that. Let us return to what my patient called 'the living world' – her living world, to be exact.

She was waiting for her boyfriend – who had one of those names so commonly associated with criminality that preventive detention at birth would be justified – to come out of prison.

'What's he in for?' I asked.

'Violent disorder.'

'Towards you?'

'He has been. But he's not in for that. He just loses it.'

'Loses what?'

'Control.'

'I suppose he strangles you.'

'And calls me names.'

'Such as?'

'Bitch, slag, slut and whore.'

I confess that, at that moment, though I should not have done, as it displays a lamentably commonplace and prejudiced mind, I could not but think of a firm of solicitors.

I asked her why her arm was in plaster.

'This bloke slashed me,' she replied.

'Which bloke?'

'I met my boyfriend's friend in a pub and he said he had nowhere to stay, so I put him up in my flat, but after a couple of days he wanted sex and I wouldn't give it to him so he threatened to throw my dog out of the window and he smashed a glass and slashed me up.'

'Do you want to stay with your boyfriend?'

'Yes.'

'Why?'

'Because if I left him, he'd beat me up and lock me in my flat.'

Our Government Takes
Millán Astray Seriously

SAD TO RELATE, none of our utterances will be remembered after our deaths, for all the passion with which we uttered them: unless, that is, we happen to belong to one of the very few, the elite of the elite, who have said something worth remembering.

Such a one was Millán Astray, the Nationalist Spanish Civil War general whose exclamation at Salamanca University – *Viva la muerte!* Long live death! – remains, if I may be allowed a slight pun, immortal. Less well-known, though equally worthy of committal to memory, is what he said next, which was, in a way, prophetic. Having praised death, he exclaimed '*Muera la inteligencia!*' Death to intelligence!

Little could Millán Astray have thought that his exclamation would have been taken up by successive British governments as the ruling, indeed the whole, principle of its education policy, devised to keep the lower classes low. Formal education is thus no counter-influence to the nightmare world of British domestic arrangements, which no doubt explains why the British are frivolous without gaiety and insouciant without charm.

Last week a girl of 16 tried to end her brief existence by taking her mother's antidepressants. Her mother took antidepressants much as Transylvanian peasants wore garlic flowers to ward off the attentions of revenants; in her case, though, she indulged in pharmaceutical magic to avoid the blows of her daughter's latest stepfather. The girl took the pills because of a row with her boyfriend, who was aged 23 and was continuing to see the three mothers of his five children. She was consumed by jealousy: she did not want to share her treasure with anyone. Moreover, he didn't agree with her decision to abort their child: he believed in the sanctity of life.

Her experience of love until she met him had not been altogether happy, either. She had had an affair with her mother's boyfriend (halfway in age between her and her mother) for about three years, from her 13th to her 16th birthday. When she decided to end it, he became violent and forced himself upon her, not once but repeatedly. Towards the end – of the affair, that is – he confined himself simply to beating her up, and eventually even her mother had had enough of his behaviour and called the police.

'But of course you dropped the charges,' I said.

'Yes. My mum said we should.'

'Why?'

'For the sake of the kids.'

The kids in question were the two children, one of them a baby, that her mother had had by him. Her mother felt that they needed the moral guidance and stability that only a father could provide. Hence the decision to abjure the processes of the law: the family always comes first.

I spoke to the patient in as avuncular a manner as I could manage. I told her that unless she took some thought she was destined for a life of poverty and misery. Before long she would consent to have a baby by her boyfriend, and then he would abandon her. She would be housed by the council between a chronic schizophrenic of violent propensities on one side and a drug-dealer on the other, with a disposable income of £23.79 per week. She agreed that it would be a disaster.

The boyfriend arrived on the ward, a black youth in a baseball cap, with a charming smile and a lupine lope. She melted into his arms.

Later in the week, I read in one of our more intellectually sophisticated newspapers a demand that mothers such as she should be subsidised by the state – that is to say, you and me: and I thought of Millán Astray. *Muera la inteligencia!*

In Literature, Conversations
Progress Logically

SOUTH AMERICA USED to have banana boats; now it has adoption runs. On the plane home from South America recently, all the seats in front of me were taken by adoptive parents bringing their new South American babies home to Europe. The airline thoughtfully provided the rest of us with earplugs.

The adoptive parents seemed like very nice people. Though they could have known their babies for only a few days, their love for them was so radiant that even I, who do not lightly acknowledge anything good in humanity, was warmed by it. This was surely how parenthood was supposed to be.

Not in my area, however. I still haven't worked out why the English want to reproduce themselves, since their lives are so miserable and their offspring are even worse. I suppose it must be the triumph of instinct over rationality: I cannot believe it is just for the welfare payments.

Take as an example the young woman whom I saw last week. She was not quite 20 years old and had taken an overdose because, despite all her efforts, she had failed 'to catch for a baby'.

'And the man who would have been the father?' I asked, approaching the subject with the insincere, oleaginous, non-judgmental delicacy that is *de rigueur* these days.

'We've split up.'

'Then perhaps it was just as well you didn't catch for a baby by him,' I said.

'That's what you say,' she replied. 'But I would've had a piece of him then that he couldn't of took off me.'

'A kind of souvenir, then?' I said.

'I'm only happy when he's with me,' she replied.

It is only in literature that conversations progress logically.

'And what was he like?' I asked.

Of course, I already knew the answer: a raging, egocentric psychopath. He had two children by a previous liaison, was ferociously possessive and jealous while being flagrantly unfaithful to her himself (he had left her, to try to 'make a go of it' with the other woman, on the latter's insistence), he was violent (she showed me the purple bruises he had inflicted on her with a chair, while she was drunk and drugged with heroin), and he had a criminal record.

'Why was he in prison?' I asked.

'It don't matter. It's not relevant.'

'I think it does, and it is.'

'Why?'

'It provides a clue as to his character.'

'He's very loving, very caring. Only he's got a nasty side; he can switch sometimes.'

'Suddenly. Just like that?' I snapped my fingers.

'Yes. How did you know?'

'Because in the last year I've examined more than 500 men who've just beaten up their girlfriends.'

'Well, I don't want to live no more. Without him, life's not worth living. I'm going to kill myself.'

'I don't think you will,' I said.

'No? How do you know? Why not?'

Too much make-up, I thought. It was like the icing on cheap British cakes. *And no one who wants to die spends as much time on her hairdo as she does.*

'Time is a great healer,' I said.

My next patient was a woman who had cut her wrists because her boyfriend, a nightclub bouncer (or greeter, as they are known nowadays) with a neck like a Russian woman shot-putter's thigh, had just left her.

'Why did he leave you?'

'I couldn't conceive.'

The Menagerie Of My Pet Hates

I SUPPOSE IT is a sign of advancing age that the menagerie of my pet hates enlarges by the hour. Some people grow wiser and more serene as they age; others tetchier and more intolerant. Of their lamentable company, I regret to say, am I. The human race, I find, does not improve upon further acquaintance.

But, as I tell my patients who complain of life in general, there must be something rather more specific than mere existence as such to inflame their savage breasts. And the thing which is currently raising my ire – easily raised, admittedly – is the mobile telephone.

A pox (or should I say a brain tumour?) upon all those who carry this frightful instrument.

Alas, as any gimcrack psychiatrist will tell you, there is in all hatred a liberal dose of self-contempt, and so it is with my abhorrence of the mobile telephone, for I possess one myself, even though I know it makes me look a little like a Yardie drug-dealer.

At least my conversations on it are sensible and important, however. I have to keep myself contactable at all times wherever I may be, just in case one of the newspapers wants me to write a ringing denunciation of one or other of the many manifestations of modern British degradation and depravity. It is possible, after all, to make money out of depravity without being depraved oneself.

But the conversations of everyone else on their mobile telephones seem to me to be banal beyond description. How typical of modern life that the technical brilliance of engineers should result in the effortless communication of utter drivel from one end of the country to the other! By comparison with modern man, Sisyphus himself led a life full of meaning and transcendent purpose.

Enough, as they say in Russian novels, of philosophy: let us descend from the perfect Platonic world of pure irritation to the

71

impure instances of that emotion. I refer, of course, to my 12-year-old patient (she looked 20), who took an overdose intending to die, and lay on her hospital bed clutching her mobile telephone as I, at her age, would have clutched my teddy bear.

'Why did you do it?' I asked.

'I'd had enough,' she pouted.

'Of life?' I asked wearily.

I'd guessed right. But the final straw, she said, had come when her 22-year-old friend accused her of having had an affair with her 25-year-old boyfriend. Good heavens, I thought: whatever happened to the generation gap?

Brrrrrr-brrrrrr! Brrrrrr-brrrrrr! Her telephone went off just as she was relating the climactic moments of her life so far.

'Hello, Snazz... No, I can't speak just now, I'm with the doctor... I'll call you back as soon as he's finished, OK?'

'I take it from your intention to call Snazz back,' I said, once she had switched the accursed thing off, 'that you no longer wish to die?'

My surmise, in this instance, was mistaken. She was reserving the right to take future overdoses after returning his call.

But her use of the mobile telephone in the hospital was only mildly disconcerting by comparison with an instance related to me by a gynaecologist colleague. He was performing what many of my patients call 'an internal' on one of his patients when her mobile telephone rang. With admirable sangfroid, she said, 'Don't mind me, doctor,' and continued with a light conversation with a friend while he examined her – again in the words of my patients – 'down below'.

Here was further confirmation of what I have always maintained: that there is no overestimating the shallowness of the human heart.

The True Kindness Of
A Sensitive Fishmonger

PEOPLE SOMETIMES WRITE to me and ask whether I ever see any good in people. The short answer is, of course, no, though I admit there are some slight variations. In the course of my work, I see the whole spectrum of human conduct, from dreadful to appalling.

So I was rather disconcerted the other week to observe a scene in my local fishmonger's that might give heart to the sentimentalists who believe in original virtue. A very tiny old lady ahead of me in the queue, shrivelled by age and obviously not well off, bought a piece of plaice and some jellied eels, and then had difficulty in counting out the cash to pay for it (I suspect it cost more than she really could afford), and was flustered by the number of people behind her waiting to be served. She emptied the money from her purse and asked the fishmonger to take what was owing him.

With great speed, he counted some money, taking far less than he had originally asked for and returning the rest to her.

'Thank you, madam,' he said, with precisely the same courtesy as if she had been his most lucrative customer.

Here was true kindness that asked for no thanks. The fishmonger was sensitive enough to know that the old lady would rather have starved than accept his charity, and took his opportunity to do her a hidden good turn with alacrity. Withal, he treated her with that courtesy which, alas, is now rarely encountered, but once seemed so widespread as to appear almost natural.

The whole scene, you might think, should restore my faith in human beings, but I am adept at drawing the most pessimistic conclusions from all that passes before me. The fact that I found this little scene, with its kindness and courtesy, so moving established for me that it was unexpected, extraordinary, out of the way; that human relations nowadays rarely reach the fishmonger's level of decency. Once upon a time, one might have been able to take his behaviour more for granted.

I thought back to the last patient I had seen in my hospital before the weekend. He was a graceless young man of 19 years of age, who had been admitted with alcohol poisoning. He was a university student, he said (God help us), of popular culture: that is to say, he studied soap operas and pop music.

He was obviously of middle-class origin, and lay in his bed with a baseball cap on. He also chewed gum, thus establishing that British youth, unlike President Ford, can do two things at once.

He peppered the answers to my question with obscene words, and I asked him to desist.

'Why should I?' he asked me. 'Here I am, all stressed out, and you're worried about my use of a two-syllable word.'

His eyes, which appeared piggy under the peak of his baseball cap, glittered with egoistic malice.

'I mean, I've got all this shit going on in my life and you're worried about my language.'

I think I'll become a fishmonger. It would give me more opportunity to do good.

The Middle Class Wins Again!

WHEN JASON HIT Wayne with a baseball bat four years ago, Wayne applied for, and was granted, legal aid to sue Jason, though Wayne had started the fight in the first place and Jason had nothing with which to compensate Wayne in any case – except, of course, his most treasured possession, his baseball bat.

Having been present when Wayne was brought to hospital nearly half a decade ago, I was called to court last week. Unfortunately, the case was adjourned because Jason's wife – I use the word in its metaphorical sense – had just given birth, and Jason therefore didn't turn up. I should like to assure British taxpayers that, at £800, my charges for sitting in the antechamber to the court, doing nothing but watching the goings-on around me, are moderate, in the middle of the range. Perhaps this was just as well, because there were three other expert witnesses who were stood down, to say nothing of the barristers, barristers' clerks, solicitors and solicitors' clerks, on the plaintiff's side alone. Moreover, this was the third adjournment of the case so far. I've already made more out of Jason's attack on Wayne than Wayne will ever be able to extract from Jason.

The middle class wins again! First it weeps crocodile tears over the poor's lack of access to justice, or at least to the courts, then it grabs all the money for itself. It's enough to make you sick – unless you're middle class, that is.

At first the judge didn't believe that Jason's 'wife' had just given birth, as he hadn't believed last time that Jason injured the cartilage of his knee playing football, and was thus forensically indisposed. Jason's tactics seem to be to delay matters until the legal aid money runs out – as likely, it seems to me, as the Pacific being emptied by a madman with a teaspoon. In the end, however, documentary evidence was produced in court that a woman was in hospital somewhere having recently given birth – the nearest we can come these days, short of a DNA test, to proof of paternity. Somewhat reluctantly, the judge accepted it.

But what a spectacle are the antechambers to our courts, worth any number of adjournments! Daumier, thou shouldst be living at this hour, England hath need of thee! Contrast the chalkstripe, shoe-polished, plummy-accented barristers with their track-suited, Doc Marten-booted, expletive-muttering clients (the solicitors coming somewhere in between the two). The majesty of the law matters not at all to our modern-day plaintiffs and defendants, who turn up to court looking as if they've come straight from a hard night's video-watching on the sofa.

'I'm head of ethnic affairs for our chambers,' I overheard an upper-class woman barrister say to a client.

What on earth did she mean by this? That she made love to representatives of all the races of the world on behalf of her partners? Did they watch through a one-way mirror? I wish I'd gone into the law rather than medicine.

Talking of ethnicity (as the weasel word is), I couldn't help noticing the large proportion of Indians at the County Court. They're obviously as attached to civil proceedings as some Jamaicans are to criminal ones. What really saddened me, though, was to see the way young Indian males have taken young white scum as their model and imitated them in every particular, from their nose rings to their body language, from their hairstyles to their snarls. This is the first age of mass downward cultural aspiration.

I Was Very Attached
To My Phone

HAVE PATIENTS THESE days no respect for doctors? I think not. My mobile phone was stolen from my office in the ward last week, and it must have been a patient who took it. There are a lot of light-fingered patients about who do not hesitate to take souvenirs of the hospital with them when they go. A little bit of what they fancy does them good.

For example, the very day before my phone was stolen, a patient was caught by a nurse walking off with one of the ward computers.

'Where are you going with that computer?' asked the nurse.

'To the toilet,' said the patient.

This is not quite so illogical a reply as might at first appear. Many an escape from our hospital by patients in the custody of the law has been made through the lavatory windows, though usually without the latest technology as an encumbrance. He dropped the computer and fled.

When I realised that my phone had been stolen, I called the police. We have a resident policeman in our hospital, a pleasant and upright young man who has never arrested anyone as far as I know. For the first time he appeared on the ward wearing a bullet-proof vest, 'just as a trial run', as he put it, for shooting round here is on the increase. If the trend continues, we'll soon have underground shelters against our patients.

Well, I received a crime number, the *sine qua non* that enabled me to make my insurance claim. It goes without saying that the insurance company, having been perfectly happy to take my money for years, attempted to wriggle out of the contract: it is a moot point as to whether insurance companies or their customers are the more dishonest nowadays. Suffice it to say that between fraudulent claims and a reluctance to meet obligations there exists what Marxists used to call a dialectical relationship. Only by bullying and threatening did I carry the day.

It also goes without saying that a week later I received through the post the offer of Victim Support. My name had been passed on by the police to the organisation that provides such emotional support 'in a very distressing time'. It is true: I was very attached to my phone.

I was offered 'the opportunity to talk through' (that is to say, relive and keep uppermost in my mind) my 'experience'. The word 'counselling' was implied, though not actually used. I also received a pamphlet explaining how I might be able to claim incapacity benefit, if no longer able to work.

I went home to my study, my retreat from the world and my consolation for it, and quite by chance picked up a book of essays by Charles Kingsley, entitled *Health and Education*, happening upon this essay entitled 'Heroism':

'It is an open question whether the policeman is not demoralising us; and that in proportion as he does his duty well; whether the perfection of justice and safety, the complete 'preservation of body and goods', may not reduce the educated and comfortable classes into that lapdog condition in which not conscience, but comfort, doth make cowards of us all.'

Oh to be a lapdog, now that crime is here!

Next Time A Mugger Has His Knife At Your Throat, Remind Him That Existence Precedes Essence

WHEN WE WERE STUDENTS, a professor of public health once told us that the death rate declined whenever or wherever doctors went on strike. This was an even stronger argument, he implied, than the purely ethical one against doctors resorting to such action, or inaction. No profession should lightly expose its uselessness to the public gaze.

Crossing Belgium recently, at a time when it had had no government for several weeks, I could not help but notice that it looked very much the same as when it did have a government. Obviously the crisis would have to be resolved sooner or later because otherwise people would realise the redundancy of the political class.

According to one Belgian I met, the only real function of the latter is to vote a budget so that the bureaucrats got paid. For without a budget, how could their salaries and their numbers ever increase?

Of course, politicians are not the only flies in the ointment of modern society. There is the small problem of the people, too: they are constantly doing the most terrible things to one another and nobody seems able to stop them, not that anyone tries very hard. A Belgian journalist told me that his nephew, aged 15, had recently been stabbed in the throat by two young Ukrainian asylum-seekers (presumably they were fleeing democracy). It happened on his first day back at school and for some days he hovered between life and death.

At first, the Belgian newspapers expressed horror in a perfectly normal and straightforward way, but the journalist knew that it wouldn't last in what is, after all, one of the most politically-correct countries in the world. First a TV station was criticised for having shown the blood on the pavement where the boy was stabbed: we like our stabbings bloodless, it seems, like the murders in the detective stories of the golden age. Then some criminologists got going.

Two from the faculty of law of the Free University of Brussels denounced the hysteria. It made scapegoats of the perpetrators, they said, and (horror of horrors) 'created a fundamental dichotomy between them and us'.

According to the criminologists, 'the description of the victim as "completely innocent" strengthens the polarisation between perpetrator and victim'. At the very least, the victim must have been guilty of being in the wrong place at the wrong time, to quote a British police spokesman deputed to comment in public on a particularly horrible attack on a passer-by. If you insist on being in the wrong place at the wrong time, what else can you expect?

The title of the article in which the criminologists wrote was 'Stabbing in the Mirror', that is to say, look in the mirror and you will see someone who goes round stabbing 15-year-old boys in the throat. We are all innocent because we are all guilty – or is it the other way round? Anyway, it doesn't seem to leave much scope for faculties of law.

The criminologists end with a quasi-religious peroration in the imperative mood. 'We must put our hands on our hearts and have this existential learning process.'

Next time a mugger has his knife at your throat, remind him that existence precedes essence. If that doesn't stop him in his tracks, nothing will.

Why Haven't They Thought Of This?

THE BRITISH MEDICAL JOURNAL these days is obsessed with inequalities in health. The Christmas edition of that august publication was largely devoted to the subject, to which it returns with monotonous regularity, and I suspect that it will not be really happy until our entire gross domestic product is devoted to procuring equality in the life expectancy of the richest and the poorest people in Britain. Of course, we doctors will then be in clover.

But as a devotee of Dr de Bono's lateral thought, it occurred to me that, since no country in the world has managed so far to raise the life expectancy of the worst-off section of the population to that of the best-off, no matter how much it has spent on health care, the desired equality could be more easily, cheaply and enjoyably brought about by curtailing the life expectancy of, say, the richest ten per cent – by, for example, denying them medical care. This policy would have the great advantage of assuaging the feelings of the envious while reducing government expenditure. In fact, I can think of no serious objection to it.

In the same issue of the *BMJ*, as it happens, there was an article of great mathematical complexity proving that people who voted Tory lived longer than those who voted Labour. Oddly enough, the article did not go on to recommend the banning of political broadcasts on behalf of the Labour Party, as it would have done had the Labour Party been a brand of cigarette; on the contrary, it attributed the superior longevity of Tory voters to their selfishness and hardheartedness.

Talking of inequalities in health, or at least in sick leave (which, as even the most minimal acquaintance with human nature will tell you, is not precisely the same thing), we received a circular from our Department of Human Resources last week. It used to be called the

Personnel Department, but then they sacked the Personnel Manager as an economy measure and employed five people in his place. And a larger department obviously needs a longer and more elegant name.

I digress, however. The circular gave us the latest figures for sick leave. Doctors, it said, are absent through illness for three per cent of the time, while other staff are absent for ten per cent of the time. The department's target for sick leave, it added, was five per cent.

It seems that doctors in our hospital are seriously underperforming where sick leave is concerned. Either they are obstinately continuing to go to work while unwell, or they are indecently healthy. Whichever explanation holds true, it is clear that something needs to be done about it. If hospital porters, laundry and kitchen staff are really three times as unhealthy as doctors, this is evidence of a crying injustice: at the very least, doctors should increase their sick leave by sixty per cent to meet the target figure. Personally, I think I'll book some sick leave in advance.

If doctors won't increase their sick leave voluntarily, however, compulsory measures may have to be taken. I would suggest reducing their salaries to those of ward cleaners: then they will fulfil and overfulfil (by many times) their target for sick leave. In fact, they will be the Stakhanovites of sick leave.

Balm To A Misanthrope's Soul

WHERE HAS ENGLISH courtesy gone? To India, that's where. I have noticed many times that Indian doctors who come to this country have an old-fashioned English courtliness about them which is balm to a misanthrope's soul.

My present junior, who arrived in England recently, has yet to adopt the coarse and abrupt manners of our age, and was surprised when the nurses urged him to call his patients by their first name, even when they were old enough to be his grandparents.

'What should I do, Dr Dalrymple?' he asked.

'Remember always that you are in the right while they are in the wrong,' I replied. 'Even if you are one and they are many.'

I couldn't honestly recommend, however (and alas), that he continue to address boys as Master Smith and Master Jones. Apart from anything else, they wouldn't know what he was talking about: they'd wrinkle up their noses and say, 'You what?'

Sometimes I ask my junior doctor a question for the sheer pleasure of listening to his reply. It is like reading Gibbon after having received a circular from the Director of Quality Assurance, Social Services: it reassures you that all is right with the world.

Of course, my junior's not a fool: he has already discovered how degenerate are the former masters of India. His jaw drops at each new instance of their utter degradation, which means that his mouth is open most of the time. He came to my room last week. He was at a loss to know what to do for one of his patients.

'What's her problem?' I asked.

'She says she needs help. She throws ashtrays at her husband.'

'Is her aim no good?'

He called her in. She had a satin dressing-gown and the complexion of a chronic drinker. She wore fluffy slippers: always a bad sign.

'I throw ashtrays at him. I can't help it, I don't know what I'm doing.'

'You could injure him severely, or even kill him.'

'It's not my fault, I can't stop myself, I just do it.'

'You mean to say that you're an automaton, a creature with no will of your own?'

'He's there, I'm here, there's an ashtray on the table, what else do you expect?'

My junior's next patient was a woman with five children, the last two by a man with whom she had now broken, though not for the first time. A year ago, when she had had only one of his children, he had put his hands round her neck to strangle her, and she had obtained an injunction against him. But then she returned to him, had a further child by him, and now sought a further injunction against him because of his strangling ways.

'Is he a jealous man?' I asked.

'I've never give him no reason to be.'

'I'm not saying that you have. I'm only asking whether he's jealous.'

'I never go nowhere or meet no one, so he's got no reason to be.'

'But is he jealous all the same? Some men are.'

'I've never had no affairs or nothing, if that's what you mean.'

She left the room. I turned to my junior and told him that she might one day be called to perform jury service.

He was astounded. 'There's no educational test or qualification?'

'No.'

'You must be joking, Dr Dalrymple, it's simply not possible, I can't believe it. No, no, it's impossible.'

If only we could learn to see ourselves as others saw us.

Two Moral Moods

THE ENGLISH, IT SEEMS to me, are subject to two moral moods: complacency and panic. Of the two, I prefer – and, in my small way, have contributed to – the latter. At least panic encourages us to examine the important questions, such as why we don't beat our children enough.

Foreigners have always thought that the English have a special penchant for beating their children, and attribute it to their reticence over sexual matters. All I can say about foreigners, then, is that they don't know much about English children. The mere sight of a crowd of such children emerging from school these days is enough to turn a St Francis into a Bluebeard.

Needless to say, I was beaten as a child and, like anyone who has had an unpleasant experience, I persuade myself that it was all to the good. Even if this was not the case, I am convinced that the character of my fellow pupils was greatly improved by the beatings they received: they put iron in their soul.

It was Colonel D___ who administered punishment at the first school I remember. He was the proprietor and headmaster, and his appearance alone was enough to strike terror into the heart of any boy. His face was perfectly round, and he had a bristly, black moustache with which one might have brushed suede shoes. His dark eyes twinkled with malice and hatred of the puerile race. His movements were slow but inexorable, and he walked with a limp, aided by a stick: I still remember the fear inspired by the syncopated rhythm of his gait as he approached the classroom door.

We rather assumed at the time that his limp was the result of a war wound, but now, on reflection, I am not sure that he was really a colonel at all, and it was quite likely he came by his injury another way. At about 11 o'clock in the morning, he would select a boy in the class to fetch his 'tea' from the kitchen downstairs. Oddly enough, his tea – in which he took no milk – came in a large dimpled glass mug with a glass handle. It was a clear brown colour and had a slight white foam on the top. My older brother, more worldly-wise, later told me that Colonel D___'s tea was sent daily from the George Washington across the road.

The colonel would tell the unfortunate boy who had brought his tea to put it on the table, and then he grabbed the boy's hand and spread his fingers on the edge of the table. Then he picked up the blackboard ruler and brought it down with a smart thwack on the boy's fingers. I can feel the sting of it even as I write.

'What do you say?' asked the colonel.

'Thank you, sir,' said the boy, with a ready voice and tears welling in his eyes.

And the rest of us, precociously pusillanimous, would titter with laughter, as if Colonel D___ had made rather a good joke. He expected it, and we laughed because we knew that tomorrow it might be us. Perhaps if we laughed enough, we should avoid our fate.

It was a valuable lesson which Colonel D___ taught us (only in the mornings – at lunchtime he repaired to the George Washington in person and thereafter was unfit to teach). We learnt that some are born evil, some achieve evil, and some have evil thrust upon them.

The Little Boy With His Finger In The Dyke

'HOW OFTEN HAVE I said to you that when you have eliminated the impossible, whatever remains, however improbable, must be the truth?'

I quoted the great Holmes to a prison officer last week when he expressed astonishment at a deduction I had made. To me it appeared less than brilliant, even ordinary; but to him it was either a stroke of genius or a manifestation of the power of the occult.

He had come to me with a bag of pills which a newly convicted prisoner had brought with him into the prison straight from the dock. I looked at them for a moment and said, 'He is a sex offender, I perceive.'

The officer took a step backward. 'How did you know, doctor?' he asked. 'Are they drugs to take away the Urges?'

'No, not at all,' I replied, anxious to prolong the explanation of my deduction as long as possible.

'How did you know, then?'

'It's really quite simple,' I replied. 'These drugs are prescribed for high blood pressure and angina. High blood pressure and angina are predominantly diseases of those who have passed middle age. Virtually all new prisoners over the age of 50 are sex offenders. Therefore this prisoner is a sex offender.'

The officer looked at me open-mouthed. He recognised at once the truth of what I had said. He did not ask me the next question, which is why men over the age of 50 go to prison only for sex offences. As a friend of mine put it when he heard the story, 'Don't 60-year-olds steal? Don't they beat their wives? Aren't they human?'

Whether the fact that all elderly prisoners, give or take one or two, are sex offenders reflects the true pattern of geriatric offending, or whether it reflects the prejudices of the judges who sentence geriatrics, I cannot say.

I went on to make another observation which astounded the officer. 'And I shouldn't be at all surprised,' I said, 'if this prisoner had a walking-stick.'

This was a deduction too far: it caused frank disbelief.

'You must've seen him already, doctor,' said the officer. 'You must've.'

'No, I assure you, I haven't.'

'How did you know he's got a stick, then?'

'Well,' I replied, 'all prisoners with walking-sticks are sex offenders, and the great majority of sex offenders over the age of 50 carry walking-sticks.'

'Why's that, doctor?'

'I'm not sure. Most of them don't need a stick to walk with – they can manage quite well without. I suspect it is to establish their frailty in the eyes of the prison staff, so that they have to be accommodated in the hospital wing.' I paused for a moment. 'On the other hand, I have known prisoners in wheelchairs, crippled by arthritis and heart failure, who have committed rape. It's a question of mind over matter, I suppose.'

It was night when I left the prison. Loitering in a dark alleyway nearby were two shadowy youths, who made a theatrically loud spitting noise as I passed – great expectorations. I heard the phlegm hit the ground with a splat.

At moments like this, I feel as if I'm the last defender of civilisation. I feel, as one patient put it to me earlier in the day, like the little boy with his finger in the dyke, crying wolf.

My Objection To The Business Of Killing Patients

I RECOGNISE, OF COURSE, that perfectly decent people may disagree profoundly about euthanasia, just as they may disagree as to whether Bronzino was a better painter than Zurburán.

My objection to the business of killing patients is that, since the whole of life is an incurable disease ending inevitably in death, the malevolent will be provided with a ready-made slippery slope down which to slide. And my experience of mankind leads me to suppose that it cannot so much as glimpse a slippery slope without sliding down it.

But euthanasia is coming, I feel sure. If there's one thing you can't beat, it's a Zeitgeist. A Zeitgeist is a wilier, more ruthless opponent than Saddam Hussein himself. Soon there'll be a death committee in every hospital, composed of the chaplain, the director of finances, a social worker and a mortuary attendant, with monthly meetings to decide who is to shuffle off this mortal coil at his own request or otherwise.

I can already see the criteria for the granting of a merciful exit from this vale of tears spreading like mould over a cheese. Indeed, I had a moving appeal for euthanasia only the other day. The patient was already well-known to me: he haunts the hospital and the prison alike.

He had tried to commit suicide by cutting his wrists in a public place, in the full gaze of hundreds, and was brought, naturally enough, to hospital. I asked him why he'd done it.

'I've got no more will to live, doctor,' he said. 'I can't take no more.'

'More of what?' I asked.

'Life,' he replied. 'I mean, me and the missis, we was having a bit of a drink like and we'd got a couple of bottles of vodka in, like we always do. Then we started to argue, me and her like, and I gave her a slap.'

'A slap?'

'Yes, nothing serious, she only had a red mark on her lip.'

'Then what happened?'

'She called the police.'

'Is she pressing charges?'

'Yes, she says she's going ahead with it.'

'I suppose that's what's called making the slap stick,' I said.

'Without her, doctor,' he said, disregarding my little joke, 'I ain't got nothing to live for. I've just give up. If I had a tablet that'd kill me, I'd take it.'

In the secret recesses of my mind, I thought, *And if I had a tablet that'd kill you, I'd give it to you* – which is precisely why I'm against euthanasia.

'Anyway,' he continued, in a slightly more cheerful vein, 'I haven't got a pill like that, so I've decided not to eat until I just fade away.'

I looked at him for a little while. At moments like this I don't really know what to say. I feel embarrassed, so I change the subject.

'By the way,' I said, 'when were you due to appear in court?'

'This morning,' he replied. 'I must of missed it.'

Does one laugh? Does one cry? I'm still not quite sure. I think perhaps I'm in the wrong job, or trapped in the wrong existence altogether. I'm a misfit, that's what I am: something isn't right, and I'm like my patient who, confused about her personal identity, said to me, 'I've always been a bit short for my height, doctor.'

The Joy Of Fools

YOU – OR PERHAPS it would be more accurate to say I – can't get away anywhere from crime and criminality.

I was walking down a country lane in one of the most beautiful shires of England. The sun was shining, the birds were singing, the lambs were gambolling in the fields, the trees were decked out in the tender green of spring, my dog was at my side: for a moment, I felt almost glad to be alive. Then I met the local magistrate, who was also out walking his dog.

When two men in their late fifties meet, their first talk is of the wickedness – the unprecedented wickedness – of youth (lament being the consolation of age).

Then they turn on the government.

The magistrate, a man in appearance whom the French would call a typical *rosbif*, told me with indignation the latest government wheeze to mislead the public about the prevalence of crime in Britain. Henceforth, shoplifters who steal less than £200 worth of goods will be summarily fined £80, just as if they had parked on double yellow lines, and their crime not recorded anywhere. So the message of the government to the shoplifters of Britain is *enrichissez-vous*.

As it happens, I was looking over the crime statistics in the Home Office's *Research Publication No. 217* the other day, which investigated the costs of crime to the country for the year 2000. At the bottom of every column was the total, save for the column indicating the number of crimes: the figure was so appalling, more than sixty million per year, that is to say more than five times the figure usually given for general public consumption, that it was deemed better to conceal it by omission, in the full knowledge that journalists would never do the addition themselves.

Half the sixty million crimes were shoplifting: confirming my old dictum that, *pace* Napoleon, the English are a nation of shoplifters. But by removing shoplifting from the realm of crime altogether, the crime rate has been halved at a stroke.

Of course, I quite understand the predicament of the government: it wants to appeal simultaneously to the readers of *The Guardian* and of *The Daily Mail*. It appeals to the latter by having created a new criminal offence every working day for the last ten years, and to the former by letting criminals, poor abused lambs that they are, make a profit.

Not long ago I had occasion to look into the life and work of Dr William Farr, the great medical statistician of the Victorian era, and the deputy registrar-general of births, deaths and marriages who, for many years, wrote the incisive introductory essays to the annual report of the registrar general. Dr Farr, the son of a farm labourer, looked like an Old Testament prophet straight out of Shropshire, a man of iron integrity. No spin for him: just God's honest truth.

The Victorians were a bit funny about sex, no doubt, but I think they were better able in other respects to look unflinchingly at themselves and their society. Would things now improve with a change of government? I fear not: for the corruption has entered our very souls. That means that the old Romanian peasant adage now applies in Britain as in the Balkans: a change of rulers is the joy of fools.

Alien Methods

IF I HAD TO choose between spending an evening in the company
of a Cabinet minister or that of a taxi driver, I should unhesitatingly
choose the latter. How much broader is the experience of a taxi driver
than that of a Cabinet minister, who in all probability has devoted
his life to the pursuit of office – a miserably narrow business at best.
Taxi drivers, on the other hand, are fine judges of human character
– they have to be, because they must tell at a glance which would-be
passenger might prove dangerous to them or fail to pay his fare at
the end of a journey. No such responsibility devolves upon Cabinet
ministers.

When our plumber called the other day to mend a cistern I was
very pleased, therefore, that he decided afterwards to relate some of
his experiences to us. We had first met him through the Yellow Pages,
when, on Christmas Eve, our heating system most inconveniently
broke down. We had little choice but to call on one of the plumbing
companies which advertise a 24-hour-per-day, 365-day-per-year
service, and likewise to pay whatever was asked. A lack of heat on
Christmas Eve is, after all, the domestic equivalent of a heart attack.

He arrived at nine in the evening. He told us that, of the £65 per
hour we were charged for his labour, he received £26 per hour less
income tax and national insurance, plus £7.50 indemnity insurance
per job performed. When he left, two hours later, he told us that he
preferred to be paid by cheque or credit card, because if he were paid
cash the company for which he worked would deduct income tax and
national insurance from his pay without passing it on to the Revenue.
His somewhat unusual request not to be paid in cash was therefore his
small revenge upon the company.

We suggested to him that he strike out on his own, as we could
give him quite a lot of work, and would recommend him to others.

(We knew he was honest – our dog took to him at once, and he is a better judge of character even than taxi drivers.) The plumber took our advice and has been working for himself ever since. It is cheaper for his customers and he is much better paid.

He told us the other day that it wasn't only the Revenue whom the company for which he had once worked cheated unmercifully. The customers were robbed blind as a matter of company policy. For example, the plumbers were enjoined never to carry spare parts with them, but always to fetch them from a supplier's, thus extending the time each job took to complete. If the worst came to the worst, and no spare parts were required, the plumbers were to pretend that spare parts were nevertheless required and then wait around the corner in their vans for up to an hour, charging the time to the unfortunate customer.

If a job was straightforward, it was to be declared fiendishly difficult. If necessary, the plumbers were actively to carry out sabotage, by removing screws, valves and so forth. They were to take no mercy on pensioners who trembled lest the job take more than an hour, and thus consume their meagre savings. It was a company requirement that jobs should last on average three hours, with labour charges of not less than £195 plus VAT. The great ally of the crooked plumbing company is the general public's complete ignorance of plumbing.

I am glad to say that, as a member of the medical profession, none of this struck the faintest chord. Such methods, I need hardly add, are completely alien to the liberal and learned professions.

But Aristotle Knew Nothing
Of Social Services

RECENTLY, WHILE ON duty at the weekend, I had – for legal reasons which I need not detail – to call upon the services of a social worker. I therefore dialled the number for out-of-hours referrals to the social services.

'Hello,' said a recorded voice. 'You have reached the Emergency Duty Team. The office is only open out of office hours. It is now closed. Thank you and goodbye.'

Did I detect a subtle note of malicious triumph in that thank you and goodbye? I rather fancy I did.

What was I to do now? It was an emergency, and it was out of hours. I was stumped, but then I remembered the fax machine. I scrawled a note and tried to send it to the Emergency Duty Team's fax number. After a few minutes of fruitless ringing, my fax machine printed the following report: 'No contestant'.

I phoned a neighbouring borough's social services to ask for help and advice. 'You could always get the police to go round,' they said.

Surely the police had better things to do than that – victim support, for example? Much later in the day, I succeeded in getting through. I complained about the time it took.

'What number did you use, doctor?' asked the social worker.

I told him.

'Oh no,' he said. 'That's just for the public. You should have used the professionals' number.'

'I didn't know what it was,' I said.

'No, we haven't told anyone yet,' he replied. 'But we're going to soon.'

I compose many letters of complaint in my head, but rarely get round to sending them. On this occasion, however, I did write to the

Director of Social Services himself. He, of course, passed it on to someone else to answer, who began his letter:

'First I should like to apologise for the lengthy delay in answering your letter – I cannot understand why it has taken a month to reach my office. I gather you were told by recorded message that the Emergency Duty Team was not available. This issue was identified later that day. This was caused by the failure of a member of staff to log in the public telephone number to the computerised system at the beginning of the shift. The difficulty was rectified and procedures are now in place to ensure that the difficulty does not re-occur.'

Is this the language in which people actually think? No wonder patients quite often ask me to take their thoughts away.

'You advised that you had not received information regarding the telephone number to Social Services Emergency Duty Team for use by other professional agencies. In fact, some delays were experienced in sending letters of information.'

By whom were the delays experienced, I wonder? Not by me, because I was completely unaware that any such number existed and was due to be distributed. It is all very curious.

'You advised that the Emergency Duty Team fax number was switched off, but I cannot understand how this situation could have arisen because the fax number is never switched off.'

I think it was Aristotle – though I can't positively swear that it was – who said that whatever happens must be possible, but then of course Aristotle knew nothing of social services.

Deep Inside, I Am A Rebel

SOMETIMES, THOUGH NOT very often, I wish my patients were the upstanding, God-fearing, law-abiding, hard-working people I tell them they ought to be. I hold myself up as what they might have been if they'd tried a little harder, but I do so with a guilty conscience. Deep inside my conventionally-suited, thoroughly respectable exterior, there is an earringed, lazy rebel trying to get out (I draw the line at tattoos, though). If I stopped working for a day, I fear that my natural sloth might get the better of me. Only terror of falling into the cold clutches of what my patients call 'the Social' (better termed, in my experience, the Antisocial) keeps me going.

Then again, if my patients were the paragons I advise them to be, they would cease to say the wonderful things which they do say, and my life would be much duller. For by comparison with foolishness, the language of wisdom is deeply impoverished. Perhaps one day a literary critic will publish an article – or even a book – in praise of the poetry of folly.

I'm thinking of a patient of mine who, on his own admission, could 'talk until the dogs come home'.

'A lot of people don't believe I'm not well,' he said. 'I don't believe it myself, doctor, but I'm not well. They don't have to put up with my kidneys and my arthritis, or my tempers like my wife does.'

'You're bad-tempered, then?'

'No, but I'm having memory losses. They make me very disgrumpled. Usually I'm the nicest person anyone could meet – and I don't mean that in the bad sense, doctor.'

The problem, it appeared, was his wife. She was a very demanding and extravagant woman.

'I took her to the cinema, doctor. Normally I'd try to sneak in for free, through the fire escape, but with her I had to pay. And she's not like me, I just want to watch the film and leave. With my wife, doctor, she wants to eat and drink, like all women do.'

Troubles, alas, don't come singly. Not only had he had to pay for the cinema, but he had recently had a letter from the Department of Social Security. This made him angry.

'I keep getting letters from these government pigs. I don't want no more letters from the Social Security, and if they send me any more I'll take an overdose. Then I'll have to go to hospital and I won't have to fill in no more forms. Do you hear, no more letters from the Social Security!'

Next in my consulting room was a young man with multiple earrings. He asked me why he always ends up beating his girlfriends.

'You enjoy it, I expect.'

'Oh,' he said, looking relieved. 'I thought it was my head playing games with me.'

He also took drugs and drank to excess.

'They say it's easier to get me off the drugs than the drink. Is that true, doctor?'

His latest court case was about a burglary.

'When I did it, doctor, I was under the influence.'

'What of?'

'Other people.'

He Didn't See The Point
Of School

IN 1961, SIR ERNST Gombrich delivered a lecture at the London School of Economics entitled 'The Tradition of General Knowledge'. In this lecture, he said a society without the assimilation of general knowledge, starting from language and reaching out to the sources of metaphor, would cease to be a society.

What, then, is the general knowledge which welds us into a society rather than leaving us as a large number of egos sharing the same geographical space?

With Gombrich in mind, I recently spoke to a youth aged 15 whose mother had asked me to talk to him because he was going off the rails. This, perhaps, wasn't altogether surprising: his father sometimes went to prison, his mother was an alcoholic and his brother had recently had a fatal accident while burgling.

The youth in question entered my room, and was pleasant and polite in a rough, untutored way. He did not remove the baseball cap from his head, and he slouched in the chair I gave him, extending his body at an angle of 30 degrees to the floor. Indeed, it crossed my mind that, in these days when education is supposed to be 'relevant' to real life, a sensible question in trigonometry might go as follows:

> A British youth goes to see his doctor. He slouches in a chair at an angle of 30 degrees to the ground. He is five feet 10 inches tall. How far above the ground is the crown of his head?

Well, I established that the youth did not go to school because he didn't see the point in doing so. And after a brief examination of his progress in the matter of education, I must admit that I rather agreed with him. If you don't learn anything in the first ten years of schooling, it is unlikely that you'll learn much in the 11th.

I gave him a paragraph to read, and he stumbled through it like a blind man negotiating a maze. After he had finished it, I asked him what it had meant, to which he replied, as nine out of ten such youths do, 'I don't know, I was only reading it.'

On, then, to arithmetic.

'What's that?' he asked.

'Sums,' I replied.

'You mean maffs?'

'Yes. Are you good at maths?'

'Yes, my maffs is all right.'

'What's nine times six?'

You could almost see the grinding and clashing of gears in his mind. After a little bodily writhing, he announced that he did not know and could not guess.

'I'm only good on my twos, fives and tens,' he said.

'And what about history?' I asked.

'I never took that as an option.'

'But still, you must know something?'

I took his silence to indicate disagreement.

'When, for example, was the second world war?'

'I don't know.'

'Well, have a guess.'

Once more the grinding and the clashing of the mental gears.

'Nineteen-sixty?' he suggested tentatively.

'Not quite,' I said. 'Do you know a single historical date?'

'No,' he replied.

'Are you top or bottom of your class?'

'About average.'

I believe it, alas. But I should like to point out to our distinguished educationists that this boy was not of defective intelligence and was not by nature ineducable. Years of research must have gone into the formulation of an educational system in which children can attend school for so long and yet learn so little. Such a system does not arise naturally.

The words of Sir Ernst Gombrich came back to me:

'What I regret most… is the loss of the historical frame of reference, the amputation of the time dimension from our culture.'

We have indeed lost our culture. We are a nation of savages.

There Are Worse Things Than Slippers

MY FATHER WAS unable or unwilling to distinguish etiquette from good manners, and, despising the one, he never acquired the other. Indeed, he came to regard tactlessness as a rough kind of charm, except when he was himself the victim of it. He then reacted as if it were the worst kind of injustice.

In like fashion, I used to think that appearances were unimportant: what mattered was the pure gold of personality within. Now I am not so sure. The ineradicable fact of the matter is that we all judge by appearances and – so long as the majority of our social intercourse is of necessity superficial – we shall continue to do so. The clothes, the facial expression, the bodily habits, proclaim the man, at least until deeper acquaintance.

Take slippers: you can tell quite a lot about someone who wears this domestic footwear. As the generous-hearted sister of my ward put it when she tried to persuade me that the patient in the third bed was really pitiable rather than nasty, 'Bad men don't wear slippers.'

There is, however, a sub-class of slipper-wearers of which I have learnt to be wary. The sub-class consists of women – it is always women – who wear slippers in the shape of furry, sky-blue rabbits or pink kittens. I have even seen badgers, pandas and tiger cubs with long tails. These women will suck a doctor's blood more ruthlessly than a vampire bat exsanguinates its prey.

I now recognise from a hundred yards the sound of furry-animal slippers shuffling – passive-aggressively – across the hospital floor, as a prelude to some impossible small request, such as a five-bedroom house from the council which the doctor, surely, can arrange. The voice is girlish, almost pre-pubertal, the manner ever so slightly coquettish.

'Madam,' I say sternly in my mind, *'remove those slippers forthwith.'*

What I actually say is, 'I'll see what I can do.'

Before long, the slippers return, shuffling inexorably in my direction. 'Have you heard yet, doctor?'

Of course, there are worse things than slippers and passive aggression: for example, there are army boots and active aggression.

Only last week, as it happens, I was consulted by a woman who complained that her husband in common law was irritable and aggressive. If his stepchild asked for something which he did not think he should have, he didn't say 'no' but 'fucking no'. Strangulation of her whom I must call his significant other was one of his modes of self-expression.

The man himself had that short haircut which turns the scalp bristly, yet allows one to make out through the hair the contours of the scars of various battles and pub brawls. His equally bristly, prognathous chin completed the salient parts of his physiognomy, which would have given anybody of normal perceptiveness the swift impression that he was about to attack; an impression strengthened and confirmed by the swastika tattooed on one hand and the cannabis leaf on the other.

'Surely,' I asked his common-law wife, having taken her aside, 'you could have predicted what he was like by his appearance?'

'Yes, doctor,' she replied. 'But that's the look I like in a man. You know, rough.'

That Elusive Entity Called Truth

'WHAT IS TRUTH? said jesting Pilate; and would not stay for an answer' – which is just as well, because no one would have given it him anyway. Man loves truth as worms love garden spades.

These days even (or especially) the truth is libellous, for example when put in references about former employees. Last week, a man discharged from his last post because he was repeatedly drunk at work told me that his ex-employers had not been able to mention his alcoholism in his reference.

'Why not?' I asked.

'It'd be libellous.'

'But you are an alcoholic,' I said.

'Yes, I know, but it'd still be libel.'

As T.S. Eliot once remarked, *en passant*, humankind cannot bear very much reality; but its tolerance seems to have declined of late, and now it can't bear to hear anything ill of itself without recourse to law.

The avoidance of truth, indeed, is the great goal of humanity, or a large part of it. Also last week, I was sent an airline pilot who was suspected of 'abusing psychoactive substances'. I don't want to alarm airline passengers unduly – after all, by air is still much the safest way to travel – but there seemed to be some reason to suspect him of sedating and revivifying himself by artificial means. He had been warned that I should want to take a specimen of his hair for analysis – the said psychoactive substances leaving a chemical deposit therein. The time came for his haircut at my hands, and I admired his luxuriant hair. I snipped a switch with my little scissors (as close to the scalp as possible) and laid it on the special tinfoil for despatch to the laboratory. A few days later I received a call from the laboratory.

'You know Captain L___ whose sample you sent us?' asked a technician. 'Are you sure it was his hair you sent us?'

'Yes,' I replied. 'Why?'

'You see,' said the technician, 'it's not human hair.'

'Oh,' I said. There seemed to be two explanations: either Captain L___ wasn't human, or he was wearing a wig.

'In fact, it isn't hair at all. We tried boiling it for hours, but it just wouldn't digest, Then we tried the ultimate test.'

'What's that?' I asked.

'We set fire to it, to see if it smelt like hair.'

'And did it?'

'It wouldn't burn at all, it wasn't even nylon.'

I should not like to give the impression that no one is ever reliable or truthful, however. Only last week a patient – in this case a prisoner – cleaved close to that elusive entity called the truth, over the nature of which philosophers have been squabbling ever since Man first learnt to think, talk and therefore to lie. He had set fire to some paper in his cell, and though the resultant fire had been quickly extinguished, his conduct was considered dangerous and possibly the result of madness.

'Why did you burn the paper?' I asked.

'I was bored.'

He stared at me with his piercing, vacant blue eyes, the windows of his soul.

'Would you like to be burnt to death just because someone was a little bored?' I asked.

'No,' he replied.

'And would you light another fire?'

'No.'

'Why not?' I asked.

'I ain't got no more matches.'

A Little Misery Brings Back
Such Happy Memories

IT HAS BEEN shown conclusively that people who listen to the news or read a newspaper at breakfast are more miserable than those who wisely maintain themselves in ignorance.

Unfortunately, help for the former is not at hand: one of the main stories in the newspapers recently was that antidepressants do not work for the vast majority of people.

Of course, I always knew this: misery is the natural and inescapable condition of man. That is why the American psychiatrist Thomas Szasz once wrote a paper in *The Lancet* proposing that happiness be classified as a disease. Not only is it statistically aberrant, but it leads to disastrous consequences (proposals of marriage, for example) and is grossly inappropriate to man's true situation.

Anyway, why should I need to know, as I read in the paper the other morning, that three off-duty policemen were lynched in a small town in Bolivia, in an act of democratic, or perhaps I should say demotic, justice? Actually, the story affected me the way the smell of the madeleine affected Proust: it brought back a flood of memories of my visits to Bolivia.

Those were the days of coups – 'golpes', to be exact – and hyperinflation, when it took longer to pay for a meal than to eat it. I changed $50 at a bank and had to return to my lodging to fetch a bag to carry away all the pesos. Those were the salad days of Thomas de la Rue and Company.

You didn't have to wait long for a coup to come. The one while I was there was almost as violent as a democratic election in Africa, and the leader of it is now serving a 30-year jail sentence.

I did the sights, of course, including one of the national shrines: the lamp-post from which the body of President Gualberto Villarroel, a kind of Bolivian Peronist, was hanged after he had been thrown from the balcony of the presidential palace (he had offered to resign, but that wasn't good enough for the mob). It's a shrine now because the Bolivian people are said to regret their impulsive act.

Until I read about the three policemen, I hadn't thought at all about General Mariano Melgarejo, one of more colourful of the Bolivian caudillos of the 19th century. He rose in the ranks of the army by a judicious mixture of sycophancy and disloyalty, and it is said that he personally disposed of the previous tyrant, whose name the crowd outside were calling with Vivas as he was killing him.

Having disposed of him, Melgarejo went out on to the balcony, told them that the president was dead, and asked them who were they shouting for now? Viva Melgarejo! came the answer. I think Shakespeare would have savoured the moment.

When he wanted to demonstrate the loyalty and discipline of his troops to visiting dignitaries, he would march them up the stairs of the presidential palace and straight over the balcony on to the ground below. He once said that he was going to rule in Bolivia as long as he liked, and he would hang anyone from the nearest tree who thought otherwise: not great political philosophy, perhaps, but at least clear and succinct. Of course, he came to a sticky end. He was overthrown in a coup and fled to Lima, where the enraged brother of a former lover shot him dead.

It's worth a little misery each morning if it brings back such happy memories.

No More Iagos In Our Factories

OF ALL THE noble concepts in the world, perhaps the very noblest is that of social justice: but what exactly is it, and how may it be defined? I suspect that it is rather like poetry: it is easier to say what social justice isn't than to say what it is. That is why everyone can agree that the present state of affairs does not represent social justice at all; for if it did, what would there remain for idealistic politicians to do?

It goes without saying that the young, idealistic to the core as ever, are much in favour of social justice. I come across cases every day in which they demonstrate their unshakable thirst for a better world, one which is free of the historical injustices which have accumulated down the ages and which it is the fervent desire of all men of goodwill to end.

For example (and I choose at random), last week a girl of 17 came to our hospital having been punched in the eye by a boy one year younger than she who suspected her of spreading a rumour that he had robbed one of her friends; which, of course, he had, but he objected to being stigmatised in this preposterously judgmental fashion.

The girl, as it happened, was highly intelligent, despite the company she kept. Indeed, not long before, she had passed more exams than the rest of her classmates put together. As a reward, her father – separated, it goes without saying, from her mother – bought her a pair of those expensive trainers which are, for reasons which entirely escape me, the *summum bonum* of slum youth.

The possession of these deeply desirable trainers was an affront to the delicate sense of social justice of the youths of her own age who lived near her, who saw no reason why she should have them and they should not. It was only natural, therefore, that they should express their outrage at this inequality and inequity by seizing her in the street and trying to set fire to her. Not until every youth in the slum had these trainers (when, of course, they would cease to be desirable) would they desist from their righteous persecution of her.

When there is perfect justice in the world – when there is equality of opportunity and therefore of outcome – tragedy will be no more. The sordid emotion of jealousy, for example, will be extinguished from the human heart, because the very concept of personal possession will appear alien, anachronistic and even ridiculous. No longer shall I have to attend to patients such as the one who consulted me last week about his self-inflicted cut wrist.

'Why did you do it?' I asked.

'Me missis just left me.'

'Why?'

'I blacked her eye.'

'Why?'

'I got this phone call from this woman who said me missis is mucking about with the foreman at work.'

'What reason did you have for thinking she must be right?'

'This woman says they keep going for walks at dinner time together.'

'So you hit her?'

'Yes, but I wish I hadn't of now.'

When social justice comes, there will be no more Iagos in our factories.

Militantly Indifferent

UNABLE TO SLEEP one night, I started to dwell on a scene from my adolescence, about which I had not thought for many years.

On my return from a trip abroad during the summer holidays, more than 30 years ago, I went to see a school-friend who lived nearby. He was a brilliant linguist who had recently won a scholarship to a university. He was also severely asthmatic, never entirely without a wheeze, and with a chest already deformed by his condition. His skin was dry, scaly and eczematous. As soon as his mother answered the door, I knew something was wrong.

'Didn't you know? Michael died last week.'

His mother recounted what happened. Michael had woken up with a severe attack one morning, not by any means an unusual occurrence for him. He asked his mother to call an ambulance and she wondered whether it was necessary because he had had so many attacks before. But then he said something which changed her mind. 'Don't you understand, I'm dying!'

Michael was not the kind of boy to say he was dying unless he was dying, and so she called for an ambulance. The ambulance controller, however, asked her numerous questions, and then demanded that she contact her son's doctor first. She explained that her son was dying, but the ambulance controller remained adamant: no ambulance without a request from her son's doctor.

She phoned the doctor, and fortunately he was there. He agreed to call an ambulance for Michael without having examined him. In all, the delay was quite short: about three minutes. But Michael died just as the ambulance arrived. He was 17.

As I left, Michael's mother exclaimed, in the bitterness of her grief, 'Why couldn't it have been his brother? He's got no brains.'

She was separated from her husband, and was not at all well off. Michael had been her great hope for a better future. She lived through and for his achievements.

My legs felt weak as I walked home. The horror of those last few minutes, as she tried to persuade the ambulance controller of the gravity of her son's ultimately unsuccessful efforts to breathe, was very vivid in my mind. To my shame, embarrassed by death, I never returned to my friend's house; I do not know whether his mother ever recovered from the blow.

Why did this scene return to me last week? I think it was something which happened in the hospital which brought it to mind.

A patient of mine had fled to the hospital (via an overdose) to escape a man who had kept her virtually a prisoner in his flat for the last two years. He beat her, and had a long record of violence towards the women with whom he lived. He was strongly suspected of having hanged one of his previous female acquaintances, though nothing could ever be proved. It seemed to me that my patient needed some assistance to leave this man, and so I called a hospital social worker. I explained the circumstances to her, and I had hardly got halfway through when she said, 'If it's a housing issue, the patient needs to go to her Neighbourhood Office.'

I said that I thought a more active and sympathetic form of assistance was required than giving my patient the address of an office where she could stand in a line for several hours waiting to be seen by a militantly indifferent employee who was dreaming only of five o'clock.

'If it's a housing issue, she needs to go to her Neighbourhood Office,' repeated the social worker.

A couple of nights later, I thought of the death of my friend. *Plus ça change.*

Good Humour
And Terrible Food

I TOOK A DAY off from the hospital and the prison last week to do God's glorious work: helping to put a wrongdoer behind bars by testifying in court as to his guilt, or at least his absence of innocence.

The case was heard in one of those dismal provincial towns with which England is so richly endowed. You could see it had once been rather a pleasant place, but the Luftwaffe and the town council (not necessarily in that order of importance) had changed all that. You could tell it had undergone moral degeneration as well as architectural by the existence of the security cameras trained upon the entrance of the Particular Baptist Ebenezer Chapel, which was next door to the courthouse.

Needless to say, my early arrival at the court proved unnecessary. The previous case was not yet concluded. I sat in the waiting-room set aside for witnesses, but my fellow witnesses availed themselves of the television placed there for our entertainment (the Devil makes programmes for idle eyes to watch), thus driving me out into the foyer.

At lunchtime, the prosecuting barrister informed me that I should not now be needed till the afternoon session and I was therefore free to taste the delights of W___ until 2.30 p.m. 'Does W___ have any delights to offer?' I asked, but the barrister kept silent on the grounds that the answer he gave might etc. etc.

I went in search of lunch. I found a small Chinese restaurant opposite which was a charity second-hand bookshop whose takings were used to send old people on day trips to neighbouring and no doubt equally dismal towns, though admittedly by canal, which would be nice. The volunteer who ran the shop was dressed in red Santa's robes (or were they those of a High Court judge?). What treasures I found in the bookshop! First a copy of *Havannah*, Lord Thomas's historical novel, inscribed by the author to David Sheppard, former Bishop of Liverpool, 'In the hope that the first chapters [set in Liverpool] will amuse one who lives in a different city.' Note that Lord Thomas writes different, not better.

Second, I found *For the Liberation of Brazil* by the Brazilian Marxist revolutionary Carlos Marighella, published in the Penguin Latin American Library (originally at 30p, now on sale, after 26 years of unprecedented inflation, at 50p). It is a do-it-yourself manual for urban guerrillas by one who was shot dead by the Brazilian police in 1969, an event described in the introduction by the great Wykehamist revolutionary, Richard Gott, as 'an undeniably serious setback'. I must admit that, looking around W___, urban guerrilla warfare seemed quite an attractive option.

And so to the Chinese restaurant. Such was the influence of the local culture and diet that even the Chinese waiters looked like Rugby League forwards. I went for the two-month special offer Christmas lunch: snowflake hot-and-sour soup and mixed satay (with rice rather than chips), thus avoiding the char sui or turkey with peas and gravy. Having been brought up in England, I not only do not mind really bad food, but sometimes positively long for it. And I wasn't in the least disappointed: I couldn't help wondering whether bovine spongiform encephalopathy had yet reached the feline population of W___.

The two ladies at the next table got up to go.

'You should thank us,' one of them said. 'We're leaving.' She wrapped up her little boy in a coat. 'People'll look at you,' she said tenderly, 'and never forget to take their contraceptives.'

I was back in the England of my childhood: good humour and terrible food.

I returned to court. It was Napoleon (I think) who said that a man who does two things at once does neither. In the British judicial system, a witness who doesn't do two things at once does nothing. I read a book until four o'clock, when the prosecution clerk told me that

I now wouldn't be called until next day. Confound the inconvenience! There was no train home for three whole hours.

At 4.15 the clerk returned. The accused had changed his plea to guilty. God be praised! Hundreds of pounds (plus expenses) for doing nothing.

The English Are Just
Savages With Stereos

THE LATE PROFESSOR Shepherd, reviewing a volume somewhat optimistically entitled by its editor *Recent Progress in Psychiatry*, wrote that a more appropriate title, perhaps, would have been *Recent Activity in Psychiatry*.

I confess that I feel the same way about popular culture. It's popular, all right, but is it culture?

I suppose in the ecumenical sense of the word, as used by American anthropologists who make no distinction between the head-hunters of New Guinea and the first Viennese school, it is culture; and in the same loose sense, the way people live in England must be counted a civilisation. Still, whenever I hear the words 'popular culture' I reach for my earplugs.

Judge not, that ye be not judgmental, that is the first tenet of the First Church of Christ, Social Worker.

Needless to say, non-judgmentalism is both impossible in practice and disastrous when attempted. People go on making judgments, but because of official non-judgmentalism are quite unable to live according to them. For example, our slum dwellers may judge all they like that a quiet life is best, but – because the Crown Prosecution Service has decided that there is nothing to choose between an intact skull and one smashed into fragments by a baseball bat – it is quite beyond their reach. So life remains for them what it need not be, a torment.

Many of my patients are goaded by their neighbours, who use every refinement of barbarism to make their lives a misery. Sometimes I think the English are just savages with stereos.

Last week, a patient came to me to complain about his neighbours. He wanted something done about them before he took to the axe or the lunatic asylum. I asked him for the burden of his complaints against his neighbours.

'Every day, we have complete swearing and spitting out of the windows.'

Complete swearing and spitting? Complete by comparison with what? Partial swearing and spitting? Would such partial swearing and spitting constitute an amelioration?

'What do you want me to do about it?' I asked.

'There should be some tablets or injections to stop them,' he replied.

His belief in the powers of medicine and doctors did him credit, of course, but in this case was quite unjustified.

'I'm afraid there's not much I can do,' I said.

'There must be,' he continued. 'They make so much noise, they've got me running around like a pea in a pod.'

When did the English become savages? It isn't a question of education, for even the uneducated of a few decades ago behaved with more natural dignity and grace than the comparatively well-educated of today.

My next patient was a nice old gentleman, an unskilled worker retired for many years, who came to ask my advice about the medicine he was taking, of which name he could only half-remember. I guessed at the full name.

'That's education for you,' he said, good-humouredly. 'Do you think I should continue to take it?'

I said that he should; to which he replied, 'Well, I can't go against a doctor's decision.'

His quiet dignity allowed him to assume not that I was right, but that I was advising him to the best of my ability: which I was. There was no hint in him of that disappointed and enraged self-importance which lies behind present ill-manners.

My next patient, 20 years old, brought me back to modern popular culture. His 38-year-old stepfather was on holiday in Greece, and had sent him a postcard, which the patient brought with him and allowed me to read. 'Pissed every night,' it said. 'Fucking great!'

Birthday Party Entertainment

WORLDLY FAME IS all too fleeting. A name which is a household word to one generation may produce merely the wrinkled brow of puzzlement in the next. Literary celebrity is perhaps the most evanescent of all – who, apart from second-hand book dealers, has now heard of E. Phillips Oppenheim, to cite but a single example of departed glory? – yet scientific fame is also short-lived.

Who now remembers Jean Piaget, the Swiss psychologist who charted the stages of a child's mental development? At one time not so very long ago he was all the rage. I don't know whether he is forgotten because his ideas were proved wrong, or because they are now regarded as so obviously true that they needed no originator; but I recall nonetheless that one of his books was about the child's concept of death.

No child, I think he said, understood the permanence of death before the comparatively late age of ten; but a generation raised on junk food and parental neglect has turned out to be surprisingly precocious, in this as in other things. I suppose this proves the resilience of Man, and we should be thankful for it.

A patient last week mentioned to me that she was finding her children difficult to tolerate. Dixon was particularly unpleasant.

'He says the most horrible things to me, doctor.'

'Such as what?' I asked.

'I'm going to stab you in the heart with a machete and then I'm going to cut your head off.'

'How old is he?'

'Six, nearly seven.'

My guess is that Dixon understood the permanence of death only too well.

'And where do you think he gets his ideas from?' I asked.

'His dad, of course.'

Dad was no longer living at home – round here, he very seldom is – but that didn't mean that he had abandoned altogether the beating up of the mother of his children. Only a few weeks ago he had arrived at her flat while another of their mutual children, Duane, was having his birthday party. And while it is commonplace nowadays for effete middle-class parents to hire a magician to entertain children at birthday parties, round here a fight or even a shooting is the preferred way of keeping their little minds occupied. Who says people don't make their own entertainment any more?

Dad grabbed Mum by the hair, pulled her to the ground and started to kick her, all in front of the children, including Dixon. Dad's language was not pleasant, I gather, and involved several threats to kill.

The beating over, and Dad having departed, Mum told the birthday guests to go home (did they all say, 'Thank you for having me' as they left, I wonder?), and then she called the police.

'And what did the police do?' I asked

'They didn't do nothing,' she replied.

'Why not?'

'They said they couldn't do nothing because he didn't break in, I opened the door to him myself.'

'But he assaulted you and threatened to kill you in front of lots of witnesses.'

'Yes, but they said they couldn't do nothing about it because I let him in myself.'

It's amazing what lies the police will tell to avoid having to fill in the forms after they make an arrest.

Talking Of The Police

THE GREAT SECRET of life, I have discovered, is always to appear busy, whether one is or not. A reputation for ceaseless occupation is a considerable asset in the eternal struggle to avoid doing what one doesn't really want to do. How many patients have I successfully fobbed off by informing them that I am far too busy either to see or to speak to them at the moment? Such is my reputation for hard work that the patients thus brushed off at once begin to stammer their apologies for having had the temerity to interrupt me in the first place.

Naturally, doctors are not the only ones to use this invaluable tactic to avoid unpleasant tasks such as obliging the public. The police, for instance, are past masters at it. Indeed, so busy are they that – in my experience – they always claim that they ought to be somewhere else than where they are now. This means, of course, that they can never investigate fully the crime to which they have been called, or arrest the culprit, for then they would have to fill in all the forms, and would be even busier.

That the police should be overwhelmingly busy is, alas, all too plausible in this land of theft and assault. It is just that, so far at least, I haven't discovered what it is the police are busy with. The jealous are not ever jealous for the cause, says Emilia in *Othello*, but they are jealous that they are jealous. The police are busy that they are busy.

For example, last week a young man of the shaven-headed and tattooed-handed tribe arrived in our hospital complaining of a headache. Shortly afterwards, his wife arrived in his wake, whereupon – she being the cause of his headache in his opinion – he beat her up in the cubicle in which he was awaiting medical attention. The nurses, who heard the punches raining down on her face, ran to rescue her and called the police.

The police arrived comparatively promptly, but declared, once the situation had been explained to them, that they were too busy to do anything about it, and left. The night before, incidentally, the woman's seven-year-old son (not by her husband) had telephoned the police because step-papa was strangling mama while simultaneously trying to eject her from the window. This is what is known in technical terms as a 'domestic'.

One swallow doesn't make a summer, of course, nor one instance of police dereliction of duty, incompetence, laziness and stupidity a complete breakdown in law and order. But in the same week another young man, a drug addict on our ward, was observed stealing the possessions of a mentally subnormal patient opposite, and then leaving the ward. The staff called the police, not only giving his name and address, but the name and address of the pharmacy from which he collected his disgusting drugs every day. It wouldn't have required Sherlock Holmes to apprehend him; even the unaided Dr Watson could have managed it.

The police duly turned up on our ward – three hours after having been called. They agreed that, theoretically speaking, it was an open and shut case, but unfortunately they were too busy to pursue it.

'Busy with what?' asked one of the nurses.

'Serious crimes,' replied the police.

Committed by whom? By people such as the violent husband and the drug addict, of course.

Let Us Open The Morgues

THE ENLIGHTENMENT PROPOSAL that every human institution, custom and prejudice be judged by the light of reason has brought us to a pretty pass; but then, come to think of it, we were in quite a mess from the beginning. Perhaps we should just accept with a good grace that we humans are destined to wallow in a swamp of our own making, from which neither faith nor reason can extricate us.

A short while ago, I published an article in which I suggested that one day it would be argued that the problem with paedophilia was not old men in raincoats but society's prejudices against their practices. Nothing is good or bad but thinking makes it so: *ergo*, anti-paedophilia is the merest prejudice.

Sure enough, I received a letter afterwards thanking me for the clarity of my exposition and enclosing my correspondent's thoughts on the subject, which, he said, agreed with mine. One day paedophiles would be free.

After paedophilia, necrophilia. Who is harmed by it, I should like to know? It is a victimless crime, at least when carried out tactfully. Therefore, let us open our morgues: the corpses won't mind.

Naturally, it is only a matter of time before this cry is taken up by progressive (that is to say, state-subsidised) artists. In fact, it already has been taken up. A nearby art cinema, which rarely has an audience of more than eight, where the atmosphere, even in the lobby, is dark and furtive, and whose staff all appear to suffer from tics and other nervous disorders, recently showed a Canadian film called *Kissed*. This is how the cinema's programme described it: 'Sandra takes a job as a mortician, and her childhood fascination with death takes an overtly sexual edge as she repeatedly sneaks into the mortuary at night, making love to a series of freshly deceased young men... The film is at once macabre, sensuous and deeply moving, a love story in which strange desires seem logical, believable and normal.'

My wife and I took our seats (she under protest). Before the film started, a man, whose odour preceded him like a cold front on a weather map, sat near us, though the auditorium was nearly empty as usual.

'Is this the right place for *Kissed*?' he asked.

'Yes,' we replied.

'Sure?'

'Yes, quite sure.'

He relaxed in his seat, deeply satisfied. The film began: I was unsurprised to learn that it had been subsidised by Canadian public money.

The protagonist's childhood was portrayed as a series of ecstatic encounters with dead animals. When she cuddled a dead mouse which she had cut open, my wife left the auditorium in disgust to wait for me in the lobby. Another smelly man approached me soon afterwards and asked whether the seat next to me was taken.

'Yes,' I replied firmly.

He sat next to another couple who swiftly fled to the opposite side of the cinema. By now, the protagonist was stroking a corpse.

'Ah, necrophilia,' murmured the man behind me appreciatively.

I felt slightly sick. Perhaps it was the Toblerone which I had hastily consumed beforehand. Chocolate and necrophilia don't mix.

I rejoined my wife, who was sitting on an old plastic-upholstered settee, designing the wormery to make compost for our garden.

'Though worms... destroy this body, yet in my flesh shall I see God.'

At Least To An Extent, Life Is What One Makes Of It

AS WE KNOW, human life is sacred. Now, indeed, that God is dead and religion defunct – to put it mildly – there is nothing left in the universe to worship except ourselves. It follows, I think, that he who saves human life is engaged upon the holiest work which can be vouchsafed us. This sometimes makes me feel positively self-righteous.

Last week, for example, I arrived at the prison to discover that a young man had attempted to cut his wrists with a ballpoint pen. He had been put in a bare cell and deprived of all the appurtenances of suicide, such as shirt and trousers, and was now dressed in Home Office anti-suicide garb, a blue Terylene outfit with Velcro fastenings.

These are what are known as strip conditions, and the cell is called the strip cell, which, a prison officer informed me, is also known in another prison down the road as the Shrine.

'Why's that?' I asked the officer.

'I don't know, sir. Perhaps it's because it has produced so many miracle cures.'

'Why did you do it?' I asked the young man in strip conditions.

'There's nothing out there for me,' he replied. 'Life's shit.'

I explained that, at least to an extent, life was what one made it.

'You don't know nothing about me, you can't talk. It's all right for you, life's easy for you.'

'You don't know anything about me,' I said. 'You can't talk.'

'There's nothing in life for me so why can't I kill myself if I want to?'

'Because it's against prison regulations, I'm afraid. What you do outside prison is your own affair, but while you're in here you won't be allowed to kill yourself.'

I turned to go.

'Can I have a cigarette, then?' he asked.

Give me smoke or give me death.

Two days later I went into his cell.

'Hello, doctor, I feel fine now, can I go back to the wing?'

How gratified I felt that I had saved another life – or, if not a life, at least a ballpoint pen.

It's just the same in the hospital, of course. A young man was admitted deeply unconscious from the effects of what are known as recreational drugs. Some recreation! In his case, they were opiates and benzodiazepines, the effects of each of which are reversible with antidote drugs.

Let sleeping psychopaths lie, say I! No sooner was he awake than he started to create chaos. His shirt – a replica of those worn by a famous football team – had had to be cut from his supine body in order that he could be fully examined.

'Fuck you, you fat motherfucking fat pigs!' he said, in gratitude for having been snatched from the jaws of death. 'That shirt cost me 40 fucking quid and you had no fucking right to cut if off me.'

With that innate sense of justice with which, as Rousseau knew, primitive Man is by nature endowed, he picked up his drip stand and began to swing it round at the equipment near him.

'I'm gonna fucking do 50 quid of damage to your fucking ward because of what you did to my shirt.'

One of the nurses tried to calm him.

'I'm going out there to fucking kill myself,' he said menacingly, 'and you've got no fucking right to stop me.'

The nurse didn't try to stop him.

'She's not a coward,' one of the other nurses told me. 'She's quite tough. She's the one that cut Andrew B___ down when he hanged himself in the toilet. But you have to draw the line somewhere.'

He Strangled Her About Once A Week, And She Was Tired Of It

THERE IS A SCHEME AFOOT, so I am told, to teach medical students the elements of literature. Once they have walked the wards, they will turn the pages – compulsorily, as a condition of their qualification. It is hoped that labour in the salt mines of literature will make them into better doctors than they would otherwise have been.

Flaubert and Chekhov have been suggested as appropriate authors for them to study, and who could object to the choice? But when it comes to dealing with the bureaucracy of the National Health Service, I should have thought a quick course in Kafka would have stood them in more stead. It is never too soon to make the acquaintance of the twilight zone of nameless dread, infinite regress and logical contradiction in which they are going to spend the rest of their professional lives.

The young daughter of a colleague of mine required a small operation, and the local hospital had promised to let the parents know in the near future when it would be performed. Three months went by, and still there was no news, so my colleague phoned the hospital to find out what was happening. The young woman at the appointments desk tapped something into her computer, and said in a tone of slightly irritated moral superiority, 'She was supposed to have had her operation two weeks ago, but you didn't bring her to the hospital.'

'We didn't receive the appointment,' said my colleague.

'Yes,' admitted the young woman, 'appointments haven't been reaching patients lately. There's something wrong with the system.'

'Then how could we have kept the appointment?'

'You could have called earlier.'

'Earlier than what?'

'Earlier than two weeks ago, before the appointment.'

Appointment desk staff in the NHS are recruited solely on the basis of an inability to see anything from a point of view other than their own. It was clear that further conversation would not merely have failed to resolve the situation, but would have put my colleague's health at risk. It would, in the words of my prisoner patients, have done his head in.

Last week, at about a quarter to one in the afternoon, I needed to speak urgently to a patient's general practitioner. The young receptionist who answered the phone had one of those sheep-like voices, so common in England, which tell you at once, from the very first word, that the mind behind the voice is utterly sluggish and only daydreaming of the weekend, when the person to whom it belongs will go clubbing in cheap, skimpy clothes.

'Could I speak to Dr S___ about one of his patients, please?' I asked.

'Dr S___ is half-day today,' she replied.

'Could I speak to the doctor on duty, then?'

'He's not on duty yet. Duty starts at one o'clock.'

'Then could I speak to Dr S___?'

'He's half-day.'

'Then I'll speak to the doctor who will be on duty in quarter of an hour.'

'But the patient isn't his, he's Dr S___'s, and Dr S___ is half-day. And the duty doctor isn't on duty yet.'

By comparison, it is almost a relief to deal with patients. My next patient was in what he called 'bits' because his girlfriend had just called the police to remove him from the common-law matrimonial home. He strangled her about once a week, and she was tired of it.

'Have you ever strangled her to the point of unconsciousness?' I asked.

'Oh no, doctor. I know when to stop.'

We Have Lawyers To Maintain

THERE MAY BE a nation more frivolous and contemptible than the English, but somehow I doubt it. I have travelled the world and sojourned in several remote countries, but I have never encountered a people which knows so little about how to live as the English. A village in the African bush is a school of virtue and an academy of culture by comparison with an English town. Long governed by bullying incompetents, the English have given up using their brains: they have the intelligence of sheep and the morals of hyenas.

I generalise, perhaps, but from a large experience. The frivolity of the English is nowhere seen to better advantage than in officialdom's ardour to succour the guilty and humiliate the innocent. Not long ago, I received a letter from the mother of a prisoner who had tried to stab himself in the stomach. He had done so, he said, because the mother of his two children had run off with his best mate even though, according to the letter apprising him of his former girlfriend's deep new attachment, she still loved him 'to bits'.

What the prisoner's mother wanted to know was why the prison had allowed him to stab himself in the stomach when it knew he was so depressed about his girlfriend. Why had he not been prevented from doing so?

I called the prisoner into my office. He was serving his fifth sentence for burglary. In the course of our conversation I asked him, as a matter of interest, how many burglaries he had committed.

'I can't answer that,' he said.

'Why not?' I asked.

'How many worms has a bird eaten?' he replied.

I wanted to write to his mother that we had failed to prevent him from stabbing himself in the stomach for the same reason that she had failed to prevent him from burgling untold numbers of houses.

Except, of course, that she probably thought that burglary, when conducted by her son, was a fine profession. I wrote to her in my usual emollient style.

She had concluded her letter by saying that she was thinking of consulting a solicitor – on legal aid, of course. I'm sure that, the case being so completely without merit, legal aid will be instantly granted. After all, we have three times as many lawyers to maintain as in 1975.

That same afternoon I returned to the hospital to discover that one of the nurses on my ward had taken the day off because she had been so terrified by an incident which had happened the previous day. The pimp of a prostitute whose arm he had broken (but who still loved him) came to visit her in hospital. She was already black and blue from his attentions, and in the course of his visit he split her lip with a well-aimed blow out of sight of the staff, of course.

On being refused his demand to use the telephone at the nurses' station, he threatened two nurses, the first with such violence that she would become a patient in her own hospital, the second with following her home and burning her house down.

The police were called. They gave the nurses an incident number. This, of course, was completely inadequate: what they really needed was counselling.

The Whirligig Of Time

I WAS BEING escorted last Saturday from the prison gate to the prison hospital when I looked up at that little tent of blue we doctors call 'the sky'.

'Lovely weather,' I said to my escorting officer who, to judge from the proportions of his abdomen, was not a nature-lover. Indeed, I should be rather surprised if he were even aware of its existence.

'Too good to be in here, sir,' he replied.

'Tell me,' I asked, 'what is the right weather to be in prison?'

'You've got a point there, sir,' he said, unlocking the door to the hospital with its notice reminding all staff that security is their responsibility.

Before long, I went to that prison within a prison, 'the block', where inmates who are accused of having offended against prison discipline are kept until a governor hears their case, a process known as 'adjudication'.

First, however, they have to be 'fitted for adjudication' by the doctor, and declared medically suitable for solitary confinement. As usual, the question is asked the wrong way round, the real question being, Are they suitable for anything else?

'Doc,' said the first of the alleged violators of the rules, 'I need some medication.'

'What for?' I asked.

'My head's a shed,' he replied.

Insofar as a shed is usually a repository for junk, this was no doubt an accurate description; but what he really meant, I think, was that he was 'in bits', that his head needed 'sorting out'. I sympathised with him, but said I thought that medication was not the answer to his problem, whereupon he lost it and went into one, threw his dolly out of the pram and became very mouthy – almost gobby, in fact.

'What's the fucking use of a fucking doctor what won't give you fuck all?'

And thus the whirligig of time has well and truly brought in its revenges, for not so many years ago we doctors were criticised for too liberal use of the tranquilliser chlorpromazine, popularly known as the liquid cosh.

I read the charge sheets against this alleged miscreant: 'On the nth day of J___ you did use insulting language towards Officer X, namely, "Who the fuck do you think you are, cunt, you can kiss my black arse, you wanker".'

'He didn't go to finishing school, did he?' I said.

'Too fucking right, he didn't,' said one of the officers.

A short while later, I left the prison and went shopping for the usual basics, such as balsamic vinegar, rocket and ciabatta.

Having completed my subsistence shopping, I was walking in the direction of the bookshop when I noticed an energetic bicyclist in apple-green Lycra weaving his way between the traffic, of which he at length burst free. He whizzed by me and lots of other pedestrians.

'Fuck off! Fuck off!' he shouted, as he flew by.

Who or what should fuck off, I wondered. The cars? The pedestrians? The world? Existence itself?

It occurred to me then that, since past civilisations, such as the Beaker Culture, are sometimes named by archaeologists for their principal surviving cultural artefacts, our civilisation should henceforth be known as 'the Fuck Off Culture'. Anyone who disagrees with me can... well, you know...

In An Emergency, Preserve Your Maggots In Gin

I HAVE LONG observed that the only modern public buildings on which expense has not been spared, and which consequently rise above the level of the barely functional, are law courts. And this is precisely as it should be, when one considers the criminality of the English population. Going to court is the only time it emerges from the primeval swamp of its own popular culture.

Alas, mere expenditure of money, while no doubt necessary, is not sufficient to bring a beautiful building into being; and the faculty of taste and discrimination has been so long absent from these islands that an ocean of money could be spent and nothing worthwhile would be built. So it is with our law courts: they all look as though they were designed by architects whose previous commissions were for underground torture chambers in African despotisms.

It was to one of these new palaces of justice that I repaired last week, to give evidence in a murder trial. It was swiftly decided by counsel, before the proceedings began that day, that I should be of more use to the opposing side than to the one by which I had been retained, and I was free to go my way (and collect my fee). Fortunately, however, I did not do so before I had had a chat with another expert witness appearing in the case.

You can always tell an expert witness: dark blue suit, slightly grubby; grey cardigan underneath; unpolished shoes with thick rubber soles. Smartness does not come naturally to expert witnesses, and generally they make a hash of it.

This expert was an entomologist, though he felt uneasy with so grand a title, and preferred to call himself more modestly a 'fly man'. The outcome of the case depended on the age of the maggots in the deceased's body, and our fly man had found serious deficiencies, not to say outright inaccuracies, in their fly man's testimony.

He had misidentified the species of fly for a start, but that was not the most egregious of his errors. He had drawn conclusions about the length, and hence the age, of the maggots from frozen specimens; and everyone knows that defrosted maggots lose their shape, as frozen strawberries do. You can conclude nothing from frozen maggots, and here the fly man gave me a tip: in an emergency, he said, preserve your maggots in gin.

'Specifically in gin?' I asked. 'Or will any spirit do?'

'Any will do,' he replied, 'but best without colouring.'

He took out graphs to prove to me that the maggots in the body could not have been more than ten days old, and not five weeks old as the opposition fly man had alleged. Upon the age of the maggots turned the fate of a man: life imprisonment or what prisoners call a 'walk-out'.

'I'll try to let him down lightly,' said our fly man of their fly man. 'But I'll probably make an enemy of him all the same.'

I had every confidence in our fly man. His graphs looked rock-solid to me. If ever I need a fly man to testify for me, he's the fly man I'll want.

As it happens, I've been in the company of insect men a few times in my life. They are uniformly splendid people, far more interesting company than, say, politicians. I could have been an insect man myself, if I hadn't been waylaid *en route* by that two-legged insect, Man.

My View Of Our Earthly Existence Is Not Altogether Sunny

I SEEM TO HAVE an adverse effect on my patients. Far from making them feel better, I make them feel worse. For example, only the other morning I saw one of my patients walking down the street arm-in-arm with a friend, enjoying a jolly good joke. Alas, this happy situation was not brought about by any treatment of mine, quite the reverse. She has only to appear in my consulting room to be at once crippled by pain and crushed by depression so deep that she is almost speechless with misery.

It is true that my view of our earthly existence is not altogether a sunny one, but surely I do not communicate my darker thoughts so unequivocally by my very manner of being that people who encounter me are at once thrust into the abyss of despair, not to mention neuralgia and a host of other symptoms? Could there be, perhaps, another explanation of the contrast between my patient's happiness on the street and her misery in my consulting room? Reader, there could. My patient used to be a nurse who worked on a geriatric ward, but one day slipped on the hospital corridor which was being mopped by a cleaner without any notice to the effect that wet stone floors are slippery. One man's negligence is another man's opportunity, of course. The prospect of early retirement on full pay with a nice lump sum into the bargain danced before my patient's eye even before she hit the ground. No more medicine time, no more tea for fractious geriatrics to drink up for their own good; henceforth her time would be her own. Only one problem remained: to convince enough doctors that her injury was severe and permanent. In this context, permanent means when doctors have grown sick of trying to cure their patient. They'll say and sign anything then, just to get rid of him or her.

On the day on which I saw her tripping merrily down the street, my first in-patient was a young man who had taken a few too many aspirins. He was chatting happily to another patient, but when he saw me his face clouded over: the mere sight of me had pitched him into the Slough of Despond. His mood became ever blacker as he approached my room. He was wearing a T-shirt with the following legend:

No scares. No worries. No regrets. No fear. NO SHIT!

On one forearm was tattooed the letters ACAB, on the other NWA: All Coppers Are Bastards and Niggaz With Attitude. On his neck the word 'Jade' was tattooed.

'Why Jade?' I asked.

'She's one of my daughters.'

'How many do you have?'

'Three.'

'One mother?'

'Three. I don't get on with none of them.'

He was now 22.

'Why did you take too many pills?' I asked.

'I ain't got nowhere to live.'

'We could find you a hostel.'

'I don't want to go to no hostel.'

'We won't be able to find you anywhere else.'

'Well, I'll have to go on taking overdoses then, won't I?'

He left my room with a face of thunder. A few minutes later I saw him laughing and joking with another patient.

Only A Fool – Or An Intellectual – Would Expect Anything Else

TRAVEL CONFIRMS the prejudices, which is just as well: who wants jet-lag *and* the discomfort of having had his preconceptions overturned? I am glad to say that a recent trip to Colombia successfully confirmed everything I have long suspected about Britain.

Colombia is like a vast British housing estate, where intimidation is the only law. There are, of course, some differences between Britain and Colombia: for example, the Colombian middle classes are much better educated and vastly more cultivated and intelligent than their British counterparts. And because the situation in Colombia is so serious, the minds of its intellectuals have been concentrated somewhat.

Catastrophe being so close at hand, there is no time left for such intellectual frivolities as criminology, which is the construction of sophistical arguments to deny the connection between crime and punishment, in order that academics may appear more compassionate than thou. Now that the whole house of cards called society is about to collapse in Colombia, the intellectuals have discovered the virtues of law and order: alas, their brilliant discovery may have come too late.

In Medellín, the most violent city in Colombia, the police accomplish two tasks: they draw their salaries and defend themselves against direct attack. Otherwise, they serve no purpose at all; precisely the same as the British police in all working-class areas of Britain. And, needless to say, when the state has withered away, à la Marx, it is not replaced by the reign of universal brotherhood and peace, but by the reign of absolute terror and intimidation. Only a fool – or an intellectual – would have expected anything else.

I now quote from an essay by the Colombian economist, Fernando Gaitán Daza, about the causes of violence in his country, which he has studied both in detail and with passion. But is he writing about Colombia or Britain?

'A digression on the subject of impunity as a facilitating factor for crime and violence. Although an increase in punishment is positively associated with a decrease in crime and violence, this is not necessarily the case for those who are already criminal, despite it being dissuasive for those who are thinking of becoming violent or criminal.

'This is reflected in long-term frequency and prevalence. Frequency refers to the number of crimes a person commits in his life, while prevalence refers to the percentage of people in a population who dedicate themselves totally or partially to criminal activities.

'Punishment has a long-term effect on prevalence, but probably not upon frequency, other than through the time a criminal stays in prison.'

Punishment for crime in Colombia is neither prolonged nor likely, so that both frequency and prevalence (as Gaitán defines them) are extremely high. And in the absence of an increase in the rate or severity of punishment for crimes committed, there is no reason why either frequency or prevalence should decline.

The logic of the situation, alas, is all too familiar to me. But who in Britain would condescend to learn from a mere Colombian?

I arrived home safely from Colombia. The airport carousel that delivered my luggage was next to two carousels delivering the luggage from holiday flights. The exhalation of stale alcohol from the waiting passengers was stronger and more nauseating than that in my hospital's casualty late on a Saturday night. Welcome to New Britain.

Prevention Is Better Than Cure

TO WHOM DOES one turn for enlightenment about what is rather grandly known as the human condition? To priests, politicians, philosophers, psychologists or psychiatrists? I think not. I prefer eclectic sources of wisdom: rat-catchers, insurance loss-adjusters, taxi-drivers: they know what man is really like.

Rat-catchers are splendid people because they are impassioned by their work in a way that so few of us are nowadays. They do not suffer from what Marxists used to call alienation: they can talk for hours on the subject of vermin, for which they obviously have a deep affection. If only I could share their enthusiasm!

As for insurance loss-adjusters, they have no equal for sniffing out a lie. They also have the invaluable ability to make you uneasy even when you are telling them the whole truth and nothing but the truth, as if they have sniffed out the central lie that is at the heart of all human existence (whatever it is).

And much may be learnt from taxi drivers, some of it practical application. For example, last evening I was returning home from a restaurant in a taxi whose driver told me how he dealt with drunken louts – a subject of ever-increasing medical importance.

It was no good refusing to pick them up, he said, unless you had a clear bit of road for a getaway; otherwise they would run after your cab, kick out the lights, smash the windows, etc. Once they were in the cab the driver should join in with their banter and pretend to find it amusing. If, however, they became too boisterous and threatening, you should pull up outside a police station and toot your horn continuously until the cops emerge – as they always do rapidly in such circumstances (unlike when your house has been burgled) because the noise disturbs their repose. The drunken passengers never actually carry out their threat to kill the taxi-driver the next time they see him: a failure resulting less from ethical scruple, perhaps, than from alcoholic amnesia.

But there was yet a third level of response, in cases where the drunken passengers would not be calmed by the driver joining in their drunken drivel, and when there was no police station near at hand to stop outside. The driver carried chilli powder with him, ready to squirt in his passengers' eyes if they grew too menacing. He only had to use it once or twice a month, he said, but it always worked.

How perfect an idea! It seems to me that every emergency department in every hospital in the country ought to have a chilli-squirter to deal with refractory patients, since the police and the courts so adamantly refuse to do so. Many injuries to nurses could be avoided that way, and prevention is better than cure.

If only we had had chilli powder on the ward when our friend the pimp threatened to follow one of our nurses to her home and burn it down with her and her family in it after she had told him that his prostitute was not yet ready to be discharged from the ward. Didn't she realise he was losing money?

Chilli powder ought to be standard issue to all doctors and nurses.

I Went Weak At The Knuckles

THE WORLD HEALTH ORGANISATION and the American government are fond of dedicating (at whose behest, and on whose behalf?) days and even whole years and decades to some medical or paramedical cause: 'World No Smoking Day', for example, or the 'Decade of the Brain'. It is the closest we come, I suppose, to religious observance.

Well, it was definitely the Day of the Finger on my ward last Monday. By the end of the morning, fingers were much in my thoughts, for reasons that I shall now explain.

My first patient was a young man from a city 100 miles away. He had come on the train, celebrating his arrival so comprehensively that he passed out with alcohol poisoning and was brought to our hospital.

It turned out, when he awoke from his slumbers, that it was not safe for him to return whence he came because he was wanted there: not by the police, but by the drug dealers to whom he owed £2,000. They had already hit him once with an iron bar, and kidnapped him from the street and taken him to the gymnasium that they used part-time as a torture chamber for a demonstration of things to come if he did not pay up.

'What do they do to people there?' I asked.

'They tie them down and beat them with baseball bats.'

'Ah yes, of course, the sporting connection. And what if you still don't pay?'

'Then it's the machete. I've known quite a few fingers go missing.'

If it's possible to go weak at the knuckles, I went weak at the knuckles.

My next patient had tried to kill herself. The houseman had written in the notes 'overdose of weed-killer', which raised the interesting question of the correct, therapeutic dose of weed-killer: but let it pass.

The woman lived in a second-floor council flat with her two sons by a man they had never met. One day a young child from the flat above them had flung a bottle out of the window upstairs and it had smashed against the windscreen of a car parked below. As luck would have it, the car belonged to a well-known family of local thugs, and, as luck would also have it, my patient's son was standing at the window overlooking the car both when the bottle was launched and when it landed. Concluding that he was the author of this desecration of their property, the thugs immediately came upstairs, kicked the door in and tried to stab him. Parrying the knife thrust with his hand, a couple of his fingers were almost severed. Once again I went weak at the knuckles.

My patient's son was now a prisoner in the flat. The gang had threatened to get him properly next time, and the tension led my patient to the Paraquat. She couldn't go to the police, she said, because if she had done so she would have made the situation worse, and turned it from a potential stabbing to certain arson.

Our citizens are much more frightened of each other than they are of the police, and with good reason. Last week I was consulted by a prisoner who was imprisoned on charges of having damaged two police cars. I asked him why he had chosen two police cars to damage.

'Because if I'd damaged any other cars,' he said, 'the owners might've beaten me up.'

I'm Just The Baby-Father

I ONCE LIVED next door to a man whose wife was a terrific drinker. Dominating their sitting-room was the largest bottle of Scotch (or of anything else) I have ever seen. Approximately the size of a man, the level in it was perceptibly lower each day.

One day, thieves broke into the house while the memsahib was enjoying her drunken siesta and stole her very valuable sapphire ring. When her husband returned home and discovered the robbery, his first words were, 'I wish they'd taken my wife and left the ring.'

There is little doubt, I'm afraid, that alcohol taken in excess can sour the sweetest of relationships. Explaining what impelled him to twist his girlfriend's arm behind her back and bash her head against the kitchen shelf, one patient – who felt such deep remorse for his actions that he pretended to have taken an overdose – said, 'It went mad, doctor, it went completely over the top.'

'What did?' I asked.

'The drinking.'

'Are you quite sure you don't mean "I drank far too much"?'

'Fair point, doctor. It was right out of order.'

Not that it requires alcohol for people to get on badly and hate one another – far from it. All it requires, in many cases, is proximity. A patient of mine described how his liaison had broken up. Both he and she had taken lovers while they lived together.

'Then it blew up in my face, doctor.'

'What did?'

'The relationship.'

'Any children?'

'A daughter.'

'Do you see her still?'

'No. She says I'm just the biological dad, not the real dad, so there's no need for me to see her.'

'You're only a baby-father, then.'

'Yes, that's right.'

In my long-distant childhood, we played at mothers and fathers. Now adolescents play at baby-mothers and baby-fathers.

'Since we've split up, my daughter's had four daddies. She's only known the latest one for a week and she's already calling him Dad. I don't want that, doctor.'

'It's a bit late now,' I said.

'I know, but it's no good for her, living with a slag like her.'

'So you don't have any more contact with either your daughter or her mother?'

'No, doctor, because it's a war zone.'

'What is?'

'The relationship. There's a war between us, and that's no good for the babby, so I don't see neither of them.'

My next patient had tried to kill himself with pills.

'Why?' I asked.

'I'm tired of fighting.'

'Fighting whom?'

'Everybody. The world, society.'

Far be it from me to decry deep concern for the deplorable state of the world; however, long experience has taught me that few people are willing to die for it.

'You couldn't be a little more specific, could you?' I asked.

He could and he was. His baby-mother never wanted to see him again after he stabbed her with a screwdriver. Worse still, the Child Support Agency was after him for the maintenance of two children of his, aged six and eight, by a previous baby-mother.

'They are still your children,' I said mildly.

'Yeah, but that was a long time ago.'

A week is a long time in modern family life.

I Seem To Be Surrounded
By Prostitution

I SEEM TO be surrounded by prostitution these days. I don't seek it out; it comes to me, as it were. For example, last week there were two prostitutes (as patients, I hasten to add) on my ward. One had stepped straight from an Otto Dix painting. She was raddled and wormeaten; some of her teeth had fallen – or been knocked – out and no quantity of makeup could restore her to youth or beauty.

The other, only a few years younger, was fresh and young and still tender. Looking from one to the other was like looking at the beginning and end of a series of Hogarth prints. The sex industry, as we must now call prostitution, promotes rapid ageing.

Both of the sex-workers had been brought to hospital after collapsing in nightclubs, where they said their drinks had been spiked by the men with whom they were dancing. The younger of them had run away from home three years ago, when she was 14 years old.

'Me and my mum wasn't getting on.'

'Why not?'

'We just wasn't, that's all.'

She fled to a city more than 100 miles away and fell straight into the welcoming arms of a black pimp.

'He locked me up and knocked me about. He had sex with me a few times against my will. He put me on crack and took all the money that I earned.'

'So nothing out of the ordinary,' I said.

'No,' she replied.

'How long were you with him?'

'A few months, then the police found me and brought me back.'

'You went back to school?'

'No, I never bothered.'

143

'Why not?'

'I could earn a lot of money on the street, so what was the point?'

She was quite right, of course. The school would have taught her nothing, in any case; she might as well have developed her career as an underage, crack-taking prostitute. I knew that my suggestion that she undertake rehabilitation would be spurned as naive and impractical: it would mean she couldn't pay the rent of her flat.

That evening I went to the cinema – out of the frying-pan of reality into the fire of cinematographic representation, as it were. It was a Dutch film called *The Polish Bride* that was showing.

In the film, a Polish woman enters Holland on a work permit arranged by two violent pimps. She runs away from them to the Dutch countryside, where she encounters a stolid, taciturn but fundamentally decent farmer. Slowly they fall in love, but then the two pimps discover her whereabouts and come to collect her. The farmer kills one of them with a shotgun while she kills the other with an axe. Afterwards they dump the bodies and live happily ever after, much to the intended gratification of the audience.

The pimps of the story obviously deserved to die, but is it not curious that an intelligentsia as presumably opposed to capital punishment as the Dutch should be surreptitiously enjoined to favour extrajudicial execution as the means of obtaining justice?

Arriving home from the cinema, I noticed a prostitute on the corner of my street. Her pimp was standing a few yards away. I recognised him at once: he broke the jaw of one of his girls in the lavatory of my ward.

Death, Taxes And Drivel

DEATH AND TAXES: these, according to Benjamin Franklin, are the two immovables of human existence.

In modern life, however, there is a third: drivel, from which, try as one might, it is now impossible to escape.

I concede, of course, that it is possible that it's my sensitivity to drivel rather than its incidence or prevalence (to borrow two terms from epidemiology) that has increased over the years. But I don't think so: I can't go further than a few yards from my front door without encountering some. That wasn't true always.

Personally, I blame broadcasting. It insinuates itself everywhere almost without human agency, or none at any rate that dare acknowledge itself, and rots the brain utterly. You can rarely find who is responsible for the constant stream of drivel in public spaces, to which you can neither give your attention nor entirely ignore, so complaint is futile. You must accept your impotence: the medium is the message.

And when the person responsible for the presence of drivel is obvious, you dare not ask him to turn it off for fear of appearing superior and giving offence. Recently, for example, I was in a taxi from the port of Dún Laoghaire to Dublin and the radio was switched on to the state-run station. I didn't ask the driver to switch it off. So there was a long discussion, still not over when I arrived at my destination three quarters of an hour later, as a kind of Greek chorus to my thoughts, about a forthcoming football match. There were heated disputations about whether such-and-such a player was past his best or had not yet reached his peak, and whether a manager had paid too much for him or had got a bargain; then the wisest man in Ireland on the subject of football was asked who would win the match.

'Will "A" beat "B"?' he said. 'Well it really depends on the strengths and weaknesses of A, and the strengths and weaknesses of B.'

Does anyone actually feel mentally sustained by this pabulum? The terrible thing was that I couldn't get it out of my mind. What the wise man of football had said had the dual defect, that bore into my brain like a worm, of being both banal and untrue. Luck can play a large part in sporting contests. Banality-cum-Untruth: surely the heraldic motto of many a public figure.

All the pubs in Dublin, even those with the strongest literary associations, now have huge plasma screens from which sports commentators drivel at various volumes, but always at interminable length. However, it is not only on the subject of sport that state-subsidised drivel is propagated. In another taxi I listened to a famous Harvard economist being interviewed after the collapse of a bank. He was asked whether this meant there would be a recession.

'Well,' he said (I paraphrase), 'there could be, in fact I think it is likely. On the other hand there might not be, because nothing is certain.'

He also opined that the recession, if there was one, could be either long or short, and either deep or shallow, or, of course, somewhere in between. This was said with oracular portentousness.

Still, all is not quite lost. On the boat over, I heard a little boy ask his father, 'Daddy, what does sir mean?'

'It's what you call someone older than yourself,' his father answered.

Civilisation has not yet been totally extinguished by broadcasting.

I've Met Many
A Decent Murderer

WHENEVER I DISCUSS the death penalty with anyone in favour of it, who is surprised to discover that I am against it, he or she asks me whether I do not know of cases in which the death penalty would be the most, indeed the only appropriate punishment. The answer to this question is not that I know of no such cases, but that I know of many – too many, in fact – and it is precisely their number that makes the death penalty impossible to apply with any justice. For if there were any justice in the world, or at least in Britain, there would be a gibbet on every corner.

Not all, or even many, of the people who deserve to die are murderers, of course. On the contrary, I've met many a decent murderer. Sometimes they've killed people who in a state of more perfect justice (which God forbid that we should ever live in) would themselves have been hanged long ago.

It is a terrible thing to meet so many people whose death would make the world a slightly better place. It requires great self-control to treat them as if they were decent citizens whose lives were as valuable as any other. No doubt in practice they get shorter shrift in our hospital than their betters, but we try our very best to expunge our knowledge of their evil from our consciousness as we treat them. But deep inside we feel a tension, a contraction in our abdomen, a rage of frustration, as we treat them better by far than they deserve.

What penalty other than death, indeed public execution by slow torture, does a man deserve who has been imprisoned twice for attempted murder, once of his former girlfriend, once of a man whom he suspected of having an affair with another former girlfriend, who breaks the jaw of his current girlfriend, intimidates her through his violent friends into not appearing in court to testify against him, and then sends her a message on her phone after his release from court, saying, 'I'm free, ha-ha!'?

He has learnt nothing from his experience and prison holds no terrors for him. Society has at last taken to heart Winston Churchill's famous dictum that the degree of civilisation of a society can be measured by the care it takes of its prisoners – just, of course, when circumstances have changed very drastically. For what do we say of a society in which a man such as I have described, and many like him, fears no punishment that the society can inflict? What price civilisation now?

I was lamenting this only last week with a prison governor on the verge of retirement. We were standing outside, looking at a comfortable new wing in which the flicker of a television was visible through the window of every cell.

'We do everything for them now,' he said. 'It's not right.'

I said that as a society we had no guts: not like when he started, he replied. He remembered the first prison in which he worked. The nurse at the dispensary painted words on the palms of his hands, which he held up to the prisoner according to the prisoner's politeness.

'No,' said the first palm. 'Fuck off,' said the second.

You Get What You Pay For

WHAT A GLORIOUS thing it is to be a British taxpayer! And how reassuring to know that the half of one's life one devotes to earning taxes is used to bring a little succour to those less well-placed than oneself.

For example, only last week a young man was admitted to my ward having taken an overdose after hitting his mother in the course of an argument with her. He took the overdose before her very eyes, no doubt to rekindle the dying embers of her maternal instinct.

He was an unemployed heroin addict, and his mother had wanted to know what he had done with the money in her purse.

'How much do you spend on your heroin?' I asked him.

'Thirty quid a day.'

'How do you get it?'

'From a dealer.'

'No, the money, not the heroin.'

'My Job Seeker's Allowance.'

What imagination our bureaucracy displays in devising pleasant euphemisms. 'Job seekers', indeed: the phrase conjures up a reassuring image of industrious ants, temporarily idle, who busily scour the land for something constructive to do. Heroin Seeker's Allowance would be more like it.

You get what you pay for. If you subsidise bad behaviour, then bad behaviour is what you get. However, honesty compels me to admit that not everything can be attributed to social security, the welfare state, etc. We must never forget that man is the root of all evil, the being who does evil for the sheer joy of it unless prevented from doing so.

The patient next to the mother-beating heroin addict was a young woman with a black eye and a broken arm. You wouldn't have to be

Hercule Poirot to suspect an affair of the heart as the cause of these injuries.

'How did you get your broken arm?' I asked.

'My boyfriend twisted it.'

'Why?'

'When you don't give him sex, you get a slap.'

It takes little imagination to understand with what exultation in his power over his beloved he heard her screams of agony, her pleas to be let go and the crunching snap of her bone. And what joy to intimidate her into dropping charges against him, a joy far removed from the merely utilitarian purpose of avoiding jail! Round here, humiliation of others for its own sake is a Kantian categorical imperative.

The woman with the black eye and a broken arm was a drinker, of course. 'You drink too much,' I said.

'They shouldn't sell it, should they?' she replied.

'You could try not buying it,' I suggested helpfully. But as with all my best suggestions, it fell on deaf ears.

'But it's everywhere, doctor.'

I felt an urgent need to retreat from the world, and therefore went to the prison, that great monastery of the slums. I felt a deep spiritual relief as I passed through its portals.

Not that I should like to pretend that all is well in the prison, that there are no problems there, that peace of mind is always to be achieved there. My first patient, a burglar, looked unhappy.

'The trouble with prison, doctor,' he said, 'is that everyone talks shop all the time.'

Candidates For Perpetual Incarceration

EVERYONE ASSUMES THAT if there were any justice in the world, they would be better off; which is rather odd because it is perfectly clear that, if there were any justice in the world, millions of our fellow countrymen would starve to death at once and hundreds of thousands would receive life-sentences with no possibility of parole or remission.

Some people think I exaggerate, but I speak only the most literal and self-evident truth. For example, yesterday I heard about four young candidates (if justice were ever to be done) for perpetual incarceration. My patient from whom I heard about them was a meek young man with a club foot; but the world into which he was born was not one that deals kindly with those who exhibit any weakness, physical or mental. One day, while he was limping to work, he was kidnapped from the street by four young toughs, bundled into a car and a balaclava pulled over his head.

He was then driven to an unknown destination, where his ankles were tied and he was suspended upside-down from the ceiling. He was beaten from side to side for several hours by his kidnappers, with the purpose of extracting a promise from him to take a bank loan of £5,000 which he would then hand over to them: or else, of course.

Returning to his own home, an apartment in a tower block, he had from fear refused to leave it ever since, but had nevertheless grown claustrophobic in the mean proportions of its rooms. The perfect solution was to take an overdose of pills and call an ambulance; for even our thugs have not yet learnt to attack people as they are wheeled into an ambulance, though no doubt this will come soon enough.

I would hardly have believed his story had he not borne the marks of his beating, and had I not heard before on several occasions of people kidnapped and tortured in special chambers hidden in the city (mostly run by drug dealers for their clients who fail to honour their financial obligations). The British people have taken over where mediaeval witchfinders left off. What is the appropriate punishment for the four torturers of my patient's story, if not a life on the treadmill or at the oar?

Of course, justice has sometimes to be tempered by mercy and forbearance. For example, the other day in the prison I was called to the cell of a man who had just been attacked in his sleep by his cellmate. One side of his face was completely – as the prisoners themselves would put it – 'mashed'. His eye was closed, one side of his upper lip was swollen, a couple of his teeth were now missing, presumed swallowed. It had been a ferocious attack, with no holds barred. Had the officers not heard the pounding inside the cell and come to his rescue, the man could have lost his life.

By the time I reached him he was groaning.

'Are you going to prefer charges against him?' I asked.

'No,' he said.

The quality of mercy is not strained but droppeth as the gentle rain etc., I thought.

'Why not?' I asked.

'I'm not a fucking grass,' he said indignantly.

I'm Glad I Won't Be Around When My Young Patients Are Old

THE MOST IMPORTANT single question facing this country is whether its disgusting, shallow, mannerless, uncouth, egotistical young people – of whom there are hundreds of thousands, if not millions – will grow up to be disgusting, shallow, mannerless, uncouth, egotistical old people; because if so, and age fails to improve them, this country will in the years ahead be an even more unpleasant place in which to live than it already is. For it is a truth very seldom acknowledged that there are few people nastier than nasty old people.

Of course, hitherto there have been relatively few such people. But is this merely because man tends naturally to mellow with age, or is it because there was a higher proportion of decent people in the population in the first place?

Alas for the future, the latter seems to be the correct answer. Research suggests that nasty old people were nasty young people. While it does not strictly follow that nice old people were nice young people, it is likely to have been the case. I'm glad, therefore, that I won't be around when my young patients are old.

Still, it is refreshing for someone who detests youth as much as I do to meet from time to time a really despicable old person in her eighties (it is usually a she – for nasty men die early, while nasty women survive). Last week, for example, I saw on the wards of my hospital an old woman who had for years attempted to set her children against each other by telling deliberate lies about them to each other. When I arrived by her bedside, both a son and a daughter were in attendance, but later, when I talked to her on her own, she complained that her son never visited her, not even when she was in hospital.

'Who was that man by your bedside when I arrived, then?' I asked.

'What man? I didn't see a man.'

'The man who was standing beside your daughter.'

'I didn't see him. It couldn't have been my son in any case, because he never visits me. My daughter doesn't speak to him either.'

I believe that is an example of what the philosopher the late Karl Popper called a reinforced dogmatism. And I was told that this evil old woman regularly called the police to complain of the beatings she received at the hands of the son whom she claimed she never saw. She had been like this ever since her children could remember: lying, divisive, self-pitying, domineering and utterly without scruple. She would depart this world in a blaze of hatred.

It was almost a relief after her to return to the less sophisticated wickedness, stupidity and degeneracy of British youth. One young woman with rings in her nose, giving her a distinctly porcine appearance, and a tattoo of the name of a rock-music band on her self-mutilated forearm, had taken an overdose of pills (analgesics for non-existent pain) while drunk on six litres of gut-rot cider.

'I think you probably drink too much,' I said to her mildly.

'You sound like my mum.'

'And furthermore,' I continued, undeterred by the insult, 'if you continue like this, one day you will vomit in your sleep and choke to death on your own vomit.'

'Does that mean I can go home then, doctor?'

He Threatened To Kill
His Kids, That's All

THERE IS SAID to be a good evolutionary reason why there should be two sexes rather than one – or three. But whatever that reason might be, it doesn't seem to apply around here, where most of the problems seem to be traceable to trouble between men and women. If it weren't for the existence of women there would be far fewer prisoners than there are.

For example, last week I encountered a prisoner in the depths of despair. I asked him what was on his mind.

'I can't get to speak to my missis. She hasn't writ to me. I haven't heard a word off her.'

'What are you charged with?' I asked.

'Nothing to do with her, nothing at all.'

'Yes, but what was it?'

'Threatening to kill the kids, that's all. Nothing to do with her whatsoever. I didn't lay a finger on her.'

Another man had been charged with stalking his former girlfriend. He was suicidally self-pitying. He was only 21 years old and of good intelligence. I asked him about his previous girlfriends.

'My first serious one was when I was 16.'

'Why did you break up with her?'

'She was pregnant and got rid of my baby, so I got rid of her.'

'How old was she?'

'Fifteen.'

He was bitter that his current girlfriend – the one he loved and the only one, he said, he'd ever been faithful to – had gone to the police about him. It was true that he shouldn't have hit her, but she shouldn't have hit him first and, anyway, he wasn't like that till he met her.

'And what have you learnt from the whole experience?' I asked.

'Women,' he said. 'Fuck 'em and leave 'em.'

Meanwhile, back in the hospital, there was a man who had tried to kill himself with pills. He had just broken up with his girlfriend.

'Were you violent towards her?' I asked.

'No, never.'

'Would she say the same?'

'She'd tell you I had my hand round her throat a couple of times, that's all.'

It wouldn't be quite accurate, however, to say that without women all would be rosy for men. For example, in the bed next to the last patient's was a man who had been attacked with a hammer by his next-door neighbour, a drunk.

'Are you going to the police about it?' I asked him.

'No,' he replied.

'Why not?'

'Because he said that if I did he'd cut me up and put the pieces in a plastic bag.'

'And you believe him?'

'He's already done nine years in prison.'

It's awful how some people are stigmatised in this unthinking fashion.

Of course, by no means all offences are *crimes passionnels*. One young man was brought before me in the prison because he had carved the word BODGER into the flesh of his chest with a razor-blade.

'Who's Bodger?' I asked.

'My dog.'

'A bull terrier?'

'How did you know?'

There were no women in his life. He found dogs answered his emotional needs more satisfactorily than they; he was a straightforward old-fashioned burglar.

'Another thing about dogs, doctor,' he said. 'Unlike women, they guard your home.'

If You Wish To Escape The Drug Dealers, You Will Have To Kill Your Dog

IN THE 1970s, a Russian author called Vladimir Voinovich published a memoir of his efforts to secure a larger apartment from the authorities, which he entitled *The Ivankiad*. Those people in Britain who, like so many of my patients, have the misfortune to rent from the Soviet Socialist Republic of Council Housing will know just what he was writing about. Britain is a land of Ivankiads.

A patient of mine, a single woman in her thirties, has been living for several years in council-owned property which even the council's own inspectors – never very exigent when it comes to the standards they require of what is known as 'social housing' – have condemned as completely uninhabitable. Her house is at the end of a cul-de-sac, the only such house within a radius of hundreds of yards that is still inhabited. It is so damp that the electricity often short-circuits and she has to sleep on a camp bed in the kitchen.

These are but minor problems, however. The road being a virtually uninhabited dead end, it is used as a way station by the fraternity of drug-dealers: Yardies, Muslims and skinheads, the very model of a modern multicultural society, in which no outmoded prejudices are allowed to stand in the way of conduct. Quite often the drug dealers cordon off the road with their cars; at other times they firebomb stolen vehicles that are surplus to requirements. Passing drunks and drug-addicts throw the detritus of their various addictions into my patient's garden which serves also as a repository for knickers and used condoms, for there is nothing the drug-dealers appreciate more than rough sex with slatterns in the back of their cars, watched and applauded by their fellow dealers.

When my patient leaves her house, which is but rarely, the drug-dealers enter and use her telephone. Her bills subsequently list every mobile phone they have ever called, but she cannot go to the police for fear of retaliation. The dealers have several times kicked down her front door or removed an entire window frame to get into the warm out of the rain to complete their drug deals; when she asked one of them what he would do if she behaved like this at his mother's house, he replied, 'I'd chop you up.'

When she apprised the housing department of the situation, it advised her to buy a guard dog, which she did. Alas, nothing changed for the better, except that she grew to love the dog. She informed the department that she couldn't go on living like this, in constant fear of burglary, rape and murder (she had discovered that one of the drug-dealers had just served six years for manslaughter). The department replied that it was a pity she didn't have any children (illegitimate, of course) because then she could have been put in a three-bedroom house that was lying empty elsewhere. As it was, the department could offer her a hostel place.

But what about the dog, she asked? Oh, that couldn't possibly go with her to the hostel. What would happen to it, then? Well, it would have to be put down. But she loved it, she said, besides which the department had told her to get it in the first place. She was advised not to be difficult, beggars couldn't be choosers, and, if she went on like this, the department might have to wash its hands of her.

Another of my patients, also a single woman, had just been burgled for the fourth time (she had also been mugged twice). She called the police.

'And what did they say?'

'They said I shouldn't be living in this area.'

Men Who Say 'On My Baby's Life' Always Abandon Their Children In The End

WHAT ARE THE most terrible words in the English language? Without doubt, they are 'I love her (or him) to bits, doctor'. For loving someone 'to bits' in modern British parlance connotes regular strangulation, either given or received. I leave it to marriage guidance counsellors to decide whether, in this context, it is more blessed to give or to receive.

Of course, the words 'on my baby's life' are also pretty terrible, irresistibly conjuring up as they do images of Old Testament sacrifice; but, in fact, 'on my baby's life' means only that everything that follows is an unadulterated lie. Thus, 'On my baby's life, doctor, I never touched her' means, 'I beat her unconscious regularly and broke several bones in her body.' It is also a fact that men who say 'on my baby's life' always abandon their children in the end.

A man who both loved his girlfriend to bits and swore on his baby's life that he hadn't laid a finger on her took an overdose because she had left him. It seemed that he had smashed up the flat in which they lived and which he had just redecorated.

'Every time I try to do something, doctor,' he said, 'it just explodes at me.'

'And would you take another overdose, then?' I asked.

'Sod that, man,' he said. 'It's caused too much pain in my head.'

He was a strangler, of course, though only an amateur by comparison with some I have met. In any case, a true strangler needs his strangulee, for as everyone knows it takes two to strangle. And, as it happens, there was a classic strangulee in the next bed.

She, too, had tried to kill herself with pills because she had had enough. The problem was that the strangler in her life kept telephoning, and each time she weakened and let him back into her house.

'When he's not strangling me,' she said, 'he's very nice.'

'How did you meet him?' I asked.

'In a pub.'

'And how long had you known him before he moved in with you?'

'A few hours.'

'Has he a criminal record?'

'Yes.'

'Has he been to prison?'

'Yes.'

'What for?'

'He was in eight years for murder. He ran over someone with his lorry.'

'If I've understood you correctly, you met a murderer in a pub, you started to live with him a few hours later, and he has repeatedly half-strangled you.'

'Yes, doctor.'

'I hope you don't mind me asking, but why do you stay with him?'

'I love him to bits, doctor.'

I howled. I laughed. I wanted to bang my head on the wall and climb straight to the hospital roof and throw myself off. In the event, I merely clutched my head. She started to laugh.

'Silly, isn't it?' she said.

'Silly?' I replied. 'It's positively insane. It's so stupid that it's wicked.'

'I know, doctor. My kids don't like him either.'

In the next bed was a young woman who had asked social services to look after her three children by three different men. I asked her why she had delivered them up to the care of others.

'I couldn't be arsed with them no more,' she replied, with that typical British elegance of phrase which so exactly matches contemporary delicacy of feeling.

Still, I know perfectly what she meant, and I often feel that way myself.

Nostalgie De La Boue

IT IS HARDLY SURPRISING, I suppose, that in my job you cease to believe in the possibility of innocence, or even of common decency. So it was a pleasant change indeed to examine medical students last week – young people who have as yet been untouched by the evil of life. How young and fresh-faced they seemed; how full of misplaced optimism!

They divided quite naturally into two categories: the boffins, more at ease with test-tubes and computers than with people; and the saccharine, save-the-whale types, who exuded like slime the secular evangelism of the age. Still, the adult world of employment in this general *sauve-qui-peut* we call England will chasten them soon enough.

Decency is all very well in its way, of course, but after a few hours of it I began to suffer acutely from *nostalgie de la boue*. It was almost with relief that I returned to the prison; I can rely on the prisoners to tone up my nervous system and put me into a pleasant state of outrage. Recently, there has been a sudden influx of domestics into the prison. I do not mean by this butlers, handymen, chauffeurs etc., but men who are accused of a domestic. One of them told me he was aggressive in drink, though otherwise a lamb. The trouble was, he was rarely sober. While inebriated, he had attempted to strangle several women, and was now in prison for a drunken stabbing. His hands were shaking and sweat poured down his face.

'What do you conclude from all this?' I asked him.

'I've got a lot of stress,' he replied.

This is a lesson learnt only at the University of Life.

In the next cell was another domestic. He had attacked his beloved with a machete, that agricultural implement of the slums. He was outraged that his girlfriend had grassed on him.

'I put it down to the hormones,' he said.

'Whose? Hers or yours?'

'Six of one and half a dozen of the other.'

In the next cell was a young man with a red devil tattooed on the inner aspect of his thigh. On his right hand were tattooed in Indian ink the letters FTW, which stand for the succinct and profound message Fuck the World.

'What are you in for?' I asked.

'A fucking telephone call.'

Instinct told me that this was a highly edited version of the events leading to his imprisonment. It turned out that by telephoning his former girlfriend, whom he had attempted to strangle and later intimidated, he had broken the conditions of his bail.

Last, but by no means least, I entered the cell of a man who said that he would like nothing better than to be allowed into the yard to do a little gardening.

'You like gardening?' I said.

'It's gardening that got me in here,' he said.

I know that the government is beginning to show dictatorial tendencies, but surely it hasn't yet got to the stage where a man is sentenced to life imprisonment for gardening?

'He had a dispute with his neighbour over a fence post, sir,' interposed a prison officer. 'And beat him to death with a pruning hook.'

All These Mad Charges

THE VALUE OF human life is, of course, incalculable, and no mere monetary figure can be placed upon it. Certain parts of the human anatomy are not quite so sacrosanct, however, as I discovered recently while visiting prison.

My patient had what I have come to think of as pub frequenter's nose: not bulbous, but broken, often in several geometric planes at once, indicating repeated injury. On this occasion, though, my patient's nose, which was no longer in the centre of his face, had been broken in his own home by an angry visitor.

'Why did he do it?' I asked.

'I'd stolen his car and crashed it. He didn't mind, like, only it was his pride and joy.'

'How did he know it was you?'

'He only lives over the road from me.'

'And after he hit you on the nose, what happened then?'

'It was quits, like, we was friends again.'

So a crashed car is worth a broken nose and, presumably, vice versa.

I asked the young man, who was very polite, what he was in prison for.

'Just stupid, petty offences.'

'Such as?'

'Just a few little burgs.'

What a beautiful, poetic word! I was struck by it at once: affectionate and yet technical at the same time. And, of course, a verb as well as a noun, as in, for example, 'to burg a house' or 'Help! My house has just been burged.'

'Anyway,' continued the man with the off-centre nose, 'I don't think I should be in here.'

'Why not?' I asked.

'Because I'm very damaged,' he replied.

'Damaged? By what?'

'By all the time I done in here. By all the time I done behind bars.'

'You've been in prison before, then?'

'Yeah, loadsa times.'

'For burgs?' I asked, so pleased with having learnt a new word that I dropped my usual insistence upon not using drug addicts' or prisoners' argot.

'Yeah, how did you know?' he asked.

The next prisoner was depressed.

'I've lost everything,' he said.

'Such as?' I asked.

He thought for a moment. 'My girlfriend,' he replied.

'Why?' I asked.

'All these mad charges. I can't get them out of my mind, doctor.'

'What are they?'

'Rape and kidnap,' he said.

'Of your girlfriend?'

'Yes. Only three days after I was released from prison an' all.'

'When you say the charges are mad, am I to take it that you mean you're innocent?'

'Yes, doctor.'

'So you're depressed?'

'Yes, doctor. You can ask the screws. They all know me. I'm not like I normally am when I'm in prison. Normally I'm a lot of trouble, but now I can't be bothered. I've changed, I just sit in my cell quietly.'

My mind returned to a man whom I once treated for depression so successfully that he became manically elated as a result. 'Can't you make him depressed again, doctor?' asked his wife. Not better, *nota bene*, but depressed.

165

'The screws know me well, doctor, because I've done more time in prison than on the out.'

'And what were you in for?'

'The last time?'

'Yes.'

'False imprisonment.'

'Of your girlfriend?'

'Yes.'

'And the time before that?'

'Kidnap and threats to kill, I think it was.'

Infuriating Jiggling

YOU SHOULDN'T JUDGE a book by its cover, perhaps, but you'd be a fool not to take any notice of the rings a girl wears.

I am not talking about diamonds as big as the Ritz, you understand; I am referring instead to a new fashion among some girls of the lower orders for placing a ring around one of their thumbs. This ring signifies, almost without exception, that the girl is attracted to drug-addicts, criminals, psychopaths and sadists. She is usually in trouble with the police herself, or ought to be. Such girls usually apply make-up as if it were icing on a cake, and pout whenever asked a question, but that is by the by.

The rings on their thumbs often have a little pendant attached to them that jiggles as they speak, breathe or move. Needless to say, girls with rings of this kind are particularly bad girls, past all redemption. They love doormen and body-builders, and either have no conception of the dangers involved in associating with such types, or never learn from experience. And the pendant that jiggles on their rings puts them in yet graver danger.

The first murderer I ever met – in the days when I considered it an honour and a privilege to meet murderers – killed his wife because of the jiggling. Admittedly it was the jiggling of her earrings rather than of the pendant to her thumb-ring, but it was a long time ago, in the unenlightened prehistoric era when no one had even heard of thumb-rings.

'When I came home of an evening, doctor,' said the murderer, 'all I wanted to do was sit and read the paper, while all my wife wanted to do was talk, talk, talk. And when she talked, her earrings went jiggle, jiggle, jiggle, and in the end I couldn't stand it no more, so I strangled her.'

Even then, before I had ever been confronted by jiggling pendants on thumb rings, I thought I understood. It is the small things in life, after all, that arouse the deepest passions, and prove what a thoroughly trivial-minded creature Man is. Even without the jiggling, thumb-rings infuriate me.

A thumb-ringed girl was admitted to our ward last week having made a vain attempt at suicide. She left a suicide note. It read, 'Fuk u, Baz. U never beleived me.' (The rule of English spelling taught in modern schools is strictly e before i except after c.) Baz, it seemed, had betrayed her for another, and would not believe that she was prepared to die for him.

'I suppose Baz works the doors?' I asked, again adopting the lingo of the slums.

'Yeah, how did you know?'

On my way to the prison later that day, I walked for a while behind two young women, each with a baby in a pushchair. The babies were obviously on their way to visit their current fathers in the prison, it being never too early to grow acclimatised to one's future environment. I overtook the mothers and their offspring, palely loitering, and I noticed thumb rings on the right thumbs of both the mothers. I also overheard a snatch of their conversation.

'Fuck off, I goes to him. I goes, fuck off.'

His Son Needed
The Latest Trainers

EVERYONE KNOWS THAT banks are the eternal enemy of mankind; that they lend money at higher rates of interest than they pay their depositors. Has there ever been a clearer case of exploitation than this?

As a matter of fact, as I shall relate, there has. For there are some people who fall below the purview of the banks, whose financial affairs are either so trifling or so precarious that those noble institutions wish to have nothing to do with them.

The urge to borrow money, however, is what distinguishes Man from the animals; and just because a man has no income with which to pay back a loan, that does not prevent him from taking it out in the first place. The more orthodox sources of finance being unavailable to him, he finds himself obliged to turn to what are known as loan sharks. For once the zoological comparison is not inapt.

My patient, now on remand in prison, was a man whose intellect was as limited as his pocket. Alas, he had a young son whom he believed he needed to deck out in designer clothes and the latest trainers (this being what counts as good parenting in much of England). But where to obtain the money to do so?

He turned to a local landlord, the owner of many flophouses and bedsits and something of a moneylender. My patient borrowed £1,500 from him, but then, over a period of two months, failed to make his instalments on the loan. Had he done so, he would have had to pay back 'only' £2,500.

'He must be a rich man by now,' I remarked.

'Yes,' said my patient. 'He doesn't really like to have working people in his houses; he prefers to have unemployed. Then he knows he'll get their housing benefit. He doesn't trust people with jobs.'

What miracles of transformation we have wrought! The unemployed more dependable than the working: is this not a source of pride to every true Briton?

But to return to the loan shark. He began to agitate for the return of his money. Having made no repayments for a whole two months, my patient discovered that he now owed £3,000. Loan sharks do not send polite letters: they pour petrol through letter-boxes with a written warning that next time it will come with a lighted match. They also intimate through intermediaries that the borrower's six-year-old son might be kneecapped one afternoon when he leaves school.

There was only one solution for my patient: to rob a bank at knifepoint. Unfortunately for him – and perhaps for the loan shark as well – he was overcome at once and handed over to the police.

'And are you pleading guilty or not guilty?' I asked.

'Not guilty,' he replied.

'But you did do what you're accused of having done?'

'Oh yes, I can't deny it. I done it all right.'

'Then why are you pleading not guilty?'

'Because my lawyer says the Crown Prosecution Service might lose all my papers, and if they do and they don't find them in time, I'll have to be released.'

What Objection Can The Democratic Secularist Make?

THE LAST TIME I played rugby, I was sent off for reading on the field. It was my small satirical protest against the supposition that my character would be much improved by having my knees dragged along icy ground, or my hand trodden into the mud by boys who, by dint of no effort of their own, were twice as large as I.

Now I am not so sure. It appears to me that every soul should be tempered a little in the fire of humiliation and suffering: though the precise dose of laudably character-forming humiliation and suffering is, I admit, difficult to estimate and dole out.

In fact, it is impossible, which is why human beings usually turn out badly. Unfortunately, all roads lead to resentment. Too little suffering in childhood means that people resent the difficulties that they inevitably encounter later in life; too much, and no success can extinguish the embers of resentment smouldering in the depths of their souls, ready to burst into flames at the first addition of tinder.

Since my youth, I have developed a visceral distaste for sport, not as an activity for amateurs, but as a spectacle that occupies the thoughts, raises the hopes and stimulates the emotions of millions. I try to understand why it does so, but try as I might, I cannot.

Yesterday, for example, I sat on a train from Paris to Avignon opposite a young man who read a newspaper devoted to football the whole way. (As in all Western European countries, the French championship is about which team can import the best foreigners.) The TGV is fast, but it still takes nearly three hours to go from Paris to Avignon. Can a human mind really be satisfied by such pabulum? (I was irritated: the young man didn't look by any means unintelligent.) I know that Nature hates a vacuum, but surely not that much.

As it happens, I was reading with enjoyment a slim volume entitled *Barbaric Sport: Critique of a Global Plague*, by Marc Perelman. The author, an architect by training and a professor of aesthetics by occupation, is a man of the far Left, slightly too young to have taken part in the events of 1968, but who was obviously affected by the slogan, 'Be realistic: demand the impossible.' He ends his book with an uncompromising demand for a society without sport. For sport 'flattens everything in its way' and is 'the steam-roller of decadent modernity'.

Mr Perelman despises sport for the same reason that Marx despised religion: it disguises from men their true situation, and diverts them from making the revolution to overcome it. But then I thought, 'What exactly is Man's true situation that needs so violently to be overcome?' What should the young man on the train have been reading instead of his football magazine? Marc Perelman's previous book, *Le football, une peste emotionelle*, perhaps? Or his *Pekin 2008: les jeux de la honte*? Or Pascal's *Pensées*?

Once we have overcome the current regime of bread and circuses, what then?

The Haitian peasant, alluding to his endless travails, says, 'Behind the mountains, more mountains.' Modern man says, 'After the circuses, more circuses.' What objection can the democratic secularist make?

It Always Ends Up In Arguments

I RARELY HAVE occasion to travel by train in England, but the irritations caused by the patent inability of the British to run any public services properly are, to some extent, mitigated by the interest of the journeys themselves.

For example, let us try to imagine an answer to the question as to why, along railway embankments in rural areas and on the grass strip between the tracks, so vast a quantity of litter should be strewn. It cannot be easy to insinuate plastic carrier bags, squashed tins of soft drinks and extra-strength lager, used condoms and all the other detritus of daily life into such remote and inaccessible corners of our glorious homeland. Indeed, it must entail considerable danger to do so, for trains sometimes, if not quite as often as scheduled, rush by at 125 miles per hour.

I am drawn to the irresistible conclusion, therefore, that there is a large band of dedicated and single-minded Britons that believes in the aesthetic virtues of litter, just as people once believed in the moral virtues of religion, and that spreads it as the faithful once spread religious tracts, leaving them on trains and elsewhere, and that is ready to risk its life for the cause. It is, indeed, the only possible explanation for the phenomenon.

My latest journey offered a scene that encapsulated the impotence of modern society, for all its wealth and technological sophistication, in the face of bad conduct.

Near me sat a drunk with smelly feet and scabs on his face and scalp. His head lolled on his chest and looked as if it might soon fall off altogether. He snored and eructated like bubbles in the mud of a hot spring. Almost everyone else in the carriage talked of millions into their mobile phones (another irritation of modern travel).

The ticket inspector arrived and asked to see our tickets.

'I've lost it,' muttered the drunk, while contemplating the dirty trainers through which the odour of his feet penetrated like gamma radiation.

'You said that last time,' said the ticket inspector. Evidently the drunk was a regular on the line. 'You get out at the next station.'

The drunk grunted his displeasure but, to my surprise, obeyed the order. He would obviously reach his destination one stop at a time.

What would have been the point of taking sterner measures against him? He was doing little harm, even if it was clear that his existence was an entirely parasitic one. If he had been charged with an offence, he wouldn't have turned up in court, setting in motion an entire bureaucratic process as futile as it was expensive. Nothing anybody did either to him or for him would prevent him from riding the trains again.

And thus a drunk with smelly feet is able to defeat with ease the whole of society, however rich and powerful it might appear.

Meanwhile, in the seats across the aisle, a man was telling a stranger about his relationship with women. Why do people find their own emotional lives so interesting? And what are emotions for but suppression?

'At my age,' he said, 'you don't want the hassle of relationships. You want to come and go as you choose, not be nagged all the time. That's why I don't have a relationship at the moment.'

'Yes,' said his female interlocutor.

'Besides, women get so jealous of me. And then I get jealous, too. It always ends up in arguments.'

Aha, I thought: a woman-beater. He alighted at a town infamous for its high crime-rate.

Expropriating The Expropriators

I AM A GREAT admirer of Karl Marx. It took talent and learning to understand so little of the human heart. Even so, he undoubtedly had his flashes of insight. For example, only last week in the prison, his words 'the expropriators are expropriated' ran through my mind like a refrain.

I was seeing a prisoner who was threatening to hang himself. He was, he said, fed up with everything, and no one would stop him. Tomorrow he would be dead.

Experience has taught me that it is usually possible to narrow down the causes of distress a little: they are seldom of cosmic or even of continental dimensions. We each of us live in a little world of our own, and it is what happens in that little world that most engages our emotions. This is not the same as saying that the causes of our distress are entirely subjective. On the contrary, even a little world may contain more than sufficient horror to be getting on with. And so it was with the prisoner who wanted to hang himself. After a little cajoling, he told me why his life was not worth living. fear.

'They've threatened me with a slashing,' he said. 'People get slashed on the yard every day.'

'They' were five prisoners who lived near him, when they were at liberty. They had come to the conclusion that he was responsible for the burglary of one of their homes, though he denied it completely. But there is no appeal from the judgment of the criminal classes.

'And what are these five in prison for?' I asked.

'Burglary,' he replied.

So the expropriators are expropriated after all, though perhaps not quite in the Marxian sense. And they don't much care for it, to judge by their reaction.

I returned to the hospital, but there was no let-up from human misery to be found there. There was a woman waiting for me who told me that she was at the end of her tether; it was her children who had driven her to that unlikely extremity. She had four of them. The first, aged 16, was in prison for a slashing he had committed in the street. According to his mother, it was a case of slash or be slashed: 'That's how it is round where I live.'

Her 13-year-old daughter was pregnant by the next-door neighbour's 14-year-old son. She wanted the baby, her mother said; ever since the girl was 10, that was all she had talked about. Her 12-year-old daughter was the same. It was only a matter of time before she 'caught pregnant'. She wouldn't go to school: what was the point, she asked? From the results I have observed, I think she was probably right. Her six-year-old was hyperactive and destroyed everything in his path, like a tornado. His mother used to derive some relief by sending him to his paternal grandmother's, until she discovered that his 12-year-old uncle was interfering with him sexually there.

'And the fathers of these children?' I asked tentatively.

'Golden,' she replied.

'Why aren't you still with them, then?'

'Womanising.'

'And do they give you money for the children?'

'No, they say they'd rather give up work than pay for them.'

A solicitor called me. Could I assess his client in the prison for fitness to plead? I went back to the prison.

'What's the difference between guilty and not guilty?' I asked the solicitor's client.

'Guilty is when you admit what you've done. Not guilty is when you don't admit what you've done.'

One Or Two Minor Injustices Might Result

NOW THAT WE'RE abolishing the right to silence, the presumption of innocence and jury trial, and will soon have the preventive detention of psychopaths before they've done anything illegal, it is time we stopped pussyfooting around and got tough on crime. And, since prevention is better than cure, it is only reasonable that we should go to the root cause of criminality: the names that parents choose to give their children.

The barest acquaintance with prison rolls will be sufficient to convince anyone moderately numerate and acquainted with British first-names that there is a great excess of incarcerated persons with the first name of Lee. A person called Lee is, in fact, virtually predestined to commit criminal acts, and many of them. It is time, surely, to take forensic advantage of this remarkable fact.

People with the name of Lee should be arrested at birth, or at least as soon as they receive that dreadful appellation, and held in detention for the first 50 years of their life. Furthermore, any male child with a brother named Lee should be held also, as having a hereditary propensity to crime. I do not deny that one or two minor injustices might result from my scheme, but what is a little injustice to compare with a 50 per cent reduction in the crime rate?

The other day in the prison I met a Lee whose detention at birth would have reduced the crime rate considerably within a radius of 100 miles of here. He had tried to hang himself because he was under threat from prisoners in another wing. He owed them money for heroin, he said, and through the bars separating the wings they had shown him a toothbrush handle which they had melted into a razor blade, ready to slash him up at the first opportunity.

'And are they likely to carry out their threat?' I asked him.

'On the out they smash kneecaps with hammers and stab people in the eye with a screwdriver.'

I asked him what he himself was charged with.

'Burglaries,' he replied.

'How many?' I asked.

'Three.'

'And how many. have you done?'

'I've got 19 TICs.'

(Taken into considerations: or is it takens into consideration?)

'But how many have you actually done?' I persisted.

'Five hundred and eighty-nine.'

'And how much have you made from them?'

'The police took £40,000 of stuff from my flat, and I've got another £80,000 stashed away where they won't find it.'

'Why didn't you pay the dealers if you have so much money?'

'Why should I of?'

It was clearly against his principles to pay for anything that could be purloined.

'Have you ever thought of all the misery you've caused?'

'I was burgled once,' he said.

'And did you like it?'

'I didn't mind it,' he replied.

'That must have been because nothing of what was stolen was yours anyway.'

'I earned it,' he protested.

'You stole it,' I replied. 'There's a difference between earning and stealing.'

'But it was hard work. It took a lot of sweat and nerve to do all them houses.'

I Shouldn't Be Surprised If Bokassa Had Never Been On A Single Team-Building Away-Day

ALL OLD AFRICA hands have a story to tell of their narrow escape from charging elephants. I have one myself, but I know from experience that such stories are usually more interesting to the teller than to the told.

They are not quite as bad as big game hunting stories, however: they are the real conversation killers. I knew an African re-tread (as expatriates who cannot forget their time in Africa are sometimes called) who used to bore dinner parties with his claim to have shot 50 zebra in an afternoon.

'What did you use?' asked one incredulous guest (I had heard the story several times before). 'A machine gun?'

The only creature I shot on my one big game hunting expedition in Africa was a little green snake. At least, I think I shot it; it was there before I pulled the trigger and gone afterwards. I found the whole thing so distasteful that I nearly turned Jain and swept the ground before me lest I trod on insects.

France has even more old Africa hands than Britain. My sister-in-law's builder, for example, spent ten years working on Gbadolite, the palace, airport and casino complex built in the back of beyond by Marshal Mobutu Sese Seko in honour of his mother, who came from there. I suppose the jungle must have reclaimed it by now. There is a book to be written about the fate of the follies of fallen African dictators. The casinos and the airports depart.

My next-door neighbour in France worked in the Central African Republic at the time when Jean-Bédel Bokassa was merely President for Life rather than the Emperor he was soon to turn himself into.

He – my neighbour, that is – was a mathematics teacher with an administrative responsibility for the whole country. One day Bokassa summoned him and told him that next year he wanted 100 pupils to pass the baccalaureate.

My neighbour explained the difficulties to the President for Life: there were at the most 30 pupils in Central African schools who just might pass next year if they were lucky.

Bokassa insisted, however. My neighbour went to the minister of education and told him of His Excellency's impossible demand.

The minister then went to Bokassa himself, and reiterated the impossibility. He was relieved of his post and sent back to his village forthwith.

This demonstrates just how primitive and backward African thinking is by comparison with our own. Neither the Minister nor Bokassa saw the obvious solution to the problem that would have occurred at once to any British government minister or educational bureaucrat: lower the standard dramatically, but still call the exam the baccalaureate.

No wonder that Africa, unlike Britain, stagnates and makes no progress. They haven't even heard of performance targets there, or service level agreements, let alone strategic development and comprehensive reviews. I shouldn't be surprised if Bokassa didn't even know what a management consultant was, and had never been on a single team-building away-day. No wonder that the per capita gross domestic product of the Central African Republic hasn't risen as fast as ours.

Our Social Services Are Devoted To The Promotion Of Misery

THE GNOSTICS KNEW that the world is not as it seems, and therefore they would not have been altogether surprised to learn that the public institutions of this country are dedicated exclusively to the frustration of the aims for which they were set up. The Bodleian Library, for example, is devoted to the prevention of scholarly activity; while all departments of social services promote misery through the moral support and financial subsidy of wickedness and depravity.

What is a good doctor? On the surface, it might appear that he should be a man who helps his patients back to health: a healer, a curer of the sick. Nothing could be further from the truth, however. A good doctor is one who gives up his patient for lost, who harbours no illusions that he might help him to take up his bed and walk. I realised this last week, when a man with what they call a lived-in face consulted me in the hospital.

He was referred to me by Dr F___, a man known for his practice among the no-hopers of this world, or at least of this city.

'You are a patient of Dr F___'s,' I said to him.

'Yes,' he replied. 'He's a really good doctor.'

'In what way?'

'He signed me off sick for the rest of my life.'

Since there was no physical condition to prevent this man from working – the flesh was willing but the spirit was weak – we may conclude that the definition of a good doctor is one who renders a man far more ill than he ever was before.

It so happened that the very same day I telephoned a publicly-funded agency that helps patients undergoing rehabilitation to find work. It was called WorkAbility, and is dedicated – ostensibly – to the premise that handicaps should not prevent a person from finding work.

'Hello, WorkAbility.'

'Hello, this is Dr Dalrymple. Could I speak to the manager, please?'

'He's off sick.'

'When will he be back?'

'I can't say.'

'Could I speak to his deputy?'

'He's on annual leave.'

'Is there anyone else I could speak to?'

'No, I'm the only one here.'

A fine symbolic representation of the British public service: an organisation that supposedly finds work for others but in which no one works while continuing to be paid.

He who sups with the devil must have a long spoon – the devil being the state, of course. In the prison that same week I met a man who was (in the words of a prison officer) 'not your typical con'. He had a Zimmer frame, from which I concluded – wrongly, in this instance – that he was a sex-offender. Actually, he was that rarest of creatures, a man on long-term sickness benefit who had something wrong with him. There was an air of respectability about him.

'Why are you in prison?' I asked.

'Social security fraud,' he replied.

'What did you do?'

'I failed to notify them of my personal savings, which were in excess of what was allowed.'

'How did they find out?'

'My ex told them.'

He had left his common-law wife, and in revenge she had informed on him to the authorities. This, of course, is a very hopeful sign for the government – a manifestation of the British population's public spirit.

The Inversion Of Values

IT IS REASSURING to know that, contrary to what is often asserted by certain ill-disposed people, the forces of law and order in this country are sometimes extremely vigilant and effective. Only last week, for example, I stayed overnight in a London hotel, pulling up outside its front door in my car to unload my suitcase (there was nowhere else to stop within at least a hundred yards of the hotel's door). Within two minutes – quite literally – I had a parking ticket, awarded by an eagle-eyed traffic warden. When I accosted him, he agreed that his action was overzealous, but he had already written the ticket and the law must henceforth take its course.

It goes without saying that no vast apparatus such as that of justice can operate equally smoothly in all its parts. Take another example from only the week before, that of a patient who threatened (in front of two witnesses) to kill me should he ever meet me in the street. Since the particular patient had already severely assaulted several people, causing them injuries requiring attendance at hospital, his threat was not entirely to be disregarded. Indeed, it was entirely credible: he meant what he said, and I had no desire whatever to test his sincerity by meeting him in the street.

Since it is illegal to utter a threat to kill, and since I knew this man to be extremely dangerous and violent, I called the police. It was my duty to do so: those who take no notice of such threats are helping to ensure that they are later carried out, if not on themselves, then on somebody else.

The policeman who arrived in answer to my complaint gave the impression of taking the matter seriously. Unfortunately, he was not empowered to take a statement from me or from either of the two witnesses. He said he would send one of his colleagues to do so in the very near future. Two weeks later, I have heard nothing, and I know I shall hear nothing, however long I wait.

The British state is thus much more concerned to prevent parking on double yellow lines (themselves a sign of official bloody-mindedness and disregard for the public) for two minutes outside a hotel than to prevent the murder of its citizens. Parking is a mortal, but murder a venial, sin.

The inversion of official values is all but complete. The large white van that distributes contraceptives to the street sex-workers in my residential district also brings them food and drink at the NHS's expense. My valiant neighbour, who grew tired of pruning the condoms from the rose bushes in her front garden, took to photographing the sex-workers as they touted for business on nearby street corners, and so far has taken pictures of 40 who work in a radius of about a hundred yards. To judge by these photographs, neither Otto Dix nor George Grosz exaggerated: they were not so much expressionists as straightforward realists. My neighbour makes her pictorial record because she had been told by the local police inspector that the sex industry does not exist locally. She wants to prove to him that it does.

He knows it already, of course, but his job is not to catch criminals; it is to try to hoodwink the public. He knows about the local sex industry because a sex-worker was picked up by a client recently and rewarded for her services to him by a severe beating. She went to the police at the inspector's own station, where she was advised to seek compensation from the Criminal Injuries Compensation Board – and not to forget to claim for loss of earnings.

Afternoon Whisky With A 15-Year-Old Girl

WHEN I WAS a child, I had several great-aunts who on family occasions delighted in asking me whether I knew who they were. Being well-brought-up and not wishing to offend them by admitting that their names had never imprinted themselves upon my memory, I replied that I did, whereupon they called my bluff and asked me who they were.

My ignorance stood revealed: not only did I not know their names, but I hadn't the faintest idea how they were related to me.

And that was in the days when family relationships were clear, well-defined and straightforward; when uncles, generally speaking, were older than their nephews, and parents-in-law older than their children-in-law. Since then, things have changed rather. I have known of cases where a great-aunt was younger than her great-niece. And most mothers round here seem to have a child who is younger than their oldest grandchild.

Last week a patient confessed to me his murderous feelings towards his girlfriend's mother's boyfriend.

'If I'd've had a bayonet, I would've killed him,' he said.

'How old was he?' I asked (demography has always been an interest of mine).

'Thirty-six.'

'And how old are you?'

'Forty-two.'

My next patient had been accused by his step-daughter of having raped her.

'Is it true?' I asked.

'No,' he said. 'She wanted sex with me.'

'And how old is she?'

185

'Fifteen.'

'What happened?'

'She came home and asked me for some whisky and lemonade.'

'What time was it?'

'Four in the afternoon.'

'And did you give her a drink?'

'Yes.'

'Do you think you should give a 15-year-old girl whisky in the afternoon?'

'Everyone knows she drinks, doctor.'

'And then what happened?'

'She came on to me, and we went down to the car.'

'Parked outside?'

'Yes.'

'And now she's accused you of rape?'

'Yes, but it's ridiculous, the little bitch.'

'Why is it ridiculous?'

'Because everyone knows she's on the game.'

My next patient had recently had a termination of pregnancy.

'When I was pregnant, my boyfriend didn't want to know,' she said.

'You mean he didn't want the baby?'

'No, he said I shouldn't have fell pregnant.'

'So he was pleased when you had your abortion?'

'No, he called me a murderess. He still does, whenever he sees me.'

It was the end of their beautiful relationship. He was like a beast that had been cheated of its prey: normally, he liked to abandon a child and its mother soon after the birth.

In the next bed was a woman with alcohol poisoning. She was an alcoholic.

'I can't go a day without drinking, seven lunchtimes a week,' she said. 'And do you want to know why I drink, doctor?'

'Why?'

'Because I've got an abusive baby-father. He suffers from schizofrenzy.'

The last patient in the ward had been badly beaten by the relatives of his former girlfriend. They accused him of having made her pregnant.

'She can't be pregnant because it's not mine,' he said.

This was the verbal equivalent of a print by Escher. And in the afternoon, an outpatient confirmed that we live in an Escheresque world.

'I can't stop myself touching women up, doctor,' he said. 'I was arrested years ago, and now it's coming back on me. I keep thinking who's the victim? We both are really.'

Giving It The Max

I WAS BROWSING in a second-hand bookshop last week when a title caught my eye: *Man's Ascent to Civilisation*. Appropriately enough, the book was in the section devoted to ancient history, though science fiction would, perhaps, have been equally appropriate. On the other hand, a book entitled *Man's Descent into Barbarism* would properly have been placed in the section devoted to current affairs. Every day, after all, I see evidence of that descent, both in my ward and everywhere else around me. I am often accused by my detractors of drawing misanthropic conclusions from a small and selected sample of humanity, to which my reply is: selected maybe, but small by no means.

However, let me narrow the sample down yet further – to the first three patients in my ward last Wednesday, to be precise. The first of them was a woman whose arms were as purple as the sails of the barge in which Cleopatra sat as she pursed up the heart of Mark Antony. They were a fine example of what one might call 'domestic bruising'. I asked her how she had come by her discolouration.

'My daughter,' she replied. 'She's got some really hard punches on her.'

I think I must have raised an eyebrow.

'Mind you,' she said by way of extenuation of her daughter's conduct, 'I'm not the only one she hits.'

'Really?' I said. 'Who else?'

'Her boyfriend. She pumbelises him.'

'Pumbelises him?'

'Yes, every time she's with him.'

'Doesn't he retaliate?'

'No he don't; you see, he's already in foster care.'

I wasn't quite sure I followed the logic of this explanation, so I moved on to the question of why her daughter was so violent.

'I don't know. But it's always worse when she's due for her months.'

In the next bed was a fat young woman, the baby-mother of several children. She had been charged with assault on her next-door neighbour's 12-year-old daughter, and had taken an overdose to establish that she had been suffering from a mental illness at the time.

'My head just went, I was completely out of it.'

I said it wasn't clear to me what she meant by that.

'My mind's playing silly games with me.'

I asked what the fight had been about.

'She was on the stairs, mouthing off at my youngest, giving it the max, when I told her to button her lip. I can't stand lippy kids, doctor. The next thing I knew, wham, she'd smacked me in the eye, so I got her round the throat and put her up against the wall. She says I strangled her and split the back of her head open, but I never.'

'Still, she was only 12.'

'Maybe, doctor, but she was a big girl, six foot for her age, and I'm only short.'

'Either she was six foot, or she wasn't: age has nothing to do with it.'

'I think she will be six foot one day, doctor.'

'I see. A stitch in time saves nine.'

In the next bed was a Kurdish refugee. He spoke no English, but managed to indicate that he was suffering from abdominal pain. An interpreter was found: the patient turned out to be a heroin addict. I asked him – through the interpreter – where he got his heroin from. After what seemed a prolonged discussion between them, the interpreter turned to me: 'He says he gets it from Jamaicans.'

I didn't know they spoke Kurdish in Jamaica.

It All Went Wrong For Me

NOT LONG AGO I heard – or rather felt the vibrations of – the first ghetto blaster of summer. I have experienced earth tremors in Central America, but the terror they inspire is not to be compared with that inspired by the ghetto blaster, whose rap and reggae first obtrude upon one's consciousness not through an assault on the ears, but through a tingling in the legs, as the ground trembles rhythmically beneath one. The volume of ghetto-blaster emissions is not to be measured in decibels, therefore, but on the Richter scale.

If ghetto-blaster comes, can riot be far behind? The riot season is upon us, after all. The time is surely nigh when the impoverished cane-cutters of Brixton, Handsworth and Toxteth, provoked beyond endurance once again by the warm weather and the unjust accumulation of unliberated goods in shops owned largely by Indian traders, will take up their machetes, their Stanley knives and their baseball bats, and try to right the wrongs that oppress them.

The prostitutes will be out in force to egg them on, even more scantily clad than they are when the temperature drops below freezing. (It is a curious fact that prostitutes, unlike mountaineers, never seem to die from exposure.) It must be admitted that, unlike most of the physical attributes of the slums, street-corner prostitutes do not look better in the sunshine, which on the contrary exposes them as strays from a George Grosz cartoon. But Weimar Germany is to modern Britain what Guildford is to Gomorrah.

In my car on the way home from the prison I was stuck behind a minibus that was taking some handicapped children on a summer outing. Oddly enough, the words 'Community Transport' were painted on its doors, the very words used on the buses that took the mental defectives from asylums to gas chambers in Nazi Germany. I was reminded of an advertisement for British Airways in Germany that promised its passengers *Sonderbehandlung*, special treatment – a term that not so many years before had had a severely technical meaning. This must have been one of the most unfortunate advertising slogans in the whole history of publicity.

I had met an old friend in the prison. He had just been returned on remand after three days at liberty. He had told me only 72 hours earlier that he was never coming back to prison, that he'd had enough of prison, that he was turning over a new leaf.

'I thought you weren't coming back,' I said to him.

'I wasn't. I didn't want to come back, doctor, but it all went wrong for me.'

'What did?' I asked.

'When I got home I found my girlfriend in bed with a 15-year-old boy.'

'So you assaulted him?'

'No, doctor. She hit me first' – he rolled up his trouser legs to show the bruises – 'so I hit her back. And so here I am.'

'That's a shame.'

He smiled: most of his front teeth had been removed by dentistry performed with a baseball bat.

'I need a prescription, doctor,' he said.

'What for?' I asked.

'My diazzies and my meffadone.'

'But you weren't taking any when you left prison.'

'Yes, I know, but my doctor outside put me back on them.'

'Why?'

'I couldn't get no sleep. Because of the heat, doctor.'

I Am In Favour Of Respectability Relieved By Secret Vice

ONCE, WHEN I WENT to Delhi, I stayed with a general in the Indian army. His house was opposite some wasteland on which stood Moghul ruins. No sooner had I arrived than I wanted to explore these ruins – something which the general, as a good Hindu, had never done.

Somewhat reluctantly, he accompanied me. On the way there I noticed an encampment of low huts, constructed of detritus, in which there lived some very dark and short people.

'Who are they?' I asked the general.

He turned to look, like a man peering through binoculars.

'I don't see anyone,' he said.

The English are like that with rubbish: they don't see it. I suppose this is because they live so much in the world of their repellent vicarious entertainments that the real world is less real to them than the virtual universe in which they live and breathe and take their being – if 'being' is not too strong a word in the context.

The house next door to mine, for example, is owned by a very sweet old lady, approaching 100, who has long rented out rooms to students. The other day I saw one of them leave the house to post a letter in the pillar-box opposite. A fox had got among the rubbish and scattered it in the front garden. The young man waded through this rubbish, the packets of a thousand pre-packaged meals, looking straight ahead of him; and likewise he returned.

The old lady's house is large: she has eight tenants, all students. I waited to see whether any of them would clear up the rubbish, the work of five minutes. None did, and in the end I did it myself.

Of course, it is possible that the minds of the students were on higher things: not the dross of the sublunary world, but the glories of the Platonic realm of abstraction. I don't think so, however; looking through the window of one of the rooms in the old lady's house, I see a huge poster of a tattooed rock star. Though middle-class, the students inhabit the Hades of popular culture, among whose manifestations is the eating of fast food on the street and the discarding of packaging where the consumer stands. The retina of modern man filters out such trivia as garbage in the streets and gardens, leaving it free to concentrate on television and video.

The eternal struggle, not between good and evil but between respectability and decadence, continues close to my house. Personally, I am in favour of respectability relieved by secret vice, but this is an old-fashioned view. Sincerity and authenticity demand, we are told, that all our vices should be out in the open.

Last night I was walking my dog (as usual) around the church when I noticed some guardians of the public virtue: four middle-class ladies and gentlemen of the street-watch, clad in luminescent jackets, loitering if not with intent, at least with deliberation.

Suddenly my dog began barking furiously at the bushes around the church and a very tall prostitute broke cover, clad in extremely high boots and a leather coat with a slit up its side revealing her nakedness.

'Fuck!' she screamed as she ran off, with some difficulty because of the height of her heels. I shall always remember the click of those heels on the pavement, a sound that would bring joy to the heart of a masochist.

'We knew she was in there,' exclaimed the members of the street-watch. 'Give that dog a bone!'

A Cross Between A Ferret
And A Cretin

THE LAW OF unintended consequences has by now become so commonplace that it is mentioned even in the philosophical symposia held in our pubs and bar-rooms; but what, I think, has hitherto remained unnoticed is the fact that when a British bureaucracy undertakes to solve a problem, its actions have *only* unintended consequences. It is important in this context to bear in mind that the words 'unintended' and 'unforeseeable' are by no means synonymous. A British bureaucrat couldn't predict lava during a volcanic eruption.

These encouraging thoughts concerning the future of our beloved homeland occurred to me as I drove at four in the morning to see a man in a police cell who had barricaded himself in his flat and threatened to burn down the whole building if 'they', his persecutors, did not leave him alone. My route took me along a road notorious as the haunt of streetwalkers, pale as ghosts and attractive as corpses, who tout for custom there.

The city council's answer to the problem of kerb-crawlers along this road was recently to construct speed bumps – what used to be called 'sleeping policemen' in the days when waking policemen did something – every 20 yards or so, thus effectively eliminating the distinction between kerb-crawlers and others. We are all kerb-crawlers now.

I reached the police station. A grateful client of the police (as I suppose we must now call detainees) was banging on the iron door of his cell and screaming the one word in his vocabulary – I need hardly say which. The police officers behind the counter were discussing Darren, a 17-year-old whom they would have to release for lack of evidence, and who did not have enough money to get home.

'He could always go and steal another car,' said one of the officers.

'Don't worry,' said another, 'he will, the little bastard.'

Darren's dad arrived. I was surprised he had one.

'Hello, Dad,' said the policeman. 'We'll just fetch your Darren from the cells.'

Dad was one of those smooth criminal types, heavy gold chain around the neck, Costa del Sol tan, blow-dried grey hair. Darren was a typical feral English youth, a cross between a ferret and a cretin. Clearly, even the criminal classes are degenerating in this country.

My patient was brought in. He at once dropped to his knees and started to kiss my feet. I like a bit of respect, but this was going too far.

'You're my saviour,' he said, 'my god.' And then he prostrated himself before me. It was all most embarrassing.

'Please get up,' I said, offering my hand to help him do so.

'Not before my god,' he replied, clinging to the ground.

It must be admitted, however, that generally speaking we doctors have more trouble with people who think *they're* God than with people who think *we're* God. For example, last week a prisoner came into my office in the prison. I was a little drowsy after lunch (as I am before and during lunch as well). He thumped the table with his fist and I woke with a start.

'I am the Son of God,' he declared.

'How do you know?' I asked, by now fully alert.

'My Father, who art in Heaven, told me so.'

'And your mother?' I asked.

'She lives in Ashton-under-Lyne.'

All Pilled Up

I HAVE LONG puzzled over the difference between 'Twoc' and 'Tada'. Twoc is Taking Without Owner's Consent, while Tada is Taking And Driving Away. Is this what philosophers call a distinction without a difference? I suppose I could settle the question by asking a professional expert – a car thief, I mean, not a philosopher or a lawyer – but somehow I always forget to do so.

There is one important and obvious respect, however, in which Twoc and Tada really do differ: the ease with which their acronyms can be turned into verbs. 'My car has just been twocked' is so much more euphonious than 'My car has just been tada-ed.' As for gerunds, there is simply no comparison. I humbly suggest, therefore, that our distinguished legislators henceforth frame laws concerning newly-created offences with regard to the syntactical flexibility of their acronyms.

New offences are created all the time. The other day, for example, I learnt of a new motoring offence. I had asked a young prisoner why he was in prison.

'Dizzy driving,' he replied.

Dizzy driving? Does that mean driving under the influence of vertigo? Surely dizziness is too subjective a sensation for anyone to be prosecuted for driving under its influence? I know that our government is eroding the rule of law, but surely this is a step too far even for it?

'Do you mean driving while dizzy?' I asked.

'No,' he said, as if I were a simpleton. 'Driving while disqualified.'

'Ah,' I said. 'And why were you disqualified?'

'This copper stopped me on a motorbike. I knocked his bike over and ran over him.'

'You ran over him. Accidentally?'

'No,' he said, indignantly, as if I were impugning both his competence and his honour. 'On purpose.'

I asked my next patient in the prison what he was charged with.

'What am I charged with?' he repeated, a frown of puzzlement wrinkling his forehead.

'Yes, what are you charged with?'

He looked around at the blank walls of the room for something to jog his memory or give him inspiration, but he did not find it.

'I don't know,' he said.

'You must be charged with something,' I persisted. 'Otherwise you wouldn't be here.'

'Nothing,' he said.

'Impossible,' I countered.

He looked at the walls one last time.

'I don't know,' he said, shaking his head. 'I can't remember.'

I tried another tack; as Emily Dickinson said, success in indirection lies.

'Do you live on your own?'

'No,' he replied.

'You're married?'

'Partner.'

'Do you have any children?'

'A daughter.'

'Will they be coming to visit you?'

'No.'

'Why not?'

'They're in intensive care.'

'That couldn't be connected in some way with you being in prison, could it?' I asked tentatively.

'I suppose so.'

'Ah,' I said.

It was my turn to look at the walls. Then I asked what had happened.

'They say I stabbed them.'

'And did you?'

'I don't know. I can't remember.'

'Why not?'

'I was all pilled up.'

I couldn't help thinking of another of my recent patients.

'Doctor,' he said, 'I can't go on like this. I'm feeling completely antidepressed.'

Who Are The Wrong Crowd?

AS INVESTORS IN the stock market know, timing is everything. This is also true of medical consultations. It so happens that everyone who consults me does so past the peak of his problems, at least with regard to smoking and drinking.

'Do you smoke?' I ask the patient.

'Yes, doctor, but not as much as I used to,' he replies.

The strange thing is that I've never met anyone who smokes as much as he used to. I can only conclude, therefore, that it is cutting down on smoking that harms people and drives them to consult their medical advisers. Heroin addicts are much the same. I ask them why they take the beastly stuff.

'I don't know,' they all reply. 'I suppose I got in with the wrong crowd.'

Who are they, the wrong crowd? I never seem to meet them in the flesh; I only hear about them through the people who get in with them. Sometimes I feel there is a vague but vast conspiracy by the Wrong Crowd to corrupt our youth, but this cannot be the case, because our youth is corrupted by the age of three at the very latest.

Perhaps you can tell that I don't love humanity, at least in its modern British instantiation. Misanthropes have the virtue at least of consistency, unlike philanthropes, who love humanity in general. Misanthropes love humanity neither in particular nor in general, and are far from supposing that an aggregate of vices, weaknesses and follies composes something noble and admirable. What a piece of work is a man, indeed: only those who know nothing of life can even pretend to love mankind.

One of my patients last week had tried to kill herself.

'I was all right,' she said, 'until I met my boyfriend.'

'What's wrong with him?' I asked.

'He's cruel, mentally cruel.'

'In what way?'

'He tells me he goes into the toilet at lunchtime at work, with the women there, and shows them his bits and pieces.'

My next patient was an attractive girl of 16 who – unlike most girls of her age and class – looked mentally alert. But her boyfriend, 17 years older than she, was a rotter: shaven-headed, tattooed, with more rings in his face than a curtain rail. This is what is known in Britain as 'being yourself'. Naturally he hit her, put his hands round her throat to throttle her and punched other men in the pub who so much as glanced at her, to prove his undying love for her. He himself was, of course, flagrantly unfaithful.

'You're thinking of having his baby,' I said.

'Yes, how did you know?'

'Girls in your situation always are.'

'I thought it might change him.'

'But, then again, it might not. Why find out?'

'Everyone deserves a second chance.'

'Even Adolf Hitler?'

'He says he wants my baby.'

'First he will try to procure an abortion by kicking you in the stomach, and then, if that doesn't work, he will abandon you either two months before or two months after the baby's birth. He wouldn't want to waste his money on his child, now would he?'

If going down on my knees would have averted her fate, I would have done it.

'I'll think about it,' she said.

She won't, of course; she'll *feel* about it.

Revenons A Nos Moutons

I OPENED MY *Guardian* the other day and saw a photograph of a man who looked like a Standard British Thug, a veritable shaven-headed tattooed monster. He was the kind of man one might expect to see in any club or pub with a reputation for violence, and whom any civilised person would go to some lengths to avoid. This shaven-headed tattooed monster, however, had written a play about to be performed at the National Theatre.

It came as no surprise to me to read that his first play had concerned the awful moral dilemma about whether sharp objects should be inserted up rectums: for there is no subject that preoccupies the British intelligentsia, the finest flower of our educational system, more. For those of us who have occasionally to deal with real sharp objects inserted up real rectums, however, there is no subject more distasteful or tedious.

But let us, as the French say, return to our sheep: that is to say, the population of Great Britain as instantiated in my hospital. There, on the same day as the *Guardian* article appeared, I saw a woman with more tattoos up her arm than I had stamps in my album as a child. The tattoos were of the names of her various children (the oldest of them now 17, and in a young offenders' institute) by equally various fathers.

I asked her why she had taken the overdose that led to her admission to hospital.

'My boyfriend left me for another woman.'

'Who?'

'My best friend's daughter.'

'And how old is your ex-boyfriend?'

'Twenty-one.'

'You must hate him now.'

'No, we're still friends, like.'

I went to the prison. There my first patient had tattoos as the Netherlands has towns and cities: that is to say, everywhere you look. He was also shaven-headed, of course.

On his right forearm was a tattooed portrait of Hitler; on the left, one of Goebbels. If one needed proof that skill is not the same as art, here it was. There were various other traditional motifs tattooed on his body, such as cannabis leaves, a policeman hanging from a lamp-post and a heart with the name of his girlfriend on it. Around his navel were the utterly supererogatory words 'Made in England', for no one, I suspect, would have doubted it for a moment. Upon the crown of his shaven scalp, he had taken the trouble to have the words 'All Coppers Are Bastards' indelibly inscribed.

'That must stand you in good stead down the station,' I said.

'I'm not a troublemaker, doctor,' he said.

Even I, who am inured to the absurd, let out an explosive little laugh.

'You'll forgive me for saying so,' I said, 'but your appearance rather belies it.'

'I don't go looking for trouble, if that's what you mean.'

'I'd be surprised if you didn't,' I said. 'On the whole, people who have Hitler and Goebbels tattooed on their skin do not have the temperament or outlook of Mother Teresa.'

'If there was a race riot in Bradford,' interposed a prison officer, 'would you go to it?'

'Of course,' he replied.

'But why, if you don't look for trouble?' I asked.

'It's what I believe in,' he said.

I Was In The Centre Of Town; Therefore, I Was Stabbed

IT IS NOT the dawn that comes up like thunder in our hospital, but the laundry trolley that passes my office window six times a day. At first but a distant rumble, it swells rapidly until it drowns out both the person speaking to me down the telephone and my own thoughts. The racket it makes turns one's mind to absolute mush – I hope only temporarily – for never in the field of human history has so much noise been generated by so small a contrivance.

You'd think it was a juggernaut at least. In fact, it is the size of the three bottom drawers of my filing cabinet. I suspect that years of research at the National Health Service's Central Laboratory for Patient Pauperisation and Humiliation have gone into developing it, for no merely natural wheels could make such a sound. Quite often the trolley is pushed round the hospital, I imagine, to ensure that no patient recovers from the disturbed night before in the Nightingale wards, complete with patients suffering from *delirium tremens* and dying of cancer. We have, after all, to let the patients know who's boss.

In the afternoon, I go to the prison for a little rest and recreation. I arrive after lunch, when the burglars are all sleeping like babies. Of course, they all then complain like hell that they cannot sleep at night, and claim to be kept awake by thoughts of various kinds.

'I can't stop thinking, doctor,' they say, as if afraid of wearing their brains out.

'Thinking what?' I ask.

'Thoughts,' they reply.

'Well, yes,' I say. 'Any particular content?'

'I think my mind's playing games with me. It does my head in.'

For some reason, at this point I can't help but recall the names of the two greatest British neurologists of their time, successively Sir Henry Head and Lord Brain.

One day last week, when the laundry trolley had been particularly active, I fled early to the prison. My first patient told me what his problem was. 'My head's scattered. It's battered to bits.'

'What do you mean?' I asked.

'I'm not well, doctor. I mean, I keep thinking.'

I tried to distract him. I had noticed that he had a thin white scar from the bottom of his ear to the corner of his mouth: evidently the work of a do-it-yourself enthusiast with a Stanley knife.

'How did you get that scar?' I asked.

'This geezer done it.'

'Why

'Well, I was in the centre of town, wasn't I?'

This seemed to him a sufficient explanation, though I doubted it was a necessary one. My instinct was right.

'I got three stab-wounds in the stomach as well.'

He lifted his shirt and, sure enough, just above the familiar supra-umbilical tattoo stating that he was made in England, were three puncture marks.

'Who did that?' I asked.

'It was a domestic that went too far.'

'Your girlfriend?'

'Ex.'

'And why did she do it?'

'It was my birthday.'

'I'm sorry,' I said. 'I don't see the connection.'

'She's diabetic, isn't she.'

'What's that got to do with it?'

'She didn't take her insulin.'

'You don't suppose it could have been the drink instead, do you?' I asked.

'Yeah, proberly.'

I returned to the hospital. My first patient there was a university student with a tongue stud. I asked him whether he had passed his recent exams.

'I'm not bigging myself up, but yeah.'

'And what are your interests?'

'You mean hobbies?'

'Yes, more or less.'

He thought for a moment.

'I like to veg out on the sofa.'

Everyone Was Doing It

A RECENT PAPER from Sweden in the *British Medical Journal* suggests that the cultured live longer than the uncultured. This is good news for the people of Sweden, no doubt, but bad news for the people round here. For if it's culture which preserves life, they're destined round here for a very early death indeed.

Unless, that is, we accept the American anthropological definition of culture, which is entirely neutral as between Beethoven's last quartets and the smashing of windows of parked cars. This rather forgiving and all-inclusive definition of culture is the one which has undoubtedly entered popular usage. A patient of mine, explaining why he was living in a dosshouse, said that wife-beating and vomiting blood in the mornings had always been part of the culture in which he was brought up.

All cultures being equal, it is wrong – indeed, impossible – to make a judgment between them as to their relative value. All manner of things are forgivable on cultural grounds, and even the Prison Service has gone over – in theory, at least – to the multicultural view of life. I found a prison officer the other day studying a sociological text for his promotion exams which required him to think about the symbolic meanings which various cultures attached to human excrement. This, said the text, would help him deal in a culturally sensitive way with what are known as 'dirty protests', in which a prisoner smears the walls of his cell with his own faeces. Of course, it all boils down to high-pressure water hoses in the end.

Just how tolerant the Prison Service has now become is illustrated by the notice which I pass almost every day at the entrance to the prison, which states that it, the Prison Service, is firmly opposed not only to discrimination on the grounds of race, sex, religion, political belief etc., but to discrimination on any grounds whatever – such as, for example, intelligence and fitness for the job. *Plus ça change…*

Far be it from me to exercise judgment of any kind, not even moral, but I feel it my duty nonetheless to mention an outbreak of near-virgin birth which seems to have afflicted our hospital of late. For example, last week I was consulted by an unmarried woman with two children.

'And the father of the two children?' I enquired mildly at the appropriate moment.

'No,' she replied, shaking her head.

'No,' I said. 'What do you mean, no? Do you mean they don't have a father?'

In which case, I should send her straight away to Medical Illustration, where all our most interesting cases end up as transparencies for display at lectures to general practitioners around the country.

'I don't have nothink to do with him.'

If ever there was a case of closing the stable door after the horse had bolted, this was it.

'Do the children see their father?'

'It was all a mistake, I was young. Everyone was doing it.'

Ah, the peer-pressure theory of undcrage sex. Peer pressure is like nuclear fusion: if only it could be harnessed to some worthwhile purpose.

'Having children was part of the culture.'

Whenever I hear the word culture…

Bored To Death

FREEDOM IS A PRECIOUS THING, as we all know. Blood has been spilled to procure it, though from my personal observation I should say that we are generally more attached to our own freedom than to that of others, which we feel quite at ease in extinguishing.

And because, by his very nature, man longs to be free, it is easy to understand with what joy prisoners must walk through the prison doors into the wide, or at least wider, world beyond. Each released prisoner must have a song in his heart and a spring in his step: free at last, free at last, thank God Almighty, free at last!

When something good happens to a man, it is only natural that he should wish to celebrate; and, as they say in Germany, every little animal has its little pleasure. So it isn't altogether surprising, given the nature of modern man's pleasures, that we in our hospital have come to recognise a released-prisoner syndrome.

This consists of an intravenous injection of heroin, administered by what passes hereabouts as a friend, followed by a cessation of breathing, plus or minus (as we doctors put it) a preliminary inhalation of vomit.

'Why do you do it?' I asked one such reveller, three days out of prison.

'Boredom,' he replied.

Round here, therefore, boredom is the first fruit of freedom.

'And does heroin relieve boredom?' I asked.

'Yes.'

This was only logical, I suppose, for it is difficult to be both bored and unconscious.

'And, having nearly died, would you do it again?'

'If I was bored.'

Bored to death, in fact.

Second Opinion

But I mustn't give the impression that everyone round here approves of heroin. On the contrary, some are most fearfully opposed.

For example (I apologise in advance for descending so swiftly from the sociologically general to the clinically particular), I saw a young man recently with only one external ear. There was a horrible angry scar where the other should have been.

'What happened to your ear?' I asked.

'My brother ripped it off.'

'Why?' This seemed the natural question to ask.

'He was trying to get me off the brown.'

I had heard of auricular acupuncture for addiction, but this was ridiculous.

'I'm sorry,' I said. 'I'm not sure I quite see the connection.'

The young man spelled it out, as if explaining to a man of defective understanding.

'My brother said to me, "Either you're coming with us, so we can get you off the brown, or I'm going to fucking make you." "You and whose army?" I said, so he grabbed me by the ear and ripped it off.'

'And did it work?' I asked.

'No.'

'Didn't you go to the hospital to try to have it sewn back on?'

'No.'

'Why not?'

'Well, I had to go and pick up some brown off my dealer, didn't I?'

His case will be included in a book I intend to write, *Injuries of the Heroin Way of Life*, a companion volume to my forthcoming *Injuries of Burglary and Escape from the Police*.

That day I met a middle-aged woman, the bones of whose forearm had been pulverised by a baseball bat wielded by two younger women. 'They was drug dealers looking for the 80 quid what my son owed them, only he was out, so they got me instead.'

Drug dealers believe in collective responsibility: of their debtors, of course.

If Hamlet Were Written Now

ONCE UPON A TIME, aspiring Britons took elocution classes; now they drop their aitches. These days, you can hardly tell an Old Etonian from an Old Borstalian; and not, I assure you, because Old Borstalians have become more refined. *Nostalgie de la boue* has become an insatiable craving; and so important has it become to prove one's democratic sentiment that everyone feels obliged to behave like scum. Bad behaviour is political virtue.

One consequence of this is that the repellent entertainments of the mob are now those of the allegedly educated as well. There is no difference in the ways in which the mentally deficient and university students amuse themselves. Stupidity is now like greatness: some are born stupid, some achieve stupidity, and some have stupidity thrust upon them.

Last week, for example, I had a patient who was a university student of languages. She would have been attractive had she been born in any country but modern Britain, but her deportment, her manners, her mode of dress cheapened her. She chewed gum, which transformed her into a kind of urban ruminant, and she put her feet up on the chair, just to let me know that she didn't believe in any old-fashioned culture of deference. It soon became evident from her answers to my questions that a large part of her problem was the emptiness, the vacuity, of her existence. I asked her about her social life, though I already knew the answer.

'I go clubbing,' she said.

'That's not socialising,' I said. 'That's antisocialising.'

Oddly enough, she agreed with me. 'You're right,' she said.

Despite her intelligence and education, she had neither intellectual nor cultural interests of any kind. I suggested that the lack of such interests was, in fact, at the root of her self-destructiveness.

'Yes,' she said. 'I've often thought that. Recently, I've been trying to get into culture.'

'What have you done?' I asked.

'I've bought tickets for the Pop Idol concert.'

My next patient was a young man who slouched in the chair beyond the call either of nature or of comfort. He yawned constantly, ontologically, much more often and broadly than a man who was merely tired, and in his right hand he clutched a plastic bottle of flavoured water with a blue dummy stopper in case he became dehydrated between yawns. He wore a baseball cap, a torn T-shirt, stained tracksuit trousers, and trainers of many colours. He was studying for a higher degree, he said. I asked him whether he enjoyed it.

'It's all right,' he said. 'They don't learn you much.'

'Obviously not,' I said, and then I asked him what he did in his spare time. I knew the answer, of course.

'I go clubbing.'

'Do you take drugs?'

'Just E and Charlie.' (NB Ecstasy and cocaine: *transl.*)

I asked him why he had tried to kill himself with an overdose of antibiotics.

'I can't be arsed to live no more.'

How charmingly put, and with what delicate sensibility! If Hamlet were written today, the famous soliloquy would begin: 'To be arsed, or not be arsed: that's the fucking question.'

'I 'ate fucking life,' he added.

'And what do your parents do?' I asked.

'My father's a barrister and my mother's a teacher.'

'And what does she teach?'

'English.'

How To Save Polonius

OF COURSE, IF HAMLET were alive today, he would probably ask for counselling; and this would save the lives of Polonius, Gertrude, Claudius, Laertes, etc. Hamlet would be helped to come to terms with the death of his father, and the final scene would consist of everyone hugging one another in reconciliation, the hug being the highest expression both of philosophy and of emotion known to modern man.

Is there anything that is beyond the power of counselling? It seems that even criminals believe in it, and 40,000 burglars can't be wrong.

A young man who came out of prison a couple of years ago took an overdose and ended up on our ward. I asked him why he had taken the overdose.

'They never gave me no counselling nor nothing,' he said. 'That's got to be wrong.'

'What were you in prison for?' I asked.

'What's that got to do with it?' he said, with surprising ferocity.

'Your counsellor might like to know,' I said, mildly, and changed the subject.

Later I discovered that he was what the layman tends carelessly to call a murderer. He had served three years for kicking a man to death, but, as it was only outside a nightclub, the court decided that the deceased probably deserved to die. Having watched the behaviour of people outside British nightclubs, I wholeheartedly concur with this view.

The one great advantage of having been in prison for killing is that it makes you irresistibly attractive to women – at least those in, or aspiring to membership of, the slut class. And this particular young man was to women what a pot of jam is to wasps: they buzzed about him in his hospital bed, waiting for him to recover so that they could go to a nightclub with him.

Of course, he had a concubine, whose departure had caused him to take the overdose. It was only after her departure that he discovered how much he loved her: before she left, he used to knock her about to the tune of 'You whore!' and 'You slut!'

I went to the prison that afternoon. My first patient had a black eye and two festering human bites on his arm.

'Where did you get those?' I asked.

'My partner.'

'Did you retaliate?'

'I don't hit women.'

'What are you in for?'

'Rape.'

Another prisoner was brought to me in an agitated state. He had been banging his head on the wall.

'I need something to calm me down,' he said.

'What's the matter?' I asked.

'My head's in bits. It's gone, cabbaged.'

'Are you being bullied?' I asked.

His manner changed to one of feral menace.

'I'd like to see anyone try,' he said. 'I'd rip his fucking frote out.'

I asked my next patient why he was in prison.

'I shouldn't be here,' he said. 'It's all wrong.'

'In what sense?'

'I was only trying to put an end to some trouble that broke out.'

'But what are you charged with?'

'Possession of a firearm.'

'And did you have a gun?'

'Yes,' he said.

'So you were in possession of a firearm?'

'Yes,' he said plaintively. 'But the others had two.'

Earners And Workers

IT MUST BE a dull dog who has never wondered what it's all about – life, I mean. It is all so very difficult and complicated, and always ends in osteoarthritis. In the circumstances, it is almost impossible to descry any meaning. Does one keep oneself busy just to avoid the question?

My patients rarely supply me with answers to man's existential problems, but last week a man in the hospital offered his answer to the question as to what life is for. I was asking him at the time how he had come by the scar that disfigured his face.

'Fighting,' he replied.

'Drunk?' I asked.

'No,' he said, mildly offended at the suggestion. 'I'm a street fighter.'

'Do you fight often?'

'Only when I have to,' he said in a tone of self-abnegation.

'How often's that?'

'If a man hits me, I hit him back. That's what you're there for, isn't it?'

Of course, I often do wonder what people are there for, especially in the public service. I have come to the conclusion that they are there so that they can pay their mortgages, in the process losing sight altogether of more ostensible ends.

For example, the last hanging we had in the prison took place on an afternoon when the vast majority of the prison officers were at a meeting – curiously enough about something known in the trade as 'Suicide Awareness'. Had there been no such meeting, the man who hanged himself might still be alive; but if there were no meetings, we'd have to employ fewer staff, particularly in the higher grades. It would be a disaster.

A paediatrician colleague of mine recently attended a case conference about a young child whose parents were suspected of cruelty. Compared with a social services conference about an abused child, the Congress of Vienna was but an informal get-together. The man-hours (or should I say person-hours?) expended would be enough to give a time-and-motion expert apoplexy.

Anyway, my colleague was asked to describe to the meeting the findings of his examination of the child. He finished by saying that the child had a black eye.

'You can't say that,' one of the social workers told him.

'Why not?' he asked. 'The child did have a black eye.'

His remark was regarded as so racially provocative that he was sent – compulsorily, of course – on a racial awareness course.

I turn to the prison as an island of comparative sanity. How calm and sensible some of the prisoners seem. For example, last week I spoke to another prisoner who was in, as he put it, for firearms.

'Did you have a gun?' I asked.

'Yes,' he replied.

'Why?'

'For protection.'

'Against what?'

'There was this man who was trying to shoot me, so I thought that if he knew I had a gun, he might not bother.'

'And why did he want to shoot you?'

'I was in this club and I accidentally trod on his foot.'

Of course, the fact that my patient had known exactly from whom to obtain a gun suggested to me that he was a criminal.

'Yes, of course,' he said. 'Everyone round by me knows I'm an earner.'

'An earner? What does that mean?'

'A criminal. There's earners and there's workers, and I'm an earner.'

'And what are workers?'

'Nine-to-fivers. You can always tell an earner from a worker.'

'How?'

'Well, if you see a man in a tracksuit and a cap, you know he's an earner. If you see a man in a shirt, you know he's a worker. You can't really miss it.'

Lombroso Was Right

LAST WEEK I HAD my day in – or perhaps it would be more accurate to say at – court. As ever, I had to wait for several hours before I was called to give my evidence, but I didn't really mind; the barrister told me to keep the meter ticking. Besides, there are few spectacles as interesting or amusing as that of British defendants, with their families, awaiting trial outside the court. One realises that the mark of Cain is no mere metaphor.

When a Briton is accused, he does everything in his power to prove that Lombroso, the great Italian criminologist, was right, and that criminals can be identified by their appearance alone. What is more, they make no attempt to pull the wool over the eyes of the judge or the jury by dressing as if a trial were a more solemn event than a football match. They appear in the dock in shiny tracksuits, unshaven and as if suffering from a hangover from the night before.

Perhaps it is a double bluff. Juries, I have noticed, don't dress up for the occasion either, but arrive in their Sunday worst. The men are worse than the women; faint traces of self-respect can still occasionally be detected in a woman juror. For the most part, however, jurors look as though they are about to settle down on the sofa at home, disgusting fast food at the ready, to watch a soap opera on what I once heard a judge call 'a television machine'.

A well-dressed defendant might therefore antagonise them and make them feel that he is a class enemy who is getting above himself. The British population is far more comfortable with people who look and behave like degenerate wrecks of low intelligence. They make them feel thoroughly at home; *chez nous* as it were. As usual, the criminals – intelligent or not – are shrewd at gauging the temper of the times. The wonder is that anyone is ever found guilty.

As everyone knows, of course, eye-witness testimony is very unreliable. Show the same event to two people, and they will describe it in a completely different way afterwards. Nowhere is this disparity in evidence more obvious than in what used to be called, when there were still marriages to be harmonious, marital disharmony. Now we have entered the era of the relationship, the 'it' of 'It didn't work out.' The question is why it did not work out, and there opinions are inclined to differ.

For example, last week I saw a man tattooed with snarling bulldogs and the word ENGLAND on his arms, a supererogatory explanation if ever there was one – who had tried to hang himself because his common-law wife of ten years had left him for the eighth time, and he was of the opinion that, on this occasion, she wasn't coming back.

'Were you ever violent to her?' I asked.

'No, doctor, I never laid a finger on her.'

I took the precaution of phoning her to obtain her views on this delicate question.

'I'm going back to work after five days off to let the bruises go down. And I had to have the police out to him twice yesterday.'

'Was this the first time?' I asked.

'No, I've had it for ten years, and I can't take no more.'

I went back to the patient.

'Why do you think your relationship failed?' I asked.

'I don't know,' he replied. 'The spark just went out of it, I suppose.'

Complaints About Me

AS IS WELL-KNOWN, complaints rise to meet the procedures set up to investigate them. Given this fact, it is not altogether surprising that, despite the many legitimate grounds for complaint with which the National Health Service so thoughtfully provides its patients, the majority of such complaints are footling or malicious, or both. The British have a genius for griping about all the wrong things.

The last time I was the subject of a complaint was about three years ago. To give the patient his due, he complained through the official channels, which proved him a man of mettle and determination, for they are not easy to find. But then he had a powerful motive to find them, for the burden of his complaint could hardly have been more serious: I had failed to provide him with a sick note. I was asked to reply to his complaint within three weeks.

I was brief and to the point. 'Mr X,' I wrote, 'is a drunk who beats his wife and I'm not writing any sick certificate for him.'

Since these facts were incontestable, I heard no more from Mr X.

Now I have heard from Mr Y. He feels aggrieved that I did not take him seriously during my consultation with him. Since he was drunk at the time and asked me whether I could fetch him some 8.4 per cent cider, I feel it was he who did not take me seriously, rather than the other way round. I have said so in no uncertain terms in my reply to his complaint; for as the Good Book would have put it, had it been written nowadays instead of several aeons ago, a soft answer turneth not away unrighteous indignation.

Despite our valiant and in some cases creative efforts to make our hospital as unwelcoming and even hostile to patients as possible, they keep coming. We make them wait in casualty; we make them wait in corridors; we make them wait in outpatients: they never surrender.

Indeed, there are some patients who want positively not to go home. There is, for example, an old man who has spent the last six weeks in our casualty department, day and night. He is not waiting for treatment; he has made it abundantly clear that he wants nothing of that kind. No, he likes the atmosphere, the human warmth, the drama, the blood and the swearing. He has resisted all attempts at ejection, with all the force of which an 80-year-old is capable. We can only hope that sooner or later he grows as bored as the lady at the front desk.

There was a young patient in our ward last week who didn't want to go home. She had been brought to hospital because she had smashed some flower-pots in the family kitchen and then taken too many pills. When I told her that she was being discharged because there was nothing wrong with her, she was very angry. 'You can't send me home,' she said.

'Why not?' I asked.

'Because I'll kill my parents.'

'You can't kill your parents,' I said.

'Why not?' she asked.

'Because I've phoned them, and they're not in.'

A Moving Encounter

A VISITOR TO OUR grey and ghastly land might easily conclude that it had just emerged from a prolonged period of severe drought and famine, for the English seem incapable these days of progressing further than a few yards, or of waiting for longer than a few minutes, without solid or liquid refreshment, or both. Evidently, we live in hungry and thirsty times.

One day last week my first patient sat outside my room accompanied by her 14-year-old daughter, who was quite pretty in an incipient slut kind of way. She had a ring through her nose (they start body-piercing early these days), and also one through her navel, which was showing despite the sub-zero temperature outside. If only such heroic self-sacrifice could be attached to a better cause!

But what I most noted about her was the packet of potato crisps which she held in one hand, and upon which she grazed with all the self-consciousness of an obligate herbivore. She ate without thinking and chewed without tasting. No doubt the empty packet would soon appear somewhere on the ground, for the English now leave litter behind them as rabbits leave pellets – though, on the whole, of course, rabbit pellets are neater and less aesthetically offensive.

My second patient arrived: a young man of high intelligence but brutal background. His slouch in the seat while waiting to see me was so exaggerated that it indicated not so much a desire to make himself comfortable as to express an attitude to life. In his hand was a bottle of mineral water from which he swigged regularly: it's thirsty work waiting in a hospital corridor for five minutes.

He brought his bottle with him into my room; no baby was ever more attached to its milk or its dummy than was this young man to his mineral water. He drank from it while he spoke to me, and while I spoke to him.

He was not a completely hopeless case. His father had been in prison for murder, but he was deeply troubled by his own propensity to violence, especially when he had been drinking. He was jealous and possessive of his girlfriend and accused her of infidelities on the slightest pretext, the absurdity of which he recognised immediately afterwards, but which seemed compelling to him at the time.

'Trifles light as air are to the jealous confirmations strong as proofs of holy writ,' I said.

'That's *Othello*,' he said. 'I really love that play.'

I cannot describe how moving it is to meet someone brought up in his environment who has discovered, through the force of his own intelligence, completely unaided by what passes for the education system and handicapped by the prevailing 'culture' surrounding him, the consolations and joys of real literature.

'My problem, doctor,' he said, 'is that my Iago is deep inside me.'

Here was a young man who was attempting genuine self-examination (a rare thing indeed in these days of easy psychobabble and exhibitionism masquerading as confession), and we discussed the origins and meaning of insensate jealousy.

'I suppose I can't really think much of myself,' he said. 'Perhaps I need more self-esteem.'

'No one needs self-esteem,' I said. 'Even to consider it is to be lost beyond redemption. What everyone needs, however, is self-respect.'

And self-respect is precisely what the English, *en masse*, lack so entirely.

I Won't Let You Down, Doctor

I MADE A MOMENTOUS discovery outside the prison last week: I discovered what God created bushes for. The illumination came to me as I was passing a little piece of waste ground. Bushes were created by God for the English to throw their crisp packets, polystyrene hamburger-containers, tabloid newspapers, used condoms, discarded chewing gum, beer cans, tins of soft drink, chocolate wrappers and empty plastic carrier bags into.

Not, of course, that empty carrier bags always find their way into the bushes. No; they are sometimes put to other uses. For example, last week in the ward there was a body-packer who swallowed £10,000-worth of cocaine in a packet wrapped in part of a Sainsbury's carrier bag. He claimed that he swallowed it accidentally when his girlfriend poked him in the ribs; he just happened to have the wrapped cocaine in his mouth at the time. The imminent arrival of the boys in blue had nothing to do with it.

'Can I go home now?' he asked.

'No,' I replied.

'Why not?'

'Because if the packet inside you bursts, well, you would be very unwell.'

I meant dead, of course. He needed an operation.

But let us return to the prison. On the day of my religious enlightenment, I examined a patient with some scars on his chest.

'What are those?' I asked.

'Gunshot wounds,' he said.

'How did you get them?'

'It's the way I live.'

'No doubt,' I said. 'Nevertheless, someone must have pulled the trigger.'

'No,' he insisted. 'When you live like me, this is what happens.'

My last patient of the day was a young drug addict, aged 21, who looked younger still. He was deeply jaundiced and had vomited some blood. He had obviously lost much weight. As he had shared needles with other addicts, he was likely to have contracted at least one viral disease. He told me that he had tried for several days to get to see a doctor in prison: but in an attempt to improve medical services, the prison had cut down the number of doctors' clinics (I am reminded of the passage in Shostakovich's Memoirs, in which he describes the closing of a theatre as 'a great cultural event').

I examined the patient.

'This is serious,' I said. 'I'm sending you to hospital.'

'Could I die, doctor?' he asked. There was a sudden anguish in his voice, as if in a flash his whole outlook on life – hitherto utterly frivolous – had changed.

'No,' I said, with a confidence I by no means felt. 'Provided that you obey doctor's orders.'

'I will,' he said.

'From now on, no more messing about.'

'You know, doctor, I'm glad they sent me to prison.'

I have heard this often. It always imparts a pang of sorrow to my heart. A life so grim that prison offers a ray of hope.

'From now on,' I said, 'a good, clean, upright life.'

'I won't let you down, doctor.'

Who knows? How easily, how lightly, is the ravelled sleeve of care knitted up. If only this young man had once known a firm but kindly authority instead of the indifference masquerading as indulgence and the sadism masquerading as discipline that are the twin poles of English child-rearing.

The Criminals Agree With The Americans, But The Intellectuals Have Other Ideas

THE AMERICANS HAVE a theory that to allow small crimes to go unremarked and unpunished is to invite bigger crimes. Needless to say, Britons of intellectual disposition despise this theory: first, because it is American; second, because it does not address the root of all crime – that is to say, the injustice of our present social and economic arrangements; and, third, because it is obviously true.

We British intellectuals prefer to think of criminals the way some people think of dormice and field mice: i.e., as harmless little furry creatures in danger of extinction. We also tend to romanticise our criminals, so long as our own houses have not been burgled and we ourselves have not been attacked in the street. In 1904, H.G. Wells said that 'a large proportion of our present-day criminals are the brightest and boldest members of families living under impossible conditions, and in many desirable qualities the average criminal is above the average of the law-abiding poor, and probably of the average respectable person'.

The criminals themselves, however, agree with the Americans. Last week, for example, I saw a young prisoner who had cut his wrist in an attempt to prove that he was suicidal, and therefore needed to be removed from his current location in the prison. I did not entirely believe his story that he was distressed over the imminent demise of his grandmother: if prisoners were to be believed, there had been a veritable holocaust of grandmothers that week. For most prisoners, a dying grandmother means insomnia, and insomnia means (they hope) a sleeping tablet 'blagged', as they call it, from the doctor. Many prisoners seem to have about 15 grandmothers, two thirds of whom are just about to die or have just died at any given moment.

I digress. I looked at the young man in question – weak and frightened – and asked him whether, perhaps, he had enemies in the prison. He did. They were drug dealers to whom he owed £50 for drugs he had bought before he came to prison. They were after him.

'How do you know?' I asked.

'They've told me that unless I give them the money, they're going to stripe me up.'

'Stripe him up' – that is to say, slash him with razor blades. It might seem excessive over a paltry £50, but they didn't want to give him the impression that he could forget the money because it was so small a sum. To disregard a small crime would be to invite a larger one.

Then I was called to another inmate's cell. He had abdominal pain. I asked his cellmate to withdraw for a moment while I examined the patient. The cellmate left a half-written letter to his girlfriend on his bed, and I could not help but notice an expression in it that I had never encountered before. I had heard of being 'lifed off' by the judge (sentenced to life imprisonment) and being 'nutted off' by the doctor (sent to the mental hospital), but in the letter were the words 'if I get birded off by the judge'.

'Birded off': sent to prison, to do bird. Eric Partridge, in his wonderful *A Dictionary of the Underworld, British and American, Being the Vocabularies of Crooks, Criminals, Racketeers, Beggars and Tramps, Convicts, the Commercial Underworld, the Drug Traffic, the White Slave Traffic, Spivs* (published in 1950 and, therefore, now sorely out of date), suggests that the term 'bird' as denoting prison is derived from the idea of a cage, and quotes Edgar Wallace as his reference.

However expressive the argot of prison, I can only hope that I am never birded off and striped up.

A Prison Without Walls
Or Warders

AS WE ALL know, mankind's most precious gift is liberty, but when, exactly, is a man free? I recall the days when, as a mere stripling, I had nothing, not a penny to my name, and thought myself imprisoned by poverty. Nowadays, I am weighed down by possessions, which act upon me as a ball and chain; but instead of concluding, as any sane man would, that I should divest myself of them, I go on accumulating them. That glorious freedom, which as a child I thought all adults enjoyed, has so far eluded me.

It certainly isn't true that everyone wants to be free, at least if freedom entails responsibility. Yesterday, for example, I was talking to a prisoner who was explaining why he needed a cell to himself.

'I've never got on with people, doctor. Not since I was a child. They've always taken advantage of me.'

I'm sure it was true. And in prison that would mean no tobacco. For most prisoners, tobacco is the meaning of life: there is no other.

We got to talking. I asked him how long he was serving.

'Four years.'

'Is this going to be your last sentence?'

'I hope not.'

I was taken aback.

'You mean you want to come back here?'

'I've only been outside prison one out of the last ten years, doctor.'

'You prefer it here?'

'I do, really.'

'Why?'

'Out there I have to do things for myself. Here everything's done for me.'

227

'But what about freedom?'

'The last time I was out they put me in a flat on my own. The front door wouldn't shut properly, so when I was sitting in the flat I was worried the burglars would come, and I wished I was back in prison because, once they shut the iron doors behind me, I'm safe.'

'And did the burglars come?'

'Yes, when I was out. They took everything, even the plates and cups. I didn't have nothing left.'

'Still,' I said, trying desperately to think of something to say in favour of liberty.

'And a prostitute who lived next door came round to borrow some money from me. She asked could she have a couple of quid, because she didn't have no money to eat, but I only had a twenty pound note, so I said I'll lend you ten quid, bring me back the change.'

'And what happened?'

'She never brought the change. Then I saw her in the street but she ignored me, so I asked her for the tenner but she started to scream that I owed her money, and then her boyfriend arrived and said I'd attacked her and I had to run away, so I never got my money back.'

It was difficult, I confess, to see what freedom could offer him. The part of the city in which he would live is nothing but a prison without walls and without warders; and there's no institution on earth worse than a prison without warders.

Macaulay wrote that 'many politicians... are in the habit of laying it down as a self-evident proposition that no people ought to be free until they are fit to use their freedom... If men are to wait for liberty till they become wise and good in slavery, they may indeed wait for ever.'

But what if they use their liberty to revert to slavery?

The Horror Of Their World

AS EVERYONE KNOWS, multiculturalism means universal tolerance and goodwill: though – in the words of St Augustine in connection with his wish that God should make him perfectly virtuous – not just yet. In the meantime, certain frictions are likely to manifest themselves, for until the lion has truly learnt to lie down with the lamb, he is quite likely to eat it.

Let us, however, descend from the noumenal to the grossly phenomenal plane. I refer to my patient last week, a young woman of Pakistani origin, who lived in a tower block of council flats with a small child by her estranged husband whom she had married by an arrangement in which she had played no active role, to put it mildly. Her parents, disapproving of her decision to leave the man whom they had selected for her, because of his continual violence towards her, disowned her completely.

Unhappily for her, the other tenants of the tower block, most of whom were of Jamaican descent, did not approve of her on racial grounds, and never saw her or her child without hurling both household detritus and abuse at her, using such multicultural expressions as, 'We don't want no fucking Paki bitches here!' (the male of a Paki bitch, of course, being a Paki bastard). She had asked the housing department to move her into a less multicultural area, but the department, true to its principles, replied that she was adequately housed – that is to say, she had four walls and a non-leaking roof.

Thereafter, three of the tenants, also true to their multicultural principles, broke down her front door and entered her flat. One of them held her while the others smashed her plates, her television and her mobile phone – indeed everything that was smashable. This was the activity known to the dwellers of all British public housing as 'trashing a flat'.

The three convinced multiculturalists left, shouting, 'Get out of here, you Paki bitch,' and she promptly took an overdose to comply with their wishes. 'The problem is, doctor,' she said, 'I'm the only Paki in the block.'

Of course, I should not like to suggest that racial hatred is the only stimulant to bad behaviour – far from it. Just as an alcoholic will use any excuse to have a drink, so modern man will use any pretext for making his own life, and that of his neighbour, a torment.

One means of doing so is to bear false witness. Indeed, the false is the only type of witness many people will bear, for they are too intimidated by criminals to bear true witness. And the patient whom I saw after the so-called Paki bitch had tried to kill himself because of a forthcoming court case in which he was accused of robbery. He said that three witnesses were conspiring to perjure themselves in court about him. I asked him why, and he thought the question naive. 'One of them's my girlfriend's ex,' he said. 'He wants to split us up.'

He spoke as if there could not be any other kind of reason for testifying in court but the pursuit of such a vendetta; the whole question of life being Lenin's: who does what to whom?

Recently, I have noticed an increase in the number of young people with marks on their skin rather like those of healed smallpox scars. Smallpox hasn't returned, however: they burn themselves with cigarettes. It is the only way in which they can express their horror of the world in which they live.

The Beer Was Immaterial

NATURE, IN HER infinite wisdom and mercy, has decreed that a goodly proportion of mankind should be born ugly: but that, of course, has not in the least discouraged mankind from supplementing her efforts. The British, it seems, are particularly talented in this direction and, for them, not only stupidity but also ugliness have taken the place of greatness: some are born ugly, some achieve ugliness and others have ugliness thrust upon them.

Last week I was consulted by a man who had had ugliness thrust upon him, not once but repeatedly. His face was criss-crossed by scars, ranging from white to livid. I pointed to the most prominent. It was a healed gash that extended from his forehead across his eye socket to his cheek below (he was blind in that eye). 'How did you get that?' I asked.

'I was defending this girl in a pub from her boyfriend who was beating her up, when she turned round and put a broken bottle in my face. It was Newcastle Brown.'

'The beer is immaterial,' I said. 'Did you call the police?'

'No.'

'Why not?' I asked.

'Well, she must've had problems of her own.'

O problems, what crimes are committed in thy name!

I pointed to a nasty-looking scar on my patient's neck. 'How did you get that?' I asked.

'That was her boyfriend. He ripped it with his teeth.'

'And he had problems too, I suppose?'

'Yeah, he must've.'

The patient in the next bed was being withdrawn from his many drugs of abuse. You name it, he took it. He looked very worried.

'Doctor,' he said, 'do you think that if I get better, I'll lose my sick pay?'

'I shouldn't think so,' I replied.

'Why not?'

'Because sick pay has nothing whatever to do with being sick,' I said.

He laughed, but then grew serious again.

'But you won't grass me up, will you, doctor?'

'No, of course not.'

'Because I don't want to get no better if I lose my sick pay.'

I reassured him that work was not around the corner.

In the next bed was an alcoholic with mild shakes. I asked him whether he took drugs. He seemed shocked by the suggestion. 'I'm not a pillhead, or nothing like that,' he said.

I asked him how he had reached his present condition.

'I lived at Hill Road — that's when the drinking really started.'

How pleasant it is after a morning in the hospital to retreat to the rational, ordered universe of the prison! If prison does not work, as so many of our intelligentsia say (without, of course, believing it for a moment), it is purely because people are not in it sufficiently long. It isn't true that you can't teach an old lag new tricks: on the contrary, you can teach only an old lag new tricks.

My first patient in the prison was an aging hippy with long, greasy hair (there's only one thing less becoming in a man than long hair, and that's short hair). He told me he was withdrawing from heroin.

'I stopped for three years, doctor,' he said. 'But then I started again after my son died.'

'And what did he die of?' I asked.

''Eroin overdose.'

232

The Tinkling Banality
Of Television

THERE IS NOTHING as boring as perpetual entertainment, and the *ennui* of those who regard life as a poor imitation of a video is like a slow wasting disease. The late Malcolm Muggeridge – a man I did not altogether admire, in large part because he always enunciated his opinions as if straining at stool – was prescient on the evils of television. He said it was the end of civilisation, and he was right.

Last week in the prison I saw a man who had tried to kill himself because of television. The instrument of the devil has been placed in almost every cell of our penal establishment, for it is now regarded as a cruel and unusual punishment to deprive our young men of the moving pictures that have emptied their minds for so many years. And a loss of freedom should not entail a loss of entertainment: that would be too harsh.

In our prison, however, there are two men to each cell. The shrewd among you will already have divined the potential for trouble that a television in a two-man cell might cause. Similar as the debased tastes of most prisoners might be, disputes can nevertheless arise as to what to watch. Since reasoned debate and compromise are not generally characteristic of this population, the question of what to watch boils down to who is the stronger and more threatening.

The prisoner who was driven to suicide by the television in his cell did not want to watch it at all – he preferred to read but he was locked up with a man, physically much stronger than he, who wanted to watch it 18 hours a day. The tinkling banality of chat shows combined with the *ersatz* excitement of sporting events and the bang-bang kapoom! violence of the dramas finally drove him to the rope. It was the only way he could escape.

I knew he was different from what the prison officers call 'your average con' the moment I stepped into his cell in the hospital wing. He was listening to a Shostakovich string quartet. Suffice it to say that this is not the favourite listening of the criminal classes, who generally prefer simpler compositions with lyrics such as 'Fuck your mother, motherfucker!' repeated over and over again to a kind of head-banging rhythm, played at a volume to make the walls vibrate.

He was a cultivated man, interested in and knowledgable about literature, art and music. At last, a kindred spirit! I sympathised with him entirely in his need to escape the evil screen and for peace and quiet. We reflected bitterly (but of course enjoyably) upon modern man's inability to be alone with his thoughts.

'What are you in prison for?' I asked, *en passant*.

'Making child porn videos,' he said.

Ah well. I never said cultivation was a sufficient condition of humanity, only a necessary one – perhaps.

I went to the next cell. The inmate had also attempted – rather feebly, as it happens – to shuffle off this mortal coil.

'What are you in for?' I asked.

'Me and me missis had a argument. I had a knife in my hand and I slashed her across the face. I never hit a woman before.'

'So you feel pretty bad about it?'

'Yeah,' he said. 'I'm all cut up.'

I Must Admit That I Have Myself Sometimes Entertained Doubts About The System

I ARRIVED AT the prison last week to find a car – a battered BMW of the no-tax-or-insurance model – parked outside. In it sat two young male AfroSaxons of the gold-front-tooth persuasion playing the car wireless so loudly that the tarmac juddered to the beat of what I suppose I must call the music. (Compared with it, the compositions of Webern were positively tuneful.) The lyrics were simple, repetitious and easily memorised, even by those with the attention span of a British government minister: FOK DA SIS-TEM, FOK DA SIS-TEM, FOK DA SIS-TEM.

I must admit that I have myself sometimes entertained doubts about the system.

Any system, after all, capable of producing such a loathsome racket must be pretty rotten, as must any system in which people can tolerate it for longer than the very briefest of moments; but any system that actually permits it so to pollute the environment is – well, near to final collapse.

Once in the prison, I came across further compelling evidence of the thorough rottenness of the system. I saw several prisoners, all in their early twenties, who were addicted to heroin, and all of them malnourished, with the purple tongues and cracked angles of the mouth that bespeak prolonged vitamin deficiency. One of them was so emaciated and rachitic that I could not refrain from saying something.

'If a press photographer took a picture of you in that condition when you left prison, everyone would conclude that we were running a concentration camp and demand its closure.'

The prisoner, who was far from stupid, told me I was right.

'Then why are there no calls to close British society down? It is a crime against humanity.'

'I can't argue with that,' said the prisoner.

The next patient had just tried to hang himself. There were red ligature marks around his neck.

'Why did you try to kill yourself?' I asked.

He handed me a letter he had just received. It was one to his girlfriend and baby-mother, and it had been returned with 'Unknown at this address' written on the envelope.

'But she opened it and read it,' he said.

'How do you know?' I asked.

'Because she took out the photograph I sent her. I don't know why she's doing this to me.'

'Why are you in prison?' I asked.

'Assault.'

'Her, by any chance?'

'Yes.'

'What did you do?'

'I strangled her. I know I shouldn't of, but she provoked me.'

'How?'

'I'd just come out after doing a 12-month. She told me this bloke she was living with while I was inside had broke the babby's arm in three places, and now it was in care and I couldn't see it. It's nearly three years old, and I only seen it once. Today is the babby's birthday.'

The next prisoner looked very angry.

'I shouldn't even be here,' he said.

'Why not?'

'I'm innocent.'

'What of?' I asked.

'Harassment. My ex says I'm harassing her. She's a liar, that's what she is, she's a liar.'

'You've split up?'

'Yeah, two months ago.'

'And did you harass her?'

'Don't be fucking stupid. How could I harass her when she's carrying my bleedin' baby?'

Prophylactic Hanging

ANYONE PLANNING TO break his leg in such a way as to require a wheelchair afterwards had better – at least if he lives in my hospital's catchment area – give plenty of notice of his intended accident, for there is a three-week waiting-list for wheelchairs. This, of course, is but the twinkling of an eye by comparison with the wait for a hernia repair, so I don't want to hear any grumbling. Remember, in today's NHS there is always someone worse off than yourself.

Of course, the very worst-off people are those who ruin their own lives: that is to say, the great bulk of mankind. For example, last week my first patient had tried to do away with himself because he said he had ruined his career.

'How's that?' I asked.

'Because I've just been convicted of GBH,' he replied. 'I never thought it would get this far.'

He sounded bitter at the injustice of it all. I asked him to explain.

'Me and my best mate, we had a bit of a fall-to. I thought he was going to have a fight on me. He came for me. I had a knife and it went in.'

'Was he injured?'

'They had to pump up his lungs and take the blood away from the bag round his heart.'

'So he very nearly died?'

'Yes, but he knows I didn't mean nothing by it. He wanted to drop the charges; he knows I get these mood swings.'

'Yes, but… '

'I never thought it would get this far, doctor. I mean, it's crazy. I'll never get the kind of job I wanted.'

'What kind of job did you want?'

'Looking after people.'

The patient in the next bed had also nearly died. He told me that, in fact, he wished he were dead.

'Why do you want to die?' I asked.

''Cause I don't want to be here no more.' It is amazing how many people think that a redescription is an explanation. 'There's nothing for me no more.'

Actually, that wasn't strictly true. He hadn't paid his drug-dealers for a few weeks, and they were threatening to beat him up. Therefore, there was most definitely something for him when he left hospital.

'I owe them five hundred pounds each and I haven't paid them for six weeks. They said, "You're taking the piss, so you owe a thousand pounds now."'

Evidently the low interest rates haven't filtered down to the drug-dealers' world.

'So I asked this geezer to inject me with heroin to kill me,' he said.

'Then he's guilty of a very serious crime,' I said. 'You might easily have died.'

'But he didn't do nothing wrong. I told him I wanted to die, and I asked him to do it, so he did it.'

My next patient had tried to hang himself, prophylactically as it were. He said he thought he had better kill himself before someone else did it for him.

'Who?' I asked.

'This Indian bloke.'

'And why does he want to kill you?'

'Because I sold him a car and it broke down. He wants his money back but I've spent it, so he's going to get me. You know how Indians all have these long knives.'

I Think The Crack
Is Keeping Me Awake

IT HAS LONG been known that, along with an inability to learn from experience, the desire to take medicine is what distinguishes man from the animals. This desire, indeed, is what kept the enterprise of medicine as a profession afloat during the many long centuries when there were plenty of drugs but no cures. The placebo effect pleased the doctor at least as much as the patient.

For many centuries, therefore, it was perfectly rational for man to be irrational, at least with regard to illness and its treatment, for the raw, unvarnished truth was insupportable. Unfortunately, irrationality cannot be switched on and off like a tap; so now that man has more control over nature than ever before, he seems to have no more control over himself than at the dawn of history. He is just as badly behaved as ever, but with a wider range of choices.

Last week, I was consulted by a female patient in a semi-Taleban outfit. Round here, most young women are dressed either as a nun or as a slut, the nuns being by far the more attractive, of course; for young white flesh raised on an exclusive diet of takeaway food and exposed to the open air is distinctly off-putting. Oddly enough, quite a few of the young women in their Muslim headgear smoke cigarettes, which I suppose could give rise one day to a charge of attempted arson with recklessness as to endangering life. So far, though, they've always got away with it.

My patient in the full costume had been admitted to hospital unconscious after having swallowed an unspecified amount of methadone, the heroin substitute that is prescribed by doctors for heroin addicts, in order that they might reduce their compulsion to steal 'to feed their habit', as the cant phrase has it, by giving them a saleable commodity free of charge. Needless to say, my patient had never been prescribed methadone by any doctor.

'What happened?' I asked.

'Well,' she said, 'I don't smoke in public, so I went behind this bus shelter and then two lads came up to me. They said they didn't have no money for fags, so they asked me whether I didn't have none to spare. I said I didn't, I was down to my last fag, so they asked me for two quid. I gave them the money, and then they said they'd just done over a chemist's and got two big bottles of methadone. They asked me whether I wanted a swig.'

'And what did you say?'

'I said no.'

'So what happened then?'

'They said, "Go on, a little methadone won't hurt you, you'll like it."'

'So you took some?'

'Well, I'd never tried it before so I thought I may as well.'

Shortly afterwards, she was found deeply unconscious and scarcely breathing near the bus stop.

That afternoon in the prison, a young man came to me complaining that he couldn't sleep.

'I think it's because I've been taking crack, doctor,' he said.

'Why do you take it?' I asked.

'Because I'm not taking weed or brown no more.'

'What about taking nothing at all?' I asked.

'Oh, I couldn't do that, doctor. My nan's just died, my girlfriend's lost a baby and my head's not thinking straight.'

A Normal Day In The Hospital

CERTAIN LINES RESONATE in the mind forever, not necessarily because they are among the greatest ever written. When first I heard Gertrude's despairing *cri de coeur*, 'O Hamlet! thou hast cleft my heart in twain', I knew that it would always express for me, more succinctly than any other words ever could, the tragic irreconcilability of the various desires of human life. Those simple monosyllables are like a stiletto to the solar plexus, and I think of them often when I am deeply moved, as I was last week.

It was a normal day in the hospital: that is to say, human folly and wickedness lay all about me for my leisurely inspection.

My first patient, for example, was a young Indian woman who was caught on the horns of a dilemma. Her mother had told her that she would kill herself unless her daughter returned to the marital home, irrespective of the fact that her father-in-law repeatedly raped her there, with the complete acquiescence of her husband, for whom filial obedience was the first principle of morality. What should she do – cause her mother's suicide or be raped continually?

It was a terrible story, of course, but I have now become too accustomed to it (or its ilk) to feel more than visceral anger for a moment or two. It was my next patient who cleft my heart in twain.

She, too, was Indian, 18 years old. She had been in England about a year, and had been married by arrangement to a man about twice her age. He wasn't a bad man, as bad men go, but he was more interested in her wages (as a sewing-machine operator in a clothing sweat shop) than in her. When she arrived home from her ill-paid work, she was expected by her in-laws to do the housework while they criticised her from the sofa as a lazy girl. The final straw came when they said she was a bad wife: she swallowed bleach.

I asked her whether she was lonely, and she replied that she was, since she had no relatives in this country.

'Would you like to go home to visit your parents?' I asked.

'No,' she replied, to my surprise.

'Why not?' I asked.

'My mother does not like me,' she said.

'Why not?' I asked.

There was a silence as she gathered up the courage to say, 'Because I am not pretty, like my sister.'

One could almost taste the bitterness of her tears as she sobbed. It was, alas, true that she was not pretty, though I see far uglier every day. By contrast, she exuded a kind of heart-rending humility that made one lower one's eyes. How cruel is the world!

My next patient was an intelligent young woman who had had an argument with the man who believed himself to be the father of her son.

'And is he?' I asked.

'To tell you the truth, doctor, I don't know.'

'And is he a good father?'

'No, he's an arsehole, doctor, excuse my language.'

'Does he work?'

Her answer was a short, explosive expulsion of air from somewhere in her respiratory system.

'He doesn't live with you?'

'No.'

'And he doesn't contribute to your son's upkeep?'

'I don't want his money.'

'But you want mine?'

She knew what I meant and laughed.

Finally, an unwashed drunk. He hadn't worked for ten years, and received sick pay so that he might continue the habit that caused his sickness in the first place. As I think I have several times remarked, it makes me proud to be a taxpayer.

I discovered to my surprise that this drunk lived with his eight-year-old son.

'You have custody of him?' I asked.

'Yes,' he replied.

'That's unusual,' I said. 'Normally the courts give custody to the mother. How did you get it?'

'I threatened to burn her house down if she didn't let me have him.'

I could not but recall at this point a passage from Macaulay: 'The history of our country during the last 160 years is eminently the history of... moral and of intellectual progress.'

Obesity: An Evolutionary Theory

HE WHO WOULD read newspapers must expect to spend his days in the darkest despair, for they contain nothing but war, murder and medical advice.

Popular wisdom, however, tells us that every cloud has a silver lining: though my experience of life leads me to conclude that, in general, the relationship between clouds and silver linings is exactly the other way around (I think Buddhists would agree). Be that as it may, I found a real reason for optimism the other day while reading the French daily, *Libération*, that started out Maoist and ended up in the hands of Edouard de Rothschild.

As everyone knows, the population, thanks to its inability to control itself, and indeed its hostility to the very idea that it ought to control itself, is growing ever fatter. We in Britain, indeed, have become a nation of Nauruans, those unfortunate South-Sea islanders who suddenly gained control of immense wealth, started to eat 7,000 calories per day each while luxuriating in a life of total immobility, and ended up with the highest rate of diabetes in the world.

However, the news is not all bad. One Friday night, a 46-year-old Frenchman who lived in a block of flats in a place called Brunoy went to his neighbour to complain about him playing his music so loud. *Libération* informs us that the only reply he received was stab wounds, two in the thigh, two in the back and two in the abdomen. (How passionately Latin! In Britain, with our typical emotional restraint, it would have been blows with a baseball bat.) 'The victim,' reads the report, 'escaped worse injury thanks to his corpulence, preventing the blade from reaching his vital organs.' No doubt this will help evolutionary theorists explain the otherwise harmful tendency to gross obesity in our society: the survival of the fattest, as it were. As more and more young people carry knives, so it makes sense, from the point of view of survival, to become fatter. The youths will eventually learn to carry longer blades, of course, in which case the obviously adaptive behaviour would be to eat more junk food; but in the meantime we should accept that, from the evolutionary point of view, obesity is not all bad (if it were, it wouldn't happen).

At more or less the same time, the French newspapers were in an effervescence of indignation about paedophilia, and the light sentences paedophiles receive. One of the most notorious recidivists, it was revealed, who had assaulted at least forty children, had been prescribed Viagra by the prison doctor, presumably on the grounds of non-discrimination and his inalienable human rights.

It is curious – is it not? – how everyone has at least one kind of criminal offence that he wants to see punished most severely, perceiving with perfect clarity the logic of long imprisonment as preventive for that particular type of crime. But he cannot see that precisely the same logic must apply to all other forms of crimes that are equally subject to recidivism, and even going so far as to deny that, in general, imprisonment does any good.

Of course it doesn't, if you keep letting recidivists out.

To Compare Le Corbusier To Mussolini Is A Gross Slur On Mussolini

FOR A BRITISH patriot, it is a great relief to go to Marseilles. At last, somewhere in Europe as filthy and littered as almost the whole of Britain! If we can't make ourselves better – and of course we won't, so long as the final purpose of our public service is to employ the people employed by the public service – we can at least rejoice in the degradation of others.

Indeed, in one respect Marseilles was worse than anywhere I have seen in Britain: for I have never seen so much graffiti anywhere in the world. Every concrete surface and, to adapt the words of a well-known song slightly, there is an awful lot of concrete in Marseilles – was covered in the handiwork of... well, of whom exactly?

Am I wrong to see in the rise of graffiti as a phenomenon the inflamed egotism of mass self-importance, the desire at all costs to impose oneself upon the world?

What else can account for the risk that young men run who deface the sides of a high bridge with their indecipherable yet supposedly unique calligraphy? Young men like risks – I was not averse to them myself, indeed still am not – but even the most pointless war seems replete with higher meaning by comparison with the ugly defacement of the inaccessible.

Of all the virtues, humility is perhaps the least in fashion. Who can admit, in these days of so many rights, that, actually, one is not very important, not only in the scheme of the universe as a whole, but in the scheme of one's own immediate surroundings? Besides, as it says in a chain of French supermarkets, a customer is sacred: and what is life if not an expedition in a vast supermarket? Every man, then, is sacred to himself.

Unfortunately, the rise of mass self-importance coincided with the rise of sub-fascist modernist architecture. (I say sub-fascist advisedly, because to compare Le Corbusier to Mussolini is a gross and unjust slur – on Mussolini.) What are buildings inspired by Le Corbusier but open invitations to young psychopaths with no way of asserting their individuality but by following the lead of a lot of other young psychopaths?

There are few laws known to sociology, but I think I have discovered one: Le Corbusier-style housing plus a sense of entitlement and low-grade consumerism equal graffiti.

This is not, of course, to say that graffiti occur nowhere else, far from it. I went on from Marseilles to Venice, and imagine my patriotic pride when I realised how far our British culture had spread, when I saw on the wall opposite my hotel the letters ACAB clearly painted in white.

My heart swelled, a choking sensation came to my throat and a tear to my eye. These letters are tattooed in blue lettering on the skin of hundreds, perhaps even thousands, of British criminals: ALL COPPERS ARE BASTARDS or (once down the station) ALWAYS CARRY A BIBLE.

Perhaps, though, they stand for something else entirely in Venetian dialect.

I am sure that one of the aesthete readers of this book will step forward to enlighten me on this point.

My Influence On The Affairs Of The Nation Had Scarcely Been Missed!

I RETURNED RECENTLY from a fortnight's break abroad – well-earned, even if I say so myself who shouldn't. To my great surprise, I discovered that my influence on the affairs of the nation had scarcely been missed and that human nature had not changed very much in my absence. In fact, to adapt very slightly the immortal words of a former poet laureate after the removal of the King's appendix, human nature was no better; it was the same.

Soon after my arrival back on the ward, I tried to speak to a colleague of mine, Dr S___, about a patient on the ward, whose medical history he knew well. A young woman, whose telephone manner was halfway between dim and pert, told me that I couldn't speak to Dr S___.

'Why not?' I asked.

'Because he's in a hospital situation.'

Some people mellow as they grow older; I don't. My fuse shortens. I almost went into one, in a manner of speaking.

'A hospital situation!' I exclaimed.

'Yes, a hospital situation.'

The English language has become the means by which we empty utterance of precise meaning.

'I'm in a hospital situation,' I spluttered. 'You're in a hospital situation. Half a million people are in a hospital situation. Thanks to the NHS, half a million people would like to be in a hospital situation, but can't be because there aren't enough hospital situations to go round. We're all in a hospital situation!'

And with that, feeling much better, I slammed down the phone.

Then I phoned the Health Authority about what a health service bureaucrat would no doubt call 'a funding issue'. An automated message replied, 'For your security, your call will be recorded.' For my security! I was reminded of when my mother used to give me translucent cod-liver oil capsules that were destined to erupt in fishy eructations: it was all for my own good, apparently. What kind of police state are we living in?

I was almost pleased to return to that haven of good sense and genuine freedom, the prison. My first patient, most of whose teeth had been evacuated by the fists of his peers, told me how much he loved prison, and was grateful to it for providing him with a haven from the world outside.

'In ten years, doctor, I done 39 days on the out.'

He so loved prison that whenever he was released he volunteered, in return for a small subvention in cash, to take the rap for people who had committed an offence that the police were eager to solve. Once he confessed, the police looked no further. He had been sentenced several times for things he hadn't done, but was outraged at the minimal terms of imprisonment. It was really very unfair on a chap who was only trying to stay in prison for good.

'Why do you love prison so much?' I asked.

He thought for a moment, and then replied, 'Because they tell me what to do, when to get up, when to eat, when to go to bed.'

My next patient told me why he had helped a man dispose of a body.

'My co-d [co-defendant] said he would show me the red card if I didn't.'

To show someone the red card is Liverpool slang for killing him. Welcome home!

A Patient Pissed Into Our Photocopier This Morning

WHAT A FINE and delicate, yet powerful instrument is the human mind! You fill it with information, and out comes the sheerest error! There is no conclusion so obvious that the human mind cannot resist it, or truth so self-evident that it cannot deny it. The human mind sets experience at naught and treats evidence as an atheist treats God: that is to say, as non-existent. Yes, compared with the human mind the average miracle is but a party trick.

Thus it is that Mr M___, who is in possession of one of these instruments, to wit a human mind, continues to attend our emergency department at least three nights a week, under the impression that he is imminently dying. No amount of experience teaches him otherwise: though of course if he persists long enough, one day he will be right. Then, human beings being what they are, he will say, 'I told you so.' In the meantime, the despairing staff have tried everything from tepid tea to hatchet-faced hostility; but nothing works. I think Mr M___ must be in the grip of two lines from John Donne:

And can there be worse sickness, than to know
That we are never well, nor can be so?

A nurse called me from the emergency department last week.

'He's here again,' she said, on the verge of hysteria. 'What can we do?'

'I'll write to his doctor,' I said. 'Perhaps he'll think of something. Can you send me a copy of his notes?'

'No,' said the nurse, but without a tone of insubordination.

'Why not?' I asked.

'Because a patient pissed into our photocopier this morning and it exploded.'

As it happened, the great urinator was in our ward, fighting off the hallucinatory demons that were attacking him because he'd omitted to drink his habitual six litres of 8.4 per cent industrial cider the day before. At the moment, he existed in two states: unconscious or violent.

In the bed opposite was a man with a large gold earring and an even larger beer belly, naked to what I suppose I must call his waist, though equator would be more accurate. He had tried to hang himself earlier in the day, but the asphyxiating pyjama cord had snapped under the weight and left him in a heap in the lavatory. In the meantime, he decided that he wanted to live after all.

What changed his mind? The arrival of his girlfriend, who herself had just been discharged from another hospital after slashing her wrists. This, I suppose, is Romeo and Juliet with the deaths removed.

Though by no means slender, she climbed on to his bed and started a long, lingering kiss full on the mouth. The happy couple might have gone much further had one of our nurses not intervened.

'Excuse me,' she said. 'This is not the place. There's a man over there already hallucinating.'

It is curious how many visitors under the age of 40 think the hospital is running some kind of bed-by-the-hour service. I went over to the man.

'Would you try again to kill yourself?' I asked.

'I might,' he replied.

'But would you?'

'I don't know,' he said. 'You're the doctor.'

'But how can I know?'

'Because you're responsible for my mental well-being.'

'No I'm not.'

'Yes you are,' he said. 'If I kill myself, it's down to you.'

What We Do Today
Will One Day Be History

ANTHROPOLOGISTS AND archaeologists, I believe, are in the habit of naming defunct societies and cultures according to a characteristic artefact that they leave behind them. For example, there was the Beaker Culture, though what it did with all those beakers history does not relate – at least to me.

Our society and its attendant culture are not yet defunct, unfortunately, but this should not prevent us from speculating upon what the anthropologists and archaeologists of a future civilisation, if there is one, will call it. I would suggest 'the Baseball Cap Culture', for I have but little doubt that the time is fast approaching when the dying will wish to die not in harness, but in their baseball caps. They will want to be buried in them, too, and thus the archaeologists of the future will find them: skulls with baseball caps, offering inscriptions that give clues as to their way of life, such as 'Aston Villa' and 'Burger King'.

I infer that people will die and be interred with their caps on from the number of young patients who now wear them in hospital beds. I encountered one such last week, a 17-year-old with the bad complexion and malevolent porcine regard of the Standard British Moron: that fine human product of a combination of parental neglect (a slut for a mother and a sloven for an absent father) and that vast and hugely expensive conspiracy to keep at least a quarter of the population in preternatural ignorance, commonly known as the British educational system. At last the liberals – in the American sense – have got their way: the environment does make the man.

The SBM had swallowed too many pills, as well as several cans of lager on the street, and, appearing unwell even by the low standards prevailing among such as he, a passer-by called an ambulance. (The availability of ambulances is the only thing that binds British society together.) He was brought to hospital and put to bed in his baseball cap.

The next day, he came into my room, the nylon of his tracksuit trousers making the sound that, round here, has completely superseded the footstep as the auditory sign of human locomotion. He did not remove his baseball cap.

I asked him why he had taken the pills.

'I don't know.'

'Anything to do with a girlfriend?' I asked, for there is one rule in cases such as this: *cherchez la slag*.

'Could be.'

'What?'

'She told me she went behind my back.'

'Anything else?'

'She told me the babby wasn't mine.'

'And now?'

'It's all right, I know she was lying. The babby's mine.'

'How do you know?'

'She told me after I took the pills.'

So all was right with the world. I asked him a few brief questions about his education: for example, was he any good at arithmetic?

'What's that?'

'Arithmetic?'

'Yes. Is it some kind of writing?'

I recalled what a Frenchman said, quoted in the pages of Helen Maria Williams's *A Narrative of the Events which Have Taken Place in France from the Landing of Napoleon Bonaparte on the 1st March, 1815, till the Restoration of Louis XVIII, With an Account of the Present State of Society and Public Opinion*: 'I have a distaste for history, when I reflect that what we do today will one day be history.'

We Lead The World
In Head-Cabbaging

IT'S A RUM WORLD: everything is upside-down or inside-out, a
mixture of Kafka and *Through the Looking-Glass*, of the sinister and the
hilarious. Horace Walpole said that the world is a tragedy to him who
feels and a comedy to him who thinks, but to him who both feels and
thinks it is a tragicomedy. One wants to do away with oneself and fall
about laughing at the same time.

Such, indeed, is my daily fate. Last week, for example (and I take
it only as an example), there was a man in my ward who had taken
an overdose of methadone. A foolish doctor had given him a week's
supply rather than a day's, and my patient, not believing his luck, had
celebrated by scoffing the lot. Then he stopped breathing. After we
revived him, I asked him why he took methadone.

'I've taken meffs for five years,' he said.

It is amazing how many people consider such an answer to be
perfectly satisfactory. I tried again.

'Yes, but why did you take it in the first place?'

'Well, if I didn't take it, I'd have to take heroin.'

'Why would you?'

'Well, I have to take something, don't I?'

I suppose that is true of us all, and since the line of questioning was
– as the prisoners would put it – doing my head in, I changed tack. I
noticed that his arms were covered in injection sites, suggesting that he
took methadone in addition to heroin rather than instead of it.

'When did you last inject yourself?' I asked.

'I haven't pinned up for three weeks,' he replied, 'thanks to the
meffs.'

'So you've been taking methadone for five years to give up heroin
for three weeks. It doesn't make a lot of sense, does it?'

He had also taken large doses of tranquillisers, known round here as diazzies, nitrazzies and temazzies.

'Where did you get them?' I asked.

'I was passing this drug clinic and a woman what I know came out. It's like a big circle.'

'I thought you were going to say it's like a big circus.'

He laughed. 'Well, it's that as well. Anyway, she shook my hand and put these pills into it, so I took them.'

You don't look a gift pill in the pharmacopoeia. Not that it would have made any difference if he had: he knew they were dangerous in conjunction with methadone, he didn't want to die, but he took them all the same. It isn't information people need, it's something to live for.

I went that afternoon to prison. My first patient was a man with a bad case of gold-front-tooth syndrome. I asked him in the course of our conversation about his schooling.

'I was expelled from every school I ever went to.'

'Why?'

'Fighting.'

'How's your arithmetic?'

'What's that?'

About half of the people under 25 round here have never heard of arithmetic. Their three Rs are Rock, Reggae and Rap. My patient explained that he had always truanted. 'That's where all the crime came in,' he said.

'Came in?' I repeated. Unbidden visitors are always unpleasant.

'Yes. I mean, I've had 139 convictions in the last five years. It's all madness.'

'What is?' I asked. 'The crimes or the convictions?'

'My head,' he said. 'It's cabbaged.'

Too Difficult For Them To Understand

IN THE OLD DAYS, whenever that was, the great advantage of stating the obvious was that one was unlikely to be flatly contradicted: but it is quite otherwise in these enlightened times of ours. Therefore, when I say that the great object of the British educational system is self-evidently to eliminate all native powers of reasoning as well as to instil an abiding hatred of knowledge, I expect there might be some who would seek to contradict me. No sensible person could deny, however, that the system is supremely successful in achieving these aims.

Last week I was talking to a prisoner about his addiction to heroin.

'Heroin addiction's not a medical problem,' I said.

He looked puzzled, so I explained further.

'During the Vietnam war, thousands of American soldiers became addicted to heroin, but when they returned home the overwhelming majority of them gave up, just like that, without any difficulty at all. Why do you suppose that was?'

'I don't know, I'm not a doctor,' he said.

'But I'm asking you to think. Try to imagine a reason.'

He tried, or appeared to try, but it was all too difficult or unfamiliar.

'I don't know, do I?' he said. 'I mean, I wasn't born then.'

You'd get a better answer from an African peasant who went to the village school for 18 months and believed that his neighbour's banana tree was so prolific because he used witchcraft.

However, current affairs do interest the prisoners, and if they know nothing of the Vietnam war, the same cannot be said of the Middle East. Last week, for example, I was asked by the officers to see an Iraqi Kurd who had been attacked by several men in the exercise yard.

257

He was an asylum-seeker who had made some kind of misrepresentation to the Home Office. Needless to say, he was vastly more cultivated, well-mannered and intelligent than the indigenous population; very good reasons why the indigenous population should hate and despise him. (I have noticed, by the way, that asylum seekers, on the whole, are precisely the kind of enterprising people that any country not in the last throes of decadence would be pleased to welcome and integrate, on condition that they expected no official assistance. Britain is not such a country, however, and never will be again.)

He had a cut lip, a black eye developing, and a few lumps on his scalp. I asked him what had happened.

'They attacked me because I am an Iraqi,' he said.

'You mean it was their contribution to the war effort?'

'Well, Britain is at war with Iraq.'

'But as a Kurd, you can hardly be much in favour of Saddam.'

'Yes, but this is too difficult for them to understand. I am Iraqi and they are British.'

It is reassuring to know that patriotic feeling, even if sometimes slightly misplaced, still exists among the burglars and crack-dealers of Britain. The death of patriotism has evidently been much exaggerated: many a man in Britain is prepared to kick someone's teeth in for his country's sake.

The Clinical Leadership Toolkit

I DON'T UNDERSTAND how anyone could ever have thought that the organ of cerebration resided anywhere other than in the head. After all, one's thoughts certainly feel as if they are located in one's skull rather than, say, in one's left foot or right elbow. I accept that in some cases I might be mistaken, but all the same…

Not everyone, of course, is in agreement with me as to the primacy of the head in the matter of personal identity. For example, last week in the ward we had a patient who took too many pills in an alleged attempt to end his life. I asked him why he had made this attempt.

'My head was just messing around with me,' he replied. 'It was playing mind games with me.'

Clearly, he considered his personal identity to be completely independent of his mentation. I was reminded of my grandmother, who thought that the key to a happy life lay in regular bowel movements.

'And why was your mind playing games with you?' I asked.

'It was all to do with the relationship. It was getting pretty crap.'

'So what happened?'

'I went back to my mum's.'

'And then?'

'We had this row. My mum wouldn't speak to her on the phone, so she said to me, "Right, you've lost your son because your mum put the phone down on me." She won't let me see him now.'

And so he took to the pills. Not, of course, that he cared any more about the child than she did, other than as a tool in the eternal war of each against all; but a wounded ego has to be soothed somehow.

I went to another ward. On the way there, I overheard two men talking. One said to the other, 'He didn't know what he fucking picked up when he went off with her – he ain't got a brain in his body.'

I arrived on the ward. At the desk I happened to find an open box into which the nurses were supposed to return a questionnaire. This questionnaire was part of the Royal College of Nursing's 'Clinical Leadership Toolkit', a phrase that makes the heart sink. It conjures up a bevy of bureaucrats, whose thirst for power and determination to achieve it is greater than their intelligence, and who imagine that, because they are doing something that no one would do in his spare time if he had the choice, they must be working.

There were 50 statements requiring a response, on a scale from 0 to 4, the former representing the response 'I never behave in this way', the latter 'I behave in this way all the time'. Needless to say, some of the statements could not property be responded to in this fashion: for example, 'Many of my ideas are unconventional, as they go against traditional thinking.' But approximate meaning is good enough for the new elite, whose attitude to truth is definitely post-modern.

I am sorry to report that the nurse at whose questionnaire I glanced never had any unconventional ideas, never expressed ideas that no one else had thought of, was never regarded by others as meticulous, never 'worked hard to give a dispassionate and objective view on proposals', never 'started to evaluate the potential' of new ideas and, perhaps not surprisingly, was never 'seen by others as a highly creative person'. Bravo!

As I returned to my own ward, I remembered the words I had found in some medical notes about a patient of mine, written by a doctor 30 years ago. 'On examination,' he wrote, 'she was miserable but conscious.' This, surely, was a mistake: what he meant, of course, was that she was miserable because conscious.

I Suffer From Legs

IN THE DAYS when relations between men and women were not so fluid or elastic that they left some room for the only cement that holds civilisation together, namely hypocrisy, it was widows and spinsters who were pitied for their condition of solitariness. Nowadays, things have changed. It is people who are not alone who are to be compassionated: that is to say, the people who are in what is known round here as a relationship. An edentate woman in her sixties explained to me last week why she was much envied by her acquaintances.

'Women are jealous of me,' she said, ''cause they've got husbands and I haven't.'

Hers had had the decency to desert her while the going was good, before the generous impulse to leave her in the lurch was inhibited by a Zimmer frame.

Of course, things hadn't turned out well for her in all respects. Life – especially round here – isn't like that. I asked her to tell me about her children. She had a son and a daughter.

'He was a busy little sod,' she said of her son, as far as I could tell without affection.

'Busy?' I asked. 'Doing what?'

'Well, he's been inside,' she said.

'Is he married?'

'Yes, but me and his wife don't get on. She give me two black eyes at the wedding.'

'And your daughter?'

'She's a slut. She only likes blacks.'

I asked her about her medical conditions. Round here, no one reaches the age of 60 without the need to take tablets.

'I'm on thyroxoid. I also take water build-up. I suffer from legs.'

My next patient was on bail. He looked unnaturally mild-mannered to me – unnatural, that is, for round here. I asked him what he had done.

'It's a long story,' he said – it always is.

He and the mother of his children had, it seems, been celebrating Christmas together. They had sent the children away to be looked after by their grandmother.

'We don't believe in mixing children with alcohol,' he said.

'Quite right,' I said. 'And then what happened?'

'I don't know. I just suddenly went upstairs and tried to hang myself.'

'Were you drunk?'

'No, not drunk. I was merry, like.'

Well, each to his own, I suppose. In any case, he had obviously not succeeded.

'And what happened next?'

'Her indoors cut me down.'

'You must have been grateful.'

'She said I threatened to kill her.'

'Hence you are on bail.'

'Yes, but she's gone to the police three time with distractions of her statement. They shouldn't of took it in the first place. She was drunk.'

'But you're still being prosecuted?'

'Yes. The police won't believe her distraction.'

I have often noticed that the police and prosecuting authorities display a determination to proceed with a case when failure is the almost certain outcome, while disregarding entirely the serious offences in which the evidence against the perpetrator is overwhelming and irrefutable. If I didn't know better, I would attribute this to the sabotage of those who used to be known in the Soviet Union as Trotskyite wreckers. In fact, they are only obeying the rules of modern British government and public administration: do what ought not to be done; do not do what ought to be done and concentrate on the trivial at the expense of the important and significant.

The Faint Echo
Of Human Decency

OUR PROBLEM IS SIMPLE: we don't know how to live. That is why modern Britain is such a torment – on the eye, on the ear, even on the nose. You can't go very far, after all, without catching a whiff of the repellent feed upon which so many of the British gorge themselves. In Britain, there is no taste, no honour, no self-respect. The British consume but do not discriminate.

So it is gratifying to be able to report one of the faint echoes of human decency that is occasionally still heard in Britain, as if emerging from far away and long ago. A patient of mine, whose life has been far from easy, told me that her father had died since I last saw her – 'passed away', were the words she used to soften the blow. And she spoke of her father with neither the justified hatred that many lower-class children now have of their progenitors, nor with the knowing disparagement and contempt that is *de rigueur* among children of the higher social classes, but rather with affection and respect.

'We gave him a good send-off,' she said. 'It was a lovely funeral, fit for a king. The service in the church lasted an hour and 100 people came. I didn't know he knew so many people.'

He died and was buried where he had lived all his life, except for war service, when he had behaved with the heroism that derives from believing in something.

'He wanted to be buried, not cremated. "Don't you go cremating me," he said, "I want to be in the ground." So we found a good plot in the cemetery for him.'

I thought of the last lines of one of Antonio Machado's poems:

Son buenas gentes que viven,
laboran, pasan y sueñan,
y en un día como tantos
descansan bajo la tierra.

(They are good people who live,/work, walk and dream,/and one day like so many others/rest in the earth.)

Is this not something we have forgotten, if we could be said ever to have known it?

'We had to choose a coffin. Mum wanted something dark and heavy, not light. It was very expensive, but it was lovely. And we bought the plot next to Dad's, so we can all be together when we go.' Then she paused for a moment. 'You don't think all this talk of death and funerals is morbid?'

'On the contrary. I think it is morbid not to talk about them. Dying well is a part of living well.'

In the afternoon, I went to the prison. There I saw the usual crop of young starvelings, sent to prison for a short while to be fattened up so that they can return to the streets in a fit state to take more heroin.

'Why do you take it?' I ask them, and they jump as if they had received an electric shock through the seat of the chair.

I went to the block that afternoon; that is to say, the segregation unit, where those who have transgressed prison rules are held for a few days.

'Doctor,' asked one of them, 'can you give me some pain-killers?'

'Are you in pain?' I asked.

'Yes.'

'Where?'

He thought for a moment.

'I've forgot,' he said.

An Outbreak Of Miracle Cures

AS ANYONE WHO reads our newspapers knows, there are in essence two medical stories: murderous doctor and miracle cure. Last week in our ward there was an outbreak of miracle cures, but it has so far not reached the press. The miracle cures involved drugs, police and paralysis.

A young man of normal criminal appearance was arrested, but managed to swallow some of the evidence before arrest, and so was brought to our hospital for his own good by the noble guardians of law and order. The evidence in question was cocaine, of which he was known to be both a wholesaler and a retailer. In these circumstances, a dose in the bowel is worth two in the hand.

We realised that he must, in fact, have been a superior type of criminal because he had three constables to watch over him at the bedside instead of the usual or customary two (sometimes there are more policemen in our ward than patients, and, indeed, than in police stations). Our patient could not complain of feeling unwanted.

Suddenly he announced that he was paralysed from the waist down. We knew that he wasn't, of course, but in these days of relativism the distinction between 'can't' and 'won't' has been dissolved out of existence; and so, when he said that he wanted to go to the lavatory, a wheelchair was brought and he was lifted into it. The constables gave him permission to go, provided that the door was left open for them to survey him during his evacuations, in whose preservation for forensic purposes they had a professional interest.

Alas, try as he might, nothing would come. As La Rochefoucauld so perceptively remarked, one cannot stare for long either at the sun or at death – or, he might have added, at a man attempting to evacuate. The attention of the constables naturally wandered, observing which our patient took a turn for the better and evacuated himself through the lavatory windows: up, up and away.

Despite a police helicopter that soon swooped over the hospital grounds, the former paraplegic was not found. Our administrators went into overdrive, suggesting that henceforth our lavatory windows should be barred to prevent further such miracle cures.

Shortly afterwards, however, there was another, similar miracle cure in our ward, though with a less happy outcome.

A young woman, caught in some kind of *flagrante delicto*, was brought to hospital under arrest but apparently unconscious. This continued for some time until one of our doctors whispered in her ear, 'We know that you're all right, so we're going to let the police take you away.'

These words produced upon her an effect little short of miraculous. She was out of the bed and the ward, running up the corridor, quicker than you could say idiopathic thrombocytopenia. Unluckily for her, however, the men deputed to prevent her general circulation in society soon outpaced her and re-established their custody over her.

How relaxing for a while to turn from miracle to natural cures! Another patient, a young man, explained to me, *sotto voce*, that he had contracted a venereal disease from a prostitute.

'You see, doctor,' he said, 'if I don't have these needs met, I might do something worser.'

'Such as what?' I asked.

He thought for a moment.

'Such as smoking, or something.'

Genes Or Environment? It Amounts To The Same Thing

IS MAN A PRODUCT more of his genes than of his environment? Oceans of ink, and even some blood, have been spilt over this question. I have thought of a new solution to this age-old puzzle: it doesn't matter in the least, at any rate with regard to man's bad habits. They get passed on one way or another.

The new solution occurred to me as I looked at the man in the first bed in our ward last week. He was deeply unconscious after taking drugs that some call 'recreational', coma being a popular form of entertainment round here (I must admit that it often immeasurably improves a patient's character). The comatose man had a tattoo of a spider's web radiating from the tip of his nose.

As he was unable to answer any questions about himself, I called his doctor.

'I can't put a face to his name,' he said.

The man's girlfriend turned up later. She looked about as pure as the beaten slut: peroxided hair, a metal spike through her eyebrow, apple-green, genital-hugging Lycra shorts. She was indeed beaten regularly by the arachnophile, and often called the police, later dropping the charges in the name of love.

She brought – or perhaps dragged would be a better way of putting it – her two young bastards with her, the malignity of whose facial expressions were fearful to behold, considering they were but two and three years old. One wouldn't have had to be a witch in *Macbeth* to predict their future: abandonment by their father, followed by tattoos as multiple as their father's, and a life of crime. Genes or environment? It amounts to the same thing.

The man in the next bed, tattooed only with a cannabis leaf on his forearm, had tried to end it all with six painkillers. I asked him why.

He told me it was because his ex (the prefix long ago became a substantive) wouldn't let him see his bastard, and the fact is that round here every man demands his human right to abandon his bastards in his own time, at the moment of his own choosing. Until then, he exercises his natural right to visit them whenever he wants, killing two birds with one stone by giving his baby-mother a good slap.

He told me that his ex had two other children, apart from his own, by different men. 'But,' he added, 'I've brought them up as their standing dad.'

Their standing dad? As opposed to what? Their sitting dad? Their lying dad?

Unfortunately, he said, his ex insisted that one of the others was his, even though he knew it wasn't. She had 'caught pregnant' by another man during what he called his 'relationship' with her; and now she demanded that, if he wanted to see his own child, he should see the other one, too. And to this he would not agree: it was a matter of principle.

I suggested that he consult a lawyer.

'There's only one problem,' he said.

'What's that?' I asked.

'He's got my name on the certificate, and the court will ask who owns him.'

'Owns him?' I asked.

'Yes,' he said. 'But how can I own him when I've never paid no maintenance?'

'Oh, easily,' I said.

A Nation Of Time-Servers

I HAVE HAD OCCASION before to observe that the English are a nation of shoplifters. But not even the most widely prevalent of characteristics is ever absolutely universal. Therefore, it is no contradiction to state also that the English are a nation of time-servers; by which I do not mean, of course, that they spend time in prison, for very few of them do that by comparison with the number of them who deserve to do so, but that they occupy posts of employment whose sole purpose, as far as they are concerned, is to supply them with a monthly cheque. This is particularly so in what is known, for lack of any other convenient name, as the public service.

Last week I had a patient who had made an above-average attempt to kill herself. The main problem, she said, was her housing situation. It was nothing short of disgusting. She was a tenant of the city's housing department, above the door of whose offices should be inscribed the words 'Abandon hope, all ye who are a renter here.'

The trouble was rats and mice. Her little son (whose father had as little intention of paying maintenance as had the housing department) was now so terrified of these creatures of the night that he refused to reside any longer in the maternal residence, but fled to his grandmother's. Apparently, he used to feel the rodents swarming over his bed as soon as his light was turned off, and not surprisingly he would scream out in terror. Of course, terrified screams are a part of normal daily life in much of England, so none of the neighbours took any notice.

'Have you reported it to the council?' I asked.

'Yes.'

'And what did they say?'

'They said I should put rat poison down, but I was afraid my little boy would eat it.'

'And what did the council say, then?'

'They said it didn't matter, that was all they could suggest.'

I yield to no one in deploring the existence of British children, of course, but even I would say that putting rat poison down for them was going a little far: sometimes, you just have to accept a *fait accompli*, however unpleasant he or she might be.

I decided to call the housing department itself, in the person of Mr Smith.

'He's interviewing,' said the telephonist, with the finality of a fatwa.

'Interrupt him, then,' I said.

'I can't. He'll call you back when he's finished.'

'But when he calls, I'll be interviewing. If I take the same line as him, we'll never speak to one another.'

As the words came out of my mouth, I realised that this was precisely what he wanted.

'That's up to you, isn't it?' said Little Miss Fatwa.

Mr Smith didn't call back, of course; or rather he did, and I was speaking to someone else. After a time, I called him again: he was interviewing again and couldn't be interrupted.

After a further round of sparring, I made it clear that it would be more trouble to Mr Smith not to speak to me than to speak to me, and he crept unwillingly to the phone.

'Your tenant says she has rats and mice.'

'Not more than anybody else,' he said.

I began to sympathise with the first patient that day, who had asked me for some Librium to calm him down. I refused on the grounds that they are addictive.

'Aren't there no tablets that aren't so potential?' he asked.

It'll Be The Heroin

THERE HAS BEEN a terrible outbreak of supposed helplessness lately, especially round here. The number of drug addicts appears to be increasing daily and, as everyone knows, drug addicts are helpless, though no one is quite sure whether the helplessness starts before or after the drug addiction. What is clear, however, is that, by the time they swim into my ken, they claim not to know what they do.

There were three drug addicts in my ward at the same time last week. One was a Standard British Moron, vacant of face and malevolent of eye, who had injected himself with a huge dose of heroin to celebrate his release from prison, and had choked on his own vomit.

'Why did you inject yourself with so much heroin?' I asked.

'For something to do,' he replied.

Ah, what we need are more youth-recreation centres: more Ping-Pong, less heroin.

I learnt that his scholastic career had not been a triumphant success: he walked out of school at the age of 12 and never returned.

'Why not?' asked.

'I didn't see the point.'

Neither did I: schools round here leave the *tabula* of the human mind strictly *rasa*.

The patient in the next bed was an aging hippie with smelly feet. He also had a blood clot in his lungs, a complication of his habit of injecting himself in the groin. He will be injecting himself in the neck, if not the eye, before he dies. He wanted me to prescribe him drugs.

'To me, doctor, withdrawal from heroin is the evilest thing in the world.'

'What a sheltered life you've led!' I exclaimed.

He laughed, revealing the blackened stumps that drug addicts, ever given to exaggeration, call teeth.

The third of the men was a body-packer: 63 condoms full of cocaine had been removed from his intestines at operation. There were complications afterwards, and he needed a nasogastric tube. He looked at the inoffensive little tube with disgust and said, 'You don't expect me to swallow that thing!'

'But you swallowed all those condoms full of cocaine,' said one of our nurses.

'I never!' he protested, deeply offended.

He denied that he had any knowledge of how the condoms full of cocaine happened to be in his intestines: presumably it was the Cocaine Fairy who inserted them by magic during the night.

The three addicts soon struck up a friendship, and were laughing and joking together.

The body-packer uttered words of encouragement to the Standard British Moron.

'What you need when you get out of here is some really good gear,' he said. 'You'd be crazy not to. I can tell you where to get it.'

I should perhaps mention that the body-packer was under arrest at the time, and there were two policemen present while he said this. He obviously enjoyed taunting them with their impotence.

'I'm going to discharge myself if you don't give me nothing, doctor,' said the man with a blood clot. 'I know it's dangerous for me, but it won't be me doing it; it'll be the heroin that makes the decision.'

Forgive them, Father, for they know exactly what they do.

An Ounce Of Prevention

AS EVERYONE KNOWS, or ought to know, abortion is a woman's right. But some men go further, and say that it is a duty. Moreover, they are prepared to put their boot where their mouth is. They can't make a woman pregnant without kicking the foetus out of her.

They do not do this because life is horrible, and they fear to bring into the world a being like themselves. Nor do they wish to evade the responsibilities of parenthood, for they have no concept of it, and usually they have already fathered several children whom they have abandoned without a second thought. No, they are motivated by something approaching an abstract ideal: no woman ought to be pregnant. And this ideal is happily united with the pleasures and immunities of domestic violence.

Thus I am perfectly familiar with the kick-started miscarriage as a form of contraception. This is a regrettably *post facto* method of family planning, however, and so last week I was pleased to learn of a man who thought ahead. He did not kick that person who now appears on all official documents as his 'partner' only after she became pregnant, he kicked her for several days every time, in her words, 'I was due my monthlies.' Better safe than sorry: an ounce of prevention is better than a pound of cure.

Of course, he was not in all other respects an ideal... I almost wrote 'husband'; my age is beginning to tell. On the contrary, he had once broken her cheekbone with a hammer, and had half-strangled her and thrown her down the stairs many times (that is what stairs are for). I have also known this used as a method of family planning, but in this case it was done without instrumental purpose, for its own sake, as the fulfilment, as it were, of a Kantian categorical imperative.

What beautiful relations subsist between British men and women! My next patient had undergone the unusual experience − unusual, that is, for round here – of marriage. It was not death, however, that had parted man and wife, but a fist's blow in the mouth after the wedding reception, in the privacy of the nuptial bed, 12 hours after the tying of the knot. The groom was drunk and angry, and with rare good sense the bride got the message and scuttled off, never to return.

'It must've been the shortest marriage ever,' she said.

'Not at all,' I said. 'It lasted six times longer than my patient whose husband tried to strangle her at the reception, two hours after the ceremony. Your marriage was comparatively successful.'

My last patient of the day was extremely nervous. She had just discovered something about her live-in lover that gave her pause for thought. It was a pity, in a way, that she had not paused before she asked him to move in with her, the day after she met him.

'He admitted to me he's just come out of prison,' she said.

'Did he tell you why he was there?' I asked.

'Yes. He said he'd been involved in a pub fight and hit this man. He fell over, banged his head and died. He was done for murder.'

'And?'

'Well, I thought he was telling me the truth.'

'But he wasn't?'

'No.'

'What is the truth?'

'He strangled his last girlfriend and had sex with her body.'

The Next Thing I Know, My Head's Gone Blank

AS I WAS WALKING through the prison last weekend shortly after the inmates had had their lunch, I was reminded very forcibly of the Strand Hotel in Rangoon. I stayed there in the glory days of Slorc, the State Law and Order Restoration Council, when taxis of vintage marque had plywood passenger windows, flat tyres and no windscreen-wipers to improve visibility during monsoons. Progress through the streets was erratic, to say the least.

The Strand Hotel was quite untouched by international cuisine: you ate either Burmese or dimly-remembered British colonial, including dreadful pink ice-cream (30 minutes to wait, said the menu). Inside the lift was a notice: 'This lift has been inspected and found safe.' It was dated 35 years before. On the ledge of the window opposite the door to my room was the night-watchman's book. The last entry read: 'All guests sleeping soundly.' It was dated 24 years before.

It was this entry that brought the Strand Hotel to my mind as I walked through the prison. As always after lunch, the guests were sleeping soundly. A kindergarten during the infants' afternoon nap is not more silent than our prison after lunch. Then there is a brief lull from the criminal music – I use the term 'music' loosely, and the term 'criminal' precisely – played at preternatural volumes, and from prisoners shouting the word 'fucking' at each other, the main substance of their communication. Silence after noise is bliss.

I was on my way, however, 'down the seg': that is to say, the segregation unit where refractory prisoners are given CC, or Cellular Confinement. I had received a telephone message that my presence was required 'down the seg' straight away, because Smith was cutting his throat again.

Smith cuts his throat quite often. I've known him for a number of years: he's in and out of prison. Usually the cuts in his neck are superficial but sometimes they are deep and need operations to repair them. Other prisoners pass him razorblades in his food so that he can make a nuisance of himself.

This time his wounds were not deep but nevertheless required stitching. He refused to allow me to do the necessary. I can't say I was sorry. I asked him what was wrong.

'Everythink,' he said, somewhat grandiosely.

'What do you mean, everything?' I said.

'Everythink,' he repeated.

'Such as?'

'My missis has just left me and won't let me see the kids.'

How very wise of her, I thought. 'Why?' I asked, my tone implying deep puzzlement.

'I don't know. I been with her 16 years, since we was 12.'

'Did you ever hit her?'

'Yes,' he said, hesitantly, as if trying to drag something from the distant recesses of his memory. 'There was violence used.'

'Is that why you're here?'

'Could be,' he said.

'What happened?'

'We was having this argument and the next thing I know my head's gone blank and I've hit her over the head with this chair.'

'That's why she doesn't want to see you any more?'

'No violence was intended. I wouldn't want to hurt her or nothing, she knows that, the fucking bitch.'

General Ne Win, thou shouldst be living at this hour. England hath need of thee.

I Seem To Be Interviewing A Lot Of Murderers These Days

THE SEARCH FOR the good has been replaced by the desire for the nice. Appearance is more real to us than any reality, and deeper judgments have become not only unfashionable but also unmentionable, as being inherently unjust and prejudiced. But it is one thing to see the best in people, no doubt a charitable attitude of which we all sometimes stand in need; it is quite another to be unable to see the evil in them or to accord it any significance.

This is the state of modern man – and woman, of course. I was reminded of it last week when a youth of the baseball-cap-wearing community (all people with anything whatever in common these days being said to belong to a community, there being no other kind of community for them to belong to) was admitted, having taken too many of the pills that his doctor had prescribed for him to get him out of the room as expeditiously as possible. This, of course, not the hope of cure, is the reason for most prescriptions round here.

The pills had made him confused and aggressive, a confusion and aggression that his tattooed mother ascribed to the absence of the heroin that she said he needed.

'He's never normally aggressive,' she said. 'He wouldn't hurt a fly.' Then she said that if we didn't give him his heroin, she would sue.

I interviewed his girlfriend. She was the barmaid type, already running to fat. Her bosom was pushed upwards by a tight bra, several sizes too small, with a force of geological proportions, and I noticed that on her right breast a multicoloured dragon had been tattooed. The black roots of her hair stood out from the bleached blond: this is the *chiaroscuro* of the slums.

I asked her what her boyfriend – who had punched a nurse on the nose and made it bleed – was like.

'He's lovely,' she said. 'You couldn't meet a nicer bloke.'

Even I, hardened misanthrope as I am, found this difficult entirely to credit.

I phoned the man's doctor. He didn't remember him very clearly, for he had few distinguishing features from the great mass of his young patients, so he looked him up on his computer.

'Ah yes,' he said, 'there's a warrant out for his arrest. More firearms offences. He did time for the same thing a couple of years ago. Also assault and GBH. Sniffs glue. Takes anything he can get, really. Never worked.'

No distinguishing features, of course, and the nicest bloke you could ever wish – or perhaps I should say expect – to meet.

That afternoon, I interviewed a murderer. I seem to be interviewing a lot of murderers these days. This one had taken his revenge on the man with whose wife he had been caught: he had stabbed him to death as a wise precaution when he met him for the second time since he had been caught *in flagrante* with her.

'Why was that?' I asked.

'Because the first time he annihilated me,' he said.

'Hold on a moment,' I said. 'I have to write it down.'

Evidently he thought I was having difficulty in spelling 'annihilated'.

'Just put he kicked my fucking head in.'

It Goes Without Saying That The Main Function Of Many People Working In The Health Service Is To Draw A Salary

I WAS OUT IN Westminster one morning last week when suddenly the streets seemed to fill with traffic wardens. It was 8.30, and I was most impressed: such signs of punctuality and efficiency are rare in the public service.

Please do not get me wrong: I do not in the least begrudge the slight pleasure that these immigrant Nigerians – for such seemed to be the national origin of a large proportion of the guardians of the public kerbs – must derive from causing a pin-prick of irritation to the owners of the shiny new BMWs and Jaguars that they themselves will never be able to afford (unless they seek a career in Nigeria's principal national industry, fraud). No: I can quite understand and even sympathise with the joy of writing all those little tickets.

As I drove down the Great West Road, the meaning of the comparatively large number of hard-working traffic wardens – three to a short street, in some places – suddenly became clear to me. As everyone knows, the speed limit on the Great West Road changes from furlong to furlong, for no reason intrinsic to the road itself, and it is also furnished with more cameras than the CIA. It is almost impossible to drive along the Great West Road and stick to the changing speed limit: the road itself, its speed limits and its cameras exist to raise revenue.

But what is this revenue for? To pay for the raising of more revenue, of course. Once this great principle has been grasped, it becomes immediately apparent why our traffic wardens are so efficient but our schools teach nothing.

It goes without saying that the main function of many people working in the health service is to draw a salary. They are certainly not paid to think, nor do they think it any part of their duty to do so.

The other day, for example, I was passed a message from a district nurse, asking me to telephone her once I had seen a patient of hers who had been admitted to the hospital. I duly called the number given, which was answered by a receptionist.

'Can I speak to Miss M___, district nurse, please?' I asked, having first introduced myself. In fact, the receptionist already knew me.

'She's out of the office.'

'Does she carry a mobile?'

'Yes.'

'Could I have the number to ring her?'

'No.'

'Why not?'

'Because we're not allowed to give out mobile phone numbers.'

'But I'm a consultant, you know who I am, I've been working here for more than 13 years.'

'It's our policy not to give out numbers.'

O policy, what crimes are committed in thy name!

I decided then and there to write what a distinguished anglophile Ceylonese physician of my acquaintance used to call 'a stinker', that is to say a letter of strongly-worded protest, to the chief executive of my hospital trust. Of course, I knew it was completely pointless, that no letter in a bottle, no time-capsule in outer space, is ever more comprehensively lost than a letter from a senior doctor to the chief executive of a National Health Service trust. But at least it relieved my feelings.

Dear Sir, I wrote, *I should be grateful if you will draw to the attention of administrative staff the necessity, however painful it may be or unnatural it may seem, occasionally to think. Yours sincerely.*

It's The Thinking
That's So Difficult

IT IS RECEIVED wisdom that the payment of tax by the very rich is voluntary. I don't know any such person myself, because I move mainly among people of the middling sort for whom taxation is lamentably compulsory; indeed, in my professional life at least I am more likely to meet the kind of person who pays no tax because, when asked what work he performs, he furrows his brow in puzzlement and says that he does not understand the question. Work, what is work? I have found it rather difficult to explain.

Just as taxation is voluntary for the rich, so imprisonment is voluntary for the criminal. You probably know many people whose house has been burgled or who have been robbed on the street, but very few, if any, who have had the satisfaction of knowing that the perpetrator has been caught. Yet there are many burglars in prison, as I can attest. How is this paradox to be resolved? The answer is that burglars who go to prison want to be caught, for without their co-operation the police can or will do nothing.

Last week, there was a patient on our ward who had taken the traditional celebratory overdose of heroin after his release from prison. (This is a tradition that dates back at least eight years, so it is now deeply etched upon the national character.) He didn't look evil, just slightly vacant. He was 21 years old.

'How many times have you been in prison?' I asked.

'Eight,' he said.

'Can I ask you something?' I said. 'Do you prefer it in prison?'

Without hesitation, he said that he did. I asked him why.

'Well, you get fed and you don't have to think about nothing.'

It's the thinking that's so difficult and painful. He said that his problem outside prison was that he thought too much, and that's why he felt so bad. I asked him what he did during his brief intervals of liberty, so-called.

'I stay at home and play with me babby.'

I asked him whether he had any interests, anything that he liked doing.

'I've lost interest in everything,' he said.

'What did you used to like doing?' I asked.

He thought for a moment, trying to recapture in his mind the joys of lost youth.

'Breaking into cars,' he said.

Anyway, he would soon be back where he was unthinkingly happy, that is to say prison. He had a couple of cases in Crown Court, and was hoping for a decent sentence this time, instead of the poxy three months he got last time.

That same day, I went to the prison myself. My first patient was a jolly Rastafarian who can't resist a woman's handbag when he sees one. Terrifying as he must be to his victims, in prison (where he has been many times) he is, as it were, the life and soul of the party. The officers like him very much, and greet him as an old friend, because he is what is called a model con. He gets his head down and does his bird.

I asked him, too, whether he liked prison.

'No, not at all, doctor,' he protested. 'I'm just not very good at what I do.'

Out There, Man, It's All Madness

WE MUST ALL move with the times, of course, or the times will move without us. I am in any case no Luddite who wishes to keep everything exactly as it was, merely from fear of the future. Technology changes, usually much for the better, and improves the quality of our lives, permitting us the time and opportunity to concentrate upon the more spiritual aspects of our earthly existence. This effect is obvious from walking down any British shopping street.

Times and technology change even in the prison. For example, in the old days (that is to say, when I started working there) prisoners would attack one another with old square batteries called PP9s, wrapped in a sock and wielded like the South American *bolas*, but then miniaturisation destroyed the market for such batteries, and in the process eliminated a transitive verb that for a time was part of prison argot: to 'PP9' someone. Thus technological advance has impoverished our language slightly.

The demise of the PP9, however, has seen the rise of the billiard ball as an instrument of attack. Last week a prisoner was hit on the side of the head with two billiard balls in a prison-issue sock, and as a result his face swelled up more or less in proportion. The reason for this attack, which could easily have done him far greater harm, was that he had once been in prison for a sexual offence.

The next prisoner I saw had been involved in a fight. He bore scratch marks on his neck and cheeks. I asked him about his assailant.

'I don't know why he done it. If it'd been on the streets, man, it would have been a different story. In here, I just didn't want to get involved, that's why I let him get on with it. But if he sees me on the streets, he's dead.'

He was a member of the gold-front-toothed community. I noticed that his face bore quite a lot of scars from wounds inflicted by machetes and even by human teeth. There was one particularly fine example of a dental impression on his cheek. I asked him how he had come by so many scars.

'Out there, man, it's madness. It's all madness.'

Fortunately, he was not badly injured and when I had finished recording my findings, he asked whether he could go on his visit. I asked him who was visiting him.

'My mother. I don't want no bitches to come, get what I mean, they only mess up your head.'

An officer interrupted, to ask me to see a prisoner urgently. The prisoner had been caught with some heroin in his possession and he had swallowed the evidence rather than face the charges. I rushed along to see him. Now he was afraid that he was going to die (a possibility in such circumstances).

'How much was it?' I said.

'I never asked,' he said. 'I don't know the price.'

'I was asking how much in quantity,' I said. 'I wasn't making an offer of purchase when it comes out the other end.'

When I Start Thinking, My Head Goes Huge

I LIKE TO HAVE a little nap in the afternoon, though I rarely have the opportunity to do so. I have reached the stage in life, though, when I rather regret waking up; I don't remember my dreams, exactly, but I know that they are better and more entertaining than reality. To wake is to die a little.

I therefore had some slight sympathy with one of my patients last week, who had taken pills above and beyond the call of therapeutics in order to kill himself. He was a young man of not altogether prepossessing *mien*, and I asked him why he wanted to end it all.

'My head, doctor,' he said, 'it's full of thoughts all the time.'

Full of thoughts? As compared with what? For some reason, an image of those polystyrene fragments that packers use to prevent damage to delicate objects in transit came to my mind's eye.

'When I start thinking, my head goes huge,' he added.

'What are you thinking about?' I asked.

'Fings in general.'

'What things?'

'Fings just aren't going right, they've all come at once, they're getting on top of me.'

I felt it was time for a leading question, otherwise we should be stuck for ever in the realms of philosophic abstraction.

'Do you have a girlfriend?' I asked.

'Yes, but she's doing mad fings. We need a break.'

'To get your head sorted?'

He looked at me with something like respect.

'Yes, that's right, how did you know?'

I modestly brushed aside the question of my psychological penetration, and asked him whether he had recently had an argument with his girlfriend and whether she had broken up with him.

'Yes.'

'Are you jealous and possessive of her?'

'I don't stop her going out.'

'Have you ever been violent to her?'

'Not much, only a slap. She's never had to go to hospital or nothing.'

I moved on to the question of drugs. Did he take crack, cannabis?

'Only when they come around me. Not all the time.'

'And how often do they come around you?'

'About three or four times a week.'

I telephoned his girlfriend. I heard the television in the background, as well as several children, not all of them his. I asked her about him.

'It's an on-off relationship and we've just had a child,' she said. 'I think I need some space.'

'To get your head sorted?'

'Yes.'

'Has he ever been violent towards you?'

'Yes.' She mentioned a number of occasions on which he had hit her: several times the number he had first thought of.

'Did you have an argument recently, just before he took the pills?'

'Yes, and he threatened to kill me.'

'Threatened to kill you?'

'Yes, but not kill as in kill.'

Kill as in what, then? Kill as in confer an inestimable benefit upon her? Kill as in offer her a box of chocolates?

'Why did he say he wanted to kill you?'

'He said I wasn't showing him enough love.'

I've always wondered what the Americans meant when they talked of Tough Love. Now I think I have some understanding. They don't mean love as in love – they mean love as in threatening to kill.

A Lot Of Social Chaos

IT IS WELL KNOWN that patients swear blind that they have never been told a thing by their doctor about their illnesses and treatment immediately they leave the consulting room. Is it that the doctor mesmerises them as a stoat mesmerises a rabbit? Many studies have shown that patients either do not listen to or do not absorb what their doctor says to them. Perhaps it is just that we doctors are very boring.

Being charged by the police also often produces such a state of amnesia in those who are so charged. If you ask them what they are charged with, they knit their brows, think hard, writhe in their chairs a bit with the effort and sometimes say that they can't remember. One might have thought that being charged was a tolerably memorable experience, but of course for some it has happened so often that one episode just runs into another. Their criminal record is a seamless robe. Is it burgs this time, or domestics? Who can say?

Last week, I asked one young remanded prisoner what he was in for. He thought for a while, ground his teeth and breathed heavily like the average school-leaver round here when asked to multiply six by seven in his head; finally, he looked relieved when the answer came to him.

'Attempted law,' he said.

Attempted law? What on earth could that be? More than one person has given the same answer. I asked him what the attempted law actually involved.

'Well, see, my ex wouldn't let me see the babby because I'm seeing my ex. But she's seeing her ex as well, so I don't see why she should be like that.'

'And why is she like that?'

'Because my ex's stepfather's brother abused her.'

287

'What did he do?'

'When I was in prison the last time, he came round and kicked the baby what she was carrying for me out of her.'

'Why was that?'

'Because my ex was jealous.'

'Your ex's stepfather's brother doesn't sound very nice.'

'He's a nutter. He's slashed someone's face. He's on the brown and on the gear. He walks around with a baseball bat. Mind you, he's gone through a lot of social chaos because of the crack.'

'Do you take drugs yourself?'

'I've had cocaine substance in my body.'

'Do you still take it?'

'Cocaine – that went out of the window a long time ago.'

I asked him whether he had any medical problems.

'I've had my spleen out.'

'Why?'

'I was arrested.'

Was this shorthand for police brutality? I noticed that he had recently shaved his head, and there were several razor cuts on his scalp.

'Why did you shave your head?' I asked.

'For something to do.'

I asked him what he would do when he was released from prison.

'I can't go back,' he said.

'Why not?

'If I was on the estate in a car, they'd chase me off.'

'And your ex, or your ex-ex?'

'Naaaah,' he said. 'They won't let me see the babbies. I think it's unfair.'

'Why?'

'Well, I think children are innocent, don't you? I mean, they haven't committed no crimes yet, have they?'

Selflessly, The Senior Bureaucrats Do Themselves Proud

WHEN ONE HAS been in the service a long time, as I have, one begins, even if one is not very clever, to recognise certain patterns. For example, when it is announced that a part of a hospital is to be refurbished, young doctors are inclined to rejoice: at last, brighter, better conditions. Older, more experienced doctors like me greet the news gloomily, however; it is more likely to be another case of the refurbishment-before-closure syndrome. Not only can no hospital be closed down without having had much spent on it immediately beforehand, but no hospital can have much money spent on it without being closed down shortly afterwards. I believe this is called 'scientific management'.

Then there is the important-visitor syndrome. This is endemic worldwide, perhaps even a universal of human nature. You can tell exactly where and how far the Important Visitor is going by which walls and floors are being cleaned and polished. The point at which an uncleaned wall or floor becomes visible is a yard or two beyond the furthest point the Important Visitor will be allowed to reach. No sense of everyday reality must ever be allowed to intrude upon the I.V.'s consciousness; and no I.V. is so interested in truth that he doesn't permit the wool to be pulled over his eyes.

Last week the Minister visited the prison. We've had ministers before, of course, as well as judges: they come and go, but the syndrome lasts for ever. The day before, a posse of prisoners scrubbed the corridors down which the ministerial feet would tread to the point when it would have been perfectly safe not only to eat off their floors, but perform operations on them as well. Staffing levels were increased to mislead him into supposing that everything was running smoothly, and altogether the visit was a great success. Only a colleague of mine

289

spoilt the party, by asking the driver of the ministerial car (with police outriders) whether it was the taxi he had called.

That afternoon, I went to the headquarters of a National Health Service Trust. Of course the building was in far better shape than any NHS hospital I have been into. The senior bureaucrats do themselves proud, I must say: but then their jobs are very stressful, finding things to do to justify their own existence. It must be very wearing after the first ten years.

I walked to the office of a senior manager through a large open-plan floor with scores of people beavering away on their computers, turning out reams of drivel. This is the new characteristic of the British: frivolity without gaiety. I waved to one of the poor bureaucrats I recognised, formerly a very good nurse, and she waved back. I couldn't get any nearer because of the maze of partitions. She looked guilty, as well she might; most of our administrators do look guilty, because they know in their hearts that they are guilty. It is a horrible way to live.

I attended the meeting. The bureaucrat outlined the plan, which was in accordance with government policy. I enumerated various objections.

'But you're going against the consensus!' expostulated the bureaucrat. Heresy! Treason! Diversity!

But Is Anyone's Mind Stable?

FAITH, HOPE AND CHARITY these days are redundant; what we need are health and safety. We safeguard them more carefully than good girls ever safeguarded their chastity. We are enjoined to do so everywhere, even on trains from Bristol to Bath. I was on one such train last weekend. A man called the Train Manager exhorted us over the public address system to be careful of the luggage in the racks above our heads, lest it should descend upon us, and advised us very strongly to 'make ourselves familiar with' (he didn't want to offend those of us who could not read, or inadvertently lessen their self-esteem by using the word 'read') the safety information in the passenger saloon.

Saloon? Was this the Orient Express, in which passengers in dinner dress, in a wood-panelled coach, are served by attendants in jackets as white as the plumage of the fairy tern or the snowy owl? No, there were two carriages, standing room only, and not much of that either; in fact, if the train had crashed, we should have been slaughtered like bacteria in a Petri dish.

But at least being squashed together allowed me to overhear the mobile telephone conversations of my fellow passengers. For example, I was next to a tall, willowy young woman with the rich, wavy, red-brown hair so favoured by the Pre-Raphaelites. In another age, she would have been a model for Burne-Jones; which proves that there has been some progress after all.

She had those loose-jointed movements that occur between adolescent awkwardness and arthritic middle age, but in her right nostril were two small rings that pinched her flesh and looked painful. She had black-painted fingernails and a ring on her thumb, and no doubt a tattoo on her shoulder, though she was dressed in clothes of a length that would have pleased even the Ayatollah Khomeini, albeit that they were of denim, the devil's cloth.

Her phone rang, and she managed to insinuate it to her ear. She clearly didn't mind being overheard; she was a well-brought up girl, who had difficulty remembering her glottal stops.

'I'm not working for Cath the psycho any more,' she said. 'There's this grocery that's all about Fair Trading. I mean it's not like it's a morally-dubious company, or anything like that.'

Then she explained why she was going to Bath. 'I'm doing some voluntary work at the theatre. It's worth it 'cause I get to hang out with the director, so I might get some design work.' Whether the proposed hanging-out with the director was morally dubious, I cannot of course positively say.

But at least the next day a man consulted me who was unequivocally beyond moral reproach. He had slit his girlfriend's throat, or rather, the knife in his pocket had done so.

'The blade came out and everything just went downhill from there.'

Well, you can't really oppose gravity, try as you might. It wasn't, as he put it, 'down to him'.

The telephone rang. It was Mrs H___.

'Hello, doctor, it's Mrs H___. Do you remember me?'

'Of course. How could I forget?'

Mrs H___ rings me whenever she is in a state of distress.

'Doctor,' she said. 'I don't think my mind's as stable as it should be.' Then she considered for a moment, and added, 'But I don't think anyone's is.'

An Emergency Casualty
Of The Serious Kind

I WAS DISCUSSING death with my closest friend recently, and we discovered that we had both caught ourselves envying the dead. They were lucky to be out of it; and neither of us would be particularly disturbed if we discovered that we had a fatal illness and had but three months to live. It wasn't that we were depressed, or anything like that: no, it was something else entirely.

'The dead don't have any forms to fill in,' I said.

'That's it,' said my friend. 'No more forms when you're dead. You don't need to seek anyone's permission to be dead.'

Of course, that may change. A single case of burial alive reported in the tabloid newspapers would result in a government regulation that corpses had to be inspected every three months to check that they were still certifiably dead.

Regulation is – well, ruling our lives. I've known military dictatorships where life is freer. It's true you couldn't shout 'Down with el Presidente' in the Plaza de Armas, but otherwise you were left more or less alone, unless you fell foul of the death squads. But now life is one long bureaucratic harassment: first you fill in the forms, and then you die.

There was an emergency in casualty last week. I don't mean of the trivial medical kind, I mean of the serious, bureaucratic kind. There was a patient who was threatening to breach the four-hour rule, and mess up our figures. The government has decreed that no patient should wait more than four hours in hospital casualty, and this character had been there for three and a half hours already. Could I come and dispose of him?

I asked for a description of the patient whose case was so urgent.

Well, they said, he's been drinking and...

'Is he drunk?' I asked.

'No, not drunk,' they said. 'Just under the influence.'

I went to casualty. I can't say I rushed. I smelt the patient from outside the cubicle: he exhaled stale alcohol. I heard him too: he was snoring so stertorously that if he had been made of metal he would have broken apart from metal fatigue. I entered the cubicle. He was on the floor, in what is known as the recovery position, to prevent him from choking to death on his own vomit. It was most unlikely that he got into that position by his own unaided efforts, or because he had decided for himself that it would be wise to do so.

'Hello, Mr Smith,' I said, quite loudly, though not really expecting an answer. And, as it says in 'The Walrus and the Carpenter', answer came there none. I tried twice more before giving him a light poke with my foot.

'Mr Smith!' I said.

There was a vague grunt, then an alcoholic eructation like a volcanic lake in Cameroon releasing poisonous gas into the atmosphere. The casualty nurse popped her head round the curtains.

'What's happening?' she said.

'This man is unrousable,' I said. 'He's completely drunk.'

'No he's not,' she said. 'He can't be. We've got to get rid of him in the next half hour. It's the four-hour rule.'

'Of course he's drunk. His history shows he's drunk a bottle and a half of whisky and a few beers.'

'He can't be. That was more than three hours ago. We've got to get him out of here.'

She was nearly hysterical. Fortunately, the consultant in charge of casualty arrived, and I explained that the patient was dead drunk and couldn't be moved. He told the nurse that such patients could be excluded from the figures. She relaxed like a balloon emptied of air. 'I do so hate these drunks,' she said. 'Don't you?'

Who Doesn't Need Counselling?

I HESITATE TO bring my own sufferings, terrible though they undoubtedly are, before the reading public, but I am actuated by a profound sense of duty in doing so. It would be wrong to withhold from the public domain information that might prove useful to my fellow beings.

A week or two ago, my mobile telephone was stolen again. I left it in a taxi, and then, remembering the following day that I had done so, called the taxi company. To my gratified surprise, I was told that the phone had been handed in by the driver, and would soon be brought back to me. Two days later I still had not received it, and after several more phone calls to the taxi company it was finally admitted that, alas, one of the company's telephonists had absconded with it.

I called the police, whom I provided with the name and address of the prime suspect. Not only that: the wretch had used the telephone to call the same number several times, and could easily be traced through the recipient of those calls. An arrest was therefore imminent, I was told.

I readied myself for my appearance in court as a prosecution witness. A few days later, however, my hopes were dashed and my dream of forensic histrionics set at naught, for I received through the post the now customary offer of victim support from the police.

Indeed I needed it. I had been on a rollercoaster of exultation and despair, enough, as they say in the prison, to do my head in. And of course there is only one remedy for a head that has been done in: counselling.

Come to think of it, I don't think I've ever met anyone who didn't need counselling. On Monday and Tuesday of last week, for example, I met two women whose heads had been done in, and who both thought they needed counselling. Their heads had been done in by their boyfriends, who had held them under water in the lavatory pan in an attempt to get them to tell the truth about the affairs with other men they weren't having at the time. One of them had nearly drowned.

'He's not like that all the time, doctor,' she said.

'I'm very glad to hear it,' I said.

'He just does silly things sometimes.'

'Like what?'

'He pulls my hair and hits my head against the wall.'

'Are you sure that silly is quite the word for it?'

'What do you mean?'

'Wouldn't evil be more accurate?'

She thought for a moment. 'I suppose you think I need counselling,' she said.

'I do assure you', I said, 'that no thought has ever been further from my mind.'

'What do you think I need, then?'

'I think you need your boyfriend to be locked up for 20 years without possibility of parole, and to be made to break rocks on a diet of bread and water.'

'But I love him, doctor.'

'In that case,' I said, 'it should be 30 years.'

She Had Elected To Have
A Child By A Psychopath

JUDGE NOT THAT ye be not judgmental, for in making a judgment you commit the worst, indeed the only, possible sin in an age of tolerance. This, perhaps, is the modern equivalent of the paradox of the Cretan liar: that we judge negatively only those who judge negatively.

It follows from moral relativism that we live in the best of all possible worlds, since every custom is equally good and each way of life equally 'valid'. There is no Archimedean moral point from which to condemn anything; only celebration of difference is permissible. Self-congratulation is the greatest, the only, virtue.

Let us therefore praise the child-rearing practices of my patient last week who had half-starved her baby and beaten it severely while under the influence of crack cocaine. The baby having been, as she put it, 'took off me', she went straight to the pills and swallowed a handful.

I asked as delicately as I could, with apology in my intonation, about the father of the baby.

'No,' she said firmly.

I was a little puzzled.

'No,' I repeated. 'What do you mean, no?'

'He don't have nothing to do with it.'

What is this 'it' of which she spoke? Whatever 'it' referred to changed rapidly.

'It was a one-night stand.' She paused. 'I've known him for ten years, it just happened, until then he'd been a kind of friend. He's a registered psychopath.'

I couldn't help but recall a patient in the prison who had introduced himself to me by saying, 'I'm one of Her Majesty's psychopaths.' You might forgive a man a lot for uttering a phrase like that – if, of course, you could make a judgment about him in the first place.

I passed on to the next patient. She, too, had elected to have a child by a psychopath, but in her case it was not a one-night stand but a 2,920-night, or eight-year, stand. She was now trying to disembarrass herself of him, but he returned to her like a dog to its vomit. He had kidnapped their child the week before in order to force her to contact him, knowing that she would be too terrified to call the police.

My next patient was a young man who had taken an overdose while under arrest. He hadn't fancied a night in the cells, and so took the pills he always had handy for the purpose. The police had obligingly de-arrested him – to use a technical term – once he had arrived in hospital.

'What did you take?' I asked.

'Triazepam.'

'Don't you mean diazepam?'

'I call it triazepam because I usually take two and stick one up my arse.'

I asked him why he took it in the first place.

'It gives me a mind for invention,' he said. 'I write songs.'

'You're an artist, then?'

'Yes, kind of. Don't get me wrong, I'm one of the best shoplifters in C___, but I don't go robbing old ladies or nothing.'

I noticed that he had a long scar on his neck, and asked him how he came by it.

'I got drunk one night and chopped myself.'

'What with?'

'A machete.'

'What happened?'

'I just went to sleep and woke up covered in blood.'

Let Us Not Cast Our Eyes
Up To The Hills

I WAS IN COURT last week, giving it large to the barrister on the other side. I love the precision, or at least the logic-chopping, of the law: it appeals to the pedant in me. It also appeals to the sophist. Few pleasures are greater than that of conjuring a specious argument out of the blue, as the occasion requires.

The case was of the usual sordid kind, I need not go into detail. It took place in one of the many provincial towns in England that seem to consist of a bus station, a ring road and a crown court. A few people move about slowly in the desolate townscape like grasshoppers in a vivarium, with cars and lorries playing the part of predatory reptiles.

Of course, there are other, more dangerous predators in this townscape as well: British youths. You don't look them in their little ferret eyes as they slope past you in their tracksuits and hoods. They are not so much hunter-gatherers as mugger-opportunists. You'd cross the road to get away from them, if the road were not the ring road, thundering constantly with large trucks delivering junk food.

Around the crown court, a new building with such dignity as modern British architects can manage, was a small fenced garden. This garden grew litter. The youths of the town, unable to control their appetites, had eaten in the streets nearby and had disposed of the wrappings, cartons and cans of what they had consumed in the little garden. It grew in little piles that were sometimes disturbed by gusts of wind, so that an empty packet of crisps blew across my face as I reached the entrance.

Inside all was clean and tidy, except for the upholstery of the seats for the public, which, though comparatively new, was deeply impregnated with Coca Cola, coffee and crumbs. There were stains on each of the seats that looked like a map of Treasure Island. As every youth in this country knows, an empty seat is for resting your trainered feet upon.

No doubt someone will pipe up that 'twas ever thus – someone who in all other respects would deride tradition. British judges, after all, carried nosegays to protect them from the exudations of the populace. I don't find this much of a consolation, even if true.

Still, there is no doubt that litter has a certain interest. It is to the contemporary social inquirer what ancient detritus is to the archaeologist. It tells us all about how people live or lived. For many years I have taught medical students to observe the litter closely on the way between the hospital and the prison. Life thus observed can be boiled down to two fundamental instinctive urges: condoms and crisps.

I suddenly realised last week, as I was walking to the prison, why people round here drop so much litter. It is to give women – who are required by their jealous male consorts to keep their eyes down to avoid the possibility of making a silent assignation with a male passer-by – something to look at. Let us not cast our eyes up to the hills; let us cast them down to the litter.

We Have No Shame

HE WHO WISHES to fathom the degradation of England must travel on our regional trains. First, of course, comes the announcement regretting 'the delay to your journey'. The delay to my journey last week was caused by the non-attendance of the driver. 'Incredible! Amazing!' exclaimed some Chinese passengers. 'Everyone says you cannot trust the trains in England. But to admit that the driver hasn't come…' Words failed them. People have been shot for less in the People's Republic. A patriot, wanting to redeem the honour of his country, piped up, 'But at least it's honest.'

Honesty is, of course, the last resort of the incompetent, and it does not follow that because dishonesty is always a vice, honesty is always a virtue.

What a spectacle is a local train in England! Weasel-faced youths regard all seats other than the one they are sitting on as footrests, their little saurian eyes (to change slightly the zoological metaphor) swivelling with glassy, paranoid malignity, on the *qui vive* for anyone who might dare to tell them to take their feet from where they are. No such person can be found, of course, for youths these days use knives in defence of their inalienable rights.

As for arrival in an English provincial town, that also presents a spectacle. I went to an ancient market town last week to examine a man who had broken into his neighbours' house and chopped up its contents, and a couple of limbs, with a machete. In like fashion, the town planners and architectural bureaucrats had inflicted terrible damage on the beautiful town, turning it in a couple of decades into a gaping urban wound fit only for garish chain stores. I had arrived without a pen and went into a store to buy one. A little boy was pulling things maliciously from the shelves on to the floor.

'Stop it!' screeched his mother, in a voice whose intonation implied 'You little bastard!' (and she should know, of course). 'You're not at home now!' An Englishman's home is his bear pit.

I was a little early for my appointment with the machete-monger, so I went into the local museum, in a splendid timbered Tudor house, next door to a concrete edifice whose hideous walls wept red and black tears of rust and pollution. I looked at this building, and thought, 'Have we no shame?' The question answers itself.

In the museum was a reconstructed dining-room. The number of minatory notices was astonishing.

'We would ask our visitors to refrain from bringing in and consuming food and drink on the premises.'

To this was appended another notice, playing bad cop to the former notice's good cop: 'These premises are protected by CCTV.'

Fixed to a door was the following notice: 'For safety reasons please keep out of the door area.'

At what distance from a door does an area become a door area, I wonder? Truly, the world is a vale not of tears, but of danger.

One corner of the room had a different notice: 'Alarmed area. Do not enter.'

I need hardly add that there was No Smoking. But that was not the only prohibition. 'Photography is not permitted in this room.'

A room, in short, fit for a nation of slaves.

I met the machete man. He was young, dressed in English folk-costume: baseball cap, shell suit and trainers whose heels lit up as he loped. I asked him why he had attacked his neighbours.

'I didn't, really. It was six of one and half a dozen of the other,' he said.

Sisyphus Had It Easy

MANY OF MY non-medical friends complain of the pointlessness of their jobs. What they do has no meaning, they say, no intrinsic worth, apart from paying the bills. My friends feel like caged mice which run incessantly inside wheels: an expense of spirit in a waste of effort.

'At least,' they say, 'your job is worthwhile.'

'In what sense?' I ask.

'You help people.'

If only they knew. Compared with the doctors in a hospital like mine, Sisyphus had it easy. Light recreation such as his would come as a relief to us.

There is, for example, a lady well-known to our hospital who attends every two weeks or so with an overdose. If she does not attend for a week or two further, we begin to wonder what is wrong with her: misjudged the dose, perhaps? She was here again last week. Actually, I rather like her; she has a sense of the absurd, which is a saving grace for all but the most determined villain.

I asked her whether it was her boyfriend again – the one she can't stand, but whom she allows into her house because he'd break in anyway if she didn't – who had driven her to the pills.

'You've got it in one,' she said.

She might have learnt nothing by her overdoses, but I had learnt something.

'What's he been up to this time?'

'He opened up the cuts on his arm again, didn't he?'

'How?'

'He sat there and pulled the stitches out.'

'In front of you?'

'He wouldn't do it otherwise.'

Of course, the original cuts were self-inflicted. I suppose this is what counts round here as a declaration of undying love: greater love hath no man than this, that he pulls out his stitches and opens up his cuts for his girl.

'Why did he cut himself in the first place?' I asked.

'Because he hit me.'

'And why did you take the tablets this time?'

'It was a stupid game,' she explained. 'Well, we got a bowl of tablets and put it on the table. Then we took it in turns to toss a coin and whoever won could say which tablet the other had to take. It was like Russian roulette, only with tablets.'

'And what happened?'

'When I won, I made him take the antibiotics what he was supposed to take for his wrist but wouldn't.'

'And when he won?'

'Painkillers.'

'How long did this go on?'

'A long time. We'd been drinking, see.'

No! You could have knocked me down with a feather.

'Then he said he wasn't feeling very well. He called an ambulance and got in. He never even asked me how I was, and I was the one taking the painkillers. So when he'd gone, I thought, fuck it, and swallowed all what was left in the bowl.'

Fortunately, her loved one had left the hospital before she arrived. He had signed the form discharging himself:

I wish to be discharged immediately. I understand that this is against medical advice. I acknowledge that I have been informed of the dangers of doing so and I accept full responsibility for the consequences of my decision.

Signed: Fuck you.

I moved on to the next patient. She had taken an overdose in front of her boyfriend.

'Did he try to stop you?' I asked.

'No.'

'Did he call an ambulance?'

'No.'

'What did he do?'

'Nothing.'

'And how would you describe him?'

She thought for a moment, as if choosing her words.

'Very caring.'

Eyes Opened To
The Existence Of Evil

MEDICAL STUDENTS ARRIVE for my tuition, fresh-faced and innocent, all eager for the treat. For the most part, they are still of conspicuously middle-class origin, despite the government's desire to destroy bourgeois science and replace it with the true proletarian variety.

The contact these students have had with the seamy side of life has been either superficial or merely theoretical. They still suppose that most people are reasonable, decent and law-abiding, that they care for their children, etc. By the time they leave me, a week afterwards, their vision of life has darkened. Their eyes are opened to the existence of evil.

Of course, I am relieved in a way that innocence should persist, despite the forces ranged against it. On the other hand, it is slightly alarming that people could go through life in a small country such as ours without any knowledge of so considerable a part of its character. Ignorance, illusion, wilful blindness and wishful thinking have ever been the guiding principles of British government.

How young the medical students look to me now! I sent one off the other day to examine a patient who was no older than himself, but who had had a rather different experience of life from his.

The patient's father – or should I say inseminator – had disappeared almost as soon as he was born. The mother took another violent drunk to her bosom, and he persecuted the child of her former lover with obsessive malignity, whipping and beating him, and even on one occasion knocking him over with his car. When he reached the age of 14, his mother decided he was *de trop* and threw him out of her home to fend for himself. Needless to say, the rest of his life had not so far been a triumph; so when he found someone willing to inject him with a would-be fatal dose of heroin, he took the opportunity.

The next patient was a Muslim girl who had been taken away from school by her father and married to a 60-year-old man in Pakistan when she was 12 years old, to prevent her from getting immoral Western ideas. Fortunately, he had died when she was still only 16, and she was brought home to marry a neighbour who was even older. Several times she had tried to escape, but she had been kidnapped on the street and returned to a proper decent life of domestic and sexual slavery.

On the way to the prison with my student that afternoon, I asked him to resolve a paradox. On the one hand, no one who is burgled or robbed on the street ever finds the police to be of any use: they seem to regard such events as beneath their august notice. On the other hand, our prisons are full of recidivists who have been caught burgling or robbing. How did he explain it?

Fortunately, the first patient in the prison helped. He had spent only three months of the last 16 years out of prison, during which months he had fathered four children.

'Do you prefer life in prison?' I asked.

'I feel safer,' he replied.

'And do you arrange to be caught when you commit a crime?'

'I don't mind being caught. I've only been out four days this time.'

My student was silent as we left the prison. It had been rather a lot to learn in a day.

Town Planners Are Very Dangerous People

I WENT TO a different prison last week, in an ancient market town, to see a man about an arson. He had set fire to a house with four of his friends – or should I say former friends (his subsequent apologies not having been accepted by them) – in it. He said that he had been under a lot of pressure lately, ever since he had discovered that his ex, the mother of his two children, was injecting herself with heroin in front of them. So was their latest stepfather, her current boyfriend.

'What has that to do with setting fire to the house?' I asked.

He answered much as Mr Blair, or any other politician, might have answered in the circumstances.

'I've never done it before,' he said. 'I don't get no buzz off of starting fires. It was a one-off.'

These days, I grow impatient when people don't answer the question. I asked it again.

'I'd turned to drink,' he said. 'It'd been a heavy day, a bottle of brandy on top of ten lagers.'

'So you were drunk?'

'Yes,' he said. 'But not out of my head with it. Since I've been in prison, I've done an Alcohol Awareness Course.'

As far as I can make out, Alcohol Awareness Courses teach people that drinking alcohol can make you drunk.

'You went to your friends' house when you were drunk?' I asked.

'It wasn't their house exactly,' he said.

'Whose house was it, then?'

'They're all registered alcoholics, like. It was a squat.'

'Why did you go there?'

'I wanted to find out why they beat me up last week.'

Round here, of course, they don't need a reason to beat you up, but perhaps it's different in ancient market towns. There, they are five or ten years behind the times as far as social decomposition is concerned.

'And why did they beat you up?'

'I never found out why.'

'And why not?'

'They was all asleep and I couldn't wake none of them up.'

'So you set fire to the house?'

'Not deliberate, like,' he said. 'I lit up a spliff and hey presto.'

'Hey presto what?' I asked.

'They said there was a fire.'

'Hey presto they said there was a fire,' I said. 'And was there?'

'So they say. I don't know. I went home.'

It was time for me to go home as well. I walked through the streets of the once beautiful old town, damaged beyond the wildest dreams of arsonists. If it's damage that should be punished, all British architects and town planners ought to have life sentences without possibility of parole. They are very dangerous people.

On the train back home, I sat opposite a shaven-headed young man with a dragon tattooed on one arm and his blood group on the other. He was O negative: the universal donor, just like Mr Brown. He put earpieces in his ears, and it was tish-ter-tish-ter-tish all the way, for over an hour.

There's going to be an epidemic of deafness in years to come. I'm glad I won't be around when it happens. Vile old people will be shouting at each other, 'What's the fucking matter with you, are you fucking deaf or something?'

Governmental Pronouncements Should Carry A Warning: 'May Contain Traces Of Untruth.'

AT MY TIME of life, and in my circumstances, I ought to be calm and unruffled. I should be like a saddhu in a Himalayan cave, whose pulse rate no merely external event in the world of appearance can raise. Instead, whenever I read *The Guardian* (which is often), a wave of irritation comes over me like a Jacksonian fit, the epileptic seizure that starts with a twitch in the toe and ends in a generalised convulsion.

The other day, for example, I was reading an article about an Indian film just released called *Water*. It is about the doleful fate of poor widows in India, and apparently the film achieved the highest of all artistic goals, the breaking of a taboo.

The writer of the article interviewed the director, Deepa Mehta, and described the difficulty she had in making the film: 'In 2000, just a few days after filming began in Varanasi… a howling mob of 15,000 turned up. Indignation quickly turned to violent protest. Death threats were issued; there was an attempted suicide. The main set was burned down and the print seized and destroyed. In the can were just five minutes of film.'

The author then lets the director take up the story: 'It was a dark time for India,' [she said]. 'Paintings were being banned and history books were being rewritten. I tried to talk to the protesters and reason with them, but it was pretty obvious that they had their own agenda about projecting themselves as the protector of the faith, in a way that is no different from Christian fundamentalists in the West.'

Is 'Christian' quite the word she is looking for here? I am myself no great admirer of certain forms of Christianity, but it is some time since rampaging mobs of fundamentalist Christians have sought to curtail artistic licence by means of violence. The protests by Christians against films and artworks that must have offended their beliefs have been genteel and restrained on the whole, rather than violent. It seems that our fearless, taboo-breaking artists are not so completely free of fear after all, and are willing to curtail their own freedom of expression.

Should I work myself up about things like this? Perhaps Deepa Mehta is merely misinformed, but in that case why was she not pulled up about it? I leave it to you to decide, ladies and gentlemen of the jury.

Having worked in the British public service for the last decade and a half, perhaps I am hypersensitive to untruth and react to it as someone who is allergic to peanuts reacts to peanuts. This is unfortunate because, like peanuts, untruth is everywhere. I think all governmental pronouncements should carry a warning for people like me: 'May contain traces of untruth.'

I read the newspaper on a train in which a young and rough-looking man argued furiously, with all the anger of the justly-accused, with the ticket collector who discovered that he had no ticket. Nothing happened, however, because the man was so aggressive; he merely got out at his destination.

Then, walking down the street, I passed two young men with the vulpine lope of the triumphantly transgressive, who were smoking dope. Behind us was a notice affixed to the window of an empty shop: 'Bill stickers will be prosecuted.'

Bill stickers will be prosecuted, indeed! I nearly had an anaphylactic shock.

The Discouraging Triumph Of Self-Esteem Over Self-Respect

PUBLIC AFFAIRS VEX no man, said Doctor Johnson, and I know what he meant. He, however, did not live as we do in an age of information in which, without retiring entirely to bed, it is next to impossible to dodge the headlines altogether.

Besides, there's something extraordinarily tonic in vexation: it is to my muse what Galvani's electrical current was to frogs' legs. Is there anyone so dull of soul that he does not enjoy a little light indignation now and then?

It would not be right – it would be advertising, in fact – to mention by name in which magnate's publication I read a story recently about a schoolteacher who took a concealed camera into her classroom and recorded pupils who, *inter alia*, smashed furniture, tried to access anal pornography on the internet and made false accusations of assault against the teacher in class.

Needless to say, there were serious consequences – for the teacher, Mrs Angela Mason. It was she, not the pupils, who faced disciplinary proceedings. I could not help but recall Evelyn Waugh's remark on Randolph Churchill's cancer, that it was typical of modern medicine that it should have removed the only part of Churchill that was not malignant.

One of the pupils whom Mrs Mason filmed was reported to have felt 'angry and upset', while another said he felt 'embarrassed and humiliated': not, of course, by his own behaviour, but by the fact of having been unfairly caught red-handed.

Didn't the little bastards – I use the word figuratively, but with a strong chance of it being apposite literally – realise that, thanks in part to young tykes such as they, Britons are now filmed 300 times a day as they go about their daily business? Did they not realise that

312

every Briton is now a star, if not of stage and screen, at least of the CCTV camera? It seems a little late in the day, and oversensitive, to complain about being filmed.

Mrs Mason is a heroine, who deserves our gratitude for trying to make us face up to what we would rather avoid: that is to say, what we have become.

What we need is more humiliation and less self-esteem.

It is curious and discouraging that people don't make the elementary distinction nowadays between self-esteem and self-respect. The other day I passed one of Anita Roddick's emporia of narcissism, and saw in the window a picture of the firm's founder telling us how she proposed to promote self-esteem in Africa, and implying strongly that it was our moral duty to go and do likewise. I suppose we are to send emergency parcels of patchouli and potpourri.

Self-esteem is odious, where it exists, for example among most criminals, and anyone who even thinks about his self-esteem has sunk into a swamp of self-regard. Self-respect imposes a discipline and obligations; self-esteem is a kind of flabby, bullying solipsism

Needless to say, self-esteem is the concern of our age. Whenever a patient claims to suffer from insufficient self-esteem, I say to him that at least he has accurately understood his own worthlessness. Far from evoking anger, my remark evokes laughter and a sigh of relief: It's a fair cop, guv, and I don't have to pretend any more.

Cascading Vision
Throughout The Team

THE MEDICAL PROFESSION used often to be twitted with the mortality of its own members: for if doctors knew so much, how came it that they died like everyone else?

I think a more interesting question is why people who study literature for a living write so badly. After all, death is a fundamental and inescapable condition of human existence; bad writing is not. It seems, however, to be almost an advantage nowadays in academic life, at least in the humanities, to write barbarously. Advancement is secure if you can veer between incomprehensibility and banality, while passing seamlessly through obvious error.

A friend of mine recently attended a conference on Sylvia Plath in Oxford. Plath was a good poet, but more remarkable for having, like Colbert, founded entire industries, in her case biographical, hagiographical, psychoanalytic and critical; though, unlike Colbert, she did not found them wittingly. If the change from coal to natural gas had been made a few years earlier than it was, quite a number of academics would have had to seek elsewhere for a subject. Needless to say, they would have found it.

Academic literary study seems these days to be ninth-rate philosophy, or drunken verbiage without the alcohol. I'd rather listen to my local pub bore than to a paper entitled 'Open Ended: Poetic Closure and the Digital Interface': 'The aim of this paper is to read Plath's work through the lens of contemporary hermeneutic discourse concerning the autonomy of the text and language, while situating it within recent developments in digital poetry and electronic means of experiencing literary texts.'

I have sometimes tried to write parodies of such language, but try as I might, clarity keeps breaking out. The habit of using language to convey meaning is too deeply ingrained in me now ever to be overcome. I am a dinosaur.

The use of arcane and meaningless language as a means of career advancement is perhaps the most salient cultural characteristic of our age. Opening a medical journal recently, an inserted glossy leaflet fell out that offered me training in leadership, management and personal development.

On the courses I could learn, *inter alia*, 'the roots of my wiring' and 'to utilise an effective communication framework to ensure clarity'. (I think I would prefer to utilise clarity to ensure an effective communication framework.) I could learn also how to 'cascade vision throughout the team', as well as 'move towards an operational environment of respect and diversity-utilisation'.

Attendance at courses that teach such skills is now obligatory for doctors who wish to advance in their careers. They must go through them as tribal boys must go through secret *rites de passage* in the bush to become men. But managers themselves are not exempt from attendance: in one of the hospitals in which I worked until my retirement, all the managers had recently to attend a two-day course, run by a Canadian, on how to bring humour into management. A better subject might have been how to bring honesty into embezzlement, had the art not already been thoroughly mastered by the new class. The business of America is business; of Britain, nowadays, the malversation of funds.

Confucius was right. 'If language is not correct, then what is said is not what is meant; if what is said is not what is meant, then what must be done remains undone; if this remains undone, morals and art will deteriorate. Hence there must be no arbitrariness in what is said. This matters above everything.'

Luckily, The Number Of Beds For Patients Is Being Reduced

THANK GOODNESS I retired in time from the National Health Service: it has cut down enormously the number of forms I have to fill in.

The latest proto-genocidal form sent out to employees by my erstwhile employers was called 'a data cleanse', though it soon became known as 'an ethnic cleanse' since it related, *inter alia*, to the staff's ethnic group. Each member of staff was asked to choose one of 17 ethnic groups to which they belonged, one of six marital statuses, five sexual orientations and nine religious affiliations.

Oh for the simple, clean lines of apartheid, when there were only blacks, whites and coloureds! This form, designed, according to the covering letter, 'to monitor our workforce effectively and to ensure we identify, tackle and eliminate discriminatory practices', divides people into 4,590 possible categories. Filling in the form will also 'help ensure that you continue to be paid correctly', that is to say according to your race and sexual practices.

But even this form is surely insufficient from every possible point of view. For example, among ethnic groups not mentioned in the form are Malays, Indochinese, Melanesians, Polynesians, Micronesians, Eskimos, Amerindians and Madagascans. Among religions not included are Buddhism, Animism, Spiritualism, Theosophy and Scientology; and, what is surely important in the context of discrimination, no mention is made of the four principal castes of Hinduism and untouchability. No distinction is made between Shia and Sunni Islam, and there is no mention of the Alawites. Among sexual affiliations not included are necrophilia, fetishism, sado-masochism, bestiality and auto-erotic asphyxia. This brings the number of categories of people not to be discriminated against to 5,508,000.

There is only one solution to this grave problem, of course: to increase drastically the number of bureaucrats. It is lucky that the number of beds for patients is being reduced, for this will free the necessary money. Luckily, also, the staff are about to be trained, yet again, on 'diversity issues'. Seven hundred of them are to be sent in batches of about 240 on three whole-day seminars on diversity to be held in a huge public arena, in the course of which they will be divided into their various religious groups (lunch, teas and coffee provided, as well as free transport).

That is the good news. The bad news is that attendance is compulsory for the staff, and those who do not obtain their certificate of attendance, signed and countersigned, will not be given a pass to the new building that is to open in the near future: that is to say, they will in effect be sacked. Thus the NHS is instituting re-education camps.

For the hospital, the seminars represent at least three man-years of labour, but that is only a small part of the cost. The arena is not cheap to hire, presumably, or the eight coaches needed twice on three different days. It is unlikely that the consultants hired to give the seminars are acting *pro bono*; and everyone suspects that there is some hidden quid-pro-quo-ing going on between the consultants and the management.

I have now described the whole principle of modern British public administration.

Doctors On The Brink

MY ONE REGRET at having retired from the National Health Service is that I no longer receive official circulars. I used for a time to derive a small secondary income from publishing them; and such was their idiocy that very little commentary on my part was required. They spoke for themselves; it was money for old rope.

I am glad to say, however, that old friends keep me in touch with Gogolio-Kafkaesque-Orwellian developments in Europe's biggest employer (now that the Gulag is no more). One of them, a senior doctor, recently passed on to me an email written about him by someone rejoicing in the title of 'Lead Nurse Manager', sent to her superior, the 'Modern Matron' (it is typical of the temper, and increasingly the biology, of the times that the Matron should be male), complaining that he had twice refused to remove his cufflinks, contrary to Department of Health policy and instructions with regard to these death-dealing sartorial accoutrements.

My friend had the email from the medical director, who had it from the Modern Matron, who had it from the Lead Nurse Manager, who had ordered two members of staff, a ward clerk and a junior nurse, to ask him to take off his cufflinks. The Medical Director informed him that the Modern Matron had told him that he, the Modern Matron, reported directly to the Department of Health, and asked the Medical Director to inform the miscreant doctor of this fact.

Six members of the hospital staff, therefore, had devoted time to this important matter: probably enough in aggregate to save a life or two, and certainly enough to relieve a little suffering. I am not sufficiently *au fait* with the procedures of the Department of Health to know how many of their staff would devote their consideration to this matter; but I am at least morally certain that they would not otherwise have been better employed, which is at least a consolation.

That same week, another doctor friend, on the brink, like most of the British medical profession, of early retirement, kindly sent me the brochure to a conference to which he had been invited, at a cost of only £399.50 to the British taxpayer, on 'Lean Management in Primary Care'. 'Lean thinking is a way of streamlining the patient journey,' said the chairman of the 'Lean Enterprise Academy'. (So, of course, was the T-4 euthanasia programme in Germany, where the patient journey was streamlined in buses marked 'Community Transport'.)

One of the talks at the conference was to be given by a person whose position was 'Lead for NHS Productive Leader', a phrase so horrible that it tortures the mind merely to read or repeat it. The main subjects of this personage's talk were 'Releasing Time to Lead' and 'Focusing on Value: Experiences of a Productive Leader Site'. Another NHS functionary was quoted as follows: 'Lean's focus on delivering care is a refreshing antidote to benchmarks, targets and the traditional approach to performance management.' It is unlikely, outside the confessional, that a franker confession of the moral, intellectual and financial nullity, not to say corruption, of professional management in the public service will ever be uttered

Perpetual bureaucratic failure is management consultancy's opportunity, of course: without wilful incompetence, inefficiency and stupidity, where would the fees come from?

'Lean is not a management fad,' said the same functionary. And, as Magritte wrote on his painting of a pipe, this is not a pipe.

What Have We Become?

THE HISTORIAN SIR Lewis Namier once said that in a drop of dew could be seen all the colours of the rainbow, presumably as a reply to those who accused him of writing more and more about less and less. However, it is definitely true that in the smallest interactions can be seen the temper of the times: in our case, the bad temper of the times.

I was waiting for my wife in a car park in France recently when I noticed that the car next to me was British. In the car, door open, was a little boy of eight or nine. He was extremely handsome, and had a heart melting smile.

While his parents went shopping – for fast food as it turned out – he had been entrusted to the care of a man, evidently the friend of his parents, of about 40 and of quite transcendent vulgarity. I am not now referring to the charming seaside postcard vulgarity of Donald McGill; rather, I am talking of something infinitely more malign. His vulgarity was aggressive, vehement and triumphal, from his flower-patterned beer-belly-bulging shorts to his Rottweiler face. No one can help being ugly, of course, but no one need look like an attack dog. His was the kind of vulgarity that is not merely the absence of refinement, but a positive contempt for refinement. Indeed, it was a principled, ideological vulgarity; and, as its bearer, he was a true modern representative of his country.

He took out a sweet, unwrapped it, opened his mouth wide enough to dislocate his jaw, and then, in front of the child, screwed the wrapper into a ball and threw it on to the ground as if trying to bomb it.

Then he took a packet of crisps. He stuffed the crisps into his mouth with what can only be called ferocity, and chewed them as if he were a starving man thrown a piece of gristle. When his fingers could no longer convey a sufficient quantity of crisps to his cement-mixing mouth, to change the metaphor slightly, he leant back and poured the rest of the contents into it, disposing of the packet immediately afterwards. The child was watching all the while.

If you look, you see this kind of lesson in how to behave being given everywhere to the children of Britain. I was for a time the vulgarity correspondent of a national newspaper: that is to say, they sent me to wherever young Britons gathered to behave badly, which is to say everywhere they gather.

Among my unpleasant duties was attendance at a football match. The man next to me, who had brought his ten-year-old son with him, seemed perfectly reasonable until suddenly he sprang to his feet, made fascist gestures at the supporters of the opposing team and screamed such vile, obscene abuse that I wanted to stop the ears of his son.

It so happened that on the day in which I witnessed the scene in the French car park, I read of the murder of a young man who had remonstrated with some youths who had thrown a half-eaten chocolate bar through an open window into his sister's car. A man who tried to intervene on his behalf was threatened with death.

What have we become? Alas, it is my generation that is responsible for it, and I have done little or nothing to stop it.

Also from Monday Books

Not With A Bang But A Whimper / **Theodore Dalrymple**
(hbk, £14.99)

In a series of penetrating and beautifully-written essays, Theodore Dalrymple explains how the liberal intelligentsia are destroying Britain. Dalrymple writes for *The Spectator, The Times, The Daily Telegraph, New Statesman, The Times Literary Supplement* and the *British Medical Journal*.

'Theodore Dalrymple's clarity of thought, precision of expression and constant, terrible disappointment give his dispatches from the frontline a tone and a quality entirely their own... their rarity makes you sit up and take notice' - **Marcus Berkmann**, *The Spectator*

'Dalrymple is a modern master' - *The Guardian*

'Dalrymple is the George Orwell of our times... he is a writer of genius' - *Dennis Dutton*

Wasting Police Time / **PC David Copperfield** (ppbk, £7.99)

The fascinating, hilarious and best-selling inside story of the madness of modern policing. A serving officer - writing deep under cover - reveals everything the government wants hushed up about life on the beat.

'Very revealing' – *The Daily Telegraph*
'Passionate, important, interesting and genuinely revealing' – *The Sunday Times*
'Graphic, entertaining and sobering' – *The Observer*
'A huge hit... will make you laugh out loud'
– *The Daily Mail*
'Hilarious... should be compulsory reading for our political masters' – *The Mail on Sunday*
'More of a fiction than Dickens'
– **Tony McNulty MP, former Police Minister**
(On a BBC *Panorama* programme about PC Copperfield, McNulty was later forced to admit that this statement, made in the House of Commons, was itself untrue)

**From all good bookshops, online from
www.mondaybooks.com or via 01455 221752.**

Perverting The Course Of Justice / **Inspector Gadget**
(ppbk, £7.99)

A senior officer picks up where *Wasting Police Time* left off. A savage, eye-opening journey through our creaking criminal justice system, which explains what it's really like at the very sharp end of British policing.

'Exposes the reality of life at the sharp end'
– *The Daily Telegraph*

'No wonder they call us Plods... A frustrated inspector speaks out on the madness of modern policing'
– *The Daily Mail*

'Staggering... exposes the bloated bureaucracy that is crushing Britain' **– *The Daily Express***

'You must buy this book... it is a fascinating insight'
– Kelvin MacKenzie, *The Sun*

From all good bookshops, online from
www.mondaybooks.com or via 01455 221752.

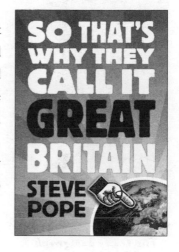